FERMANAGH

ALSO AVAILABLE IN THIS SERIES:

Sligo, Michael Farry (2012)
Tyrone, Fergal McCluskey (2014)
Waterford, Pat McCarthy (2015)
Monaghan, Terence Dooley (2017)
Derry, Adrian Grant (2018)
Limerick, John O'Callaghan (2018)
Louth, Donal Hall (2019)
Kildare, Seamus Cullen (2020)
Leitrim, Patrick McGarty (2020)
Antrim, Brian Feeney (2021)
Roscommon, John Burke (2021)
Donegal, Pauric Travers (2022)
Mayo, Joost Augusteijn (2023)

Fermanagh

The Irish Revolution, 1912–23

Daniel Purcell

FOUR COURTS PRESS

Typeset in 10.5 pt on 12.5 pt Ehrhardt by
Carrigboy Typesetting Services for
FOUR COURTS PRESS LTD
7 Malpas Street, Dublin 8, Ireland
www.fourcourtspress.ie
and in North America for
FOUR COURTS PRESS
c/o IPG, 814 N. Franklin St, Chicago, IL 60610.

A catalogue record for this title
is available from the British Library.

ISBN 978–1–84682–977–2

Printed in England
by CPI Antony Rowe, Chippenham, Wilts.

Contents

LIST OF ILLUSTRATIONS   vi

LIST OF ABBREVIATIONS   viii

ACKNOWLEDGMENTS   x

The Irish Revolution, 1912–23 series   xi

1   'Outpost of Ulster': Fermanagh in 1912   1

2   'Both sides may be said to be watching each other': the home rule crisis, 1912–14   11

3   'Bury the hatchet and take up the rifle': the First World War, 1914–16   30

4   'Rebels, traitors and pro-Germans': the rise of Sinn Féin and the unionist response, 1916–18   40

5   'There was little sign to be seen of the war': the War of Independence, 1919–20   64

6   'A unionist coup': Fermanagh and the Treaty in 1921   95

7   'Ulster is awake': the establishment of the northern state, 1922–3   116

8   Fermanagh in 1923 and beyond   142

NOTES   151

SELECT BIBLIOGRAPHY   175

INDEX   181

Illustrations

PLATES

1   William Copeland Trimble.
2   Jeremiah Jordan.
3   Edward Archdale.
4   Cahir Healy.
5   Godfrey Fetherstonhaugh.
6   Charles Falls.
7   Orange Order Derrygonnelly Star of Freedom, *c*.1910.
8   Seán O'Mahony.
9   Enniskillen Town Hall, *c*.1900.
10 Ulster Women's Unionist Council postcard, 1 August 1912.
11 Enniskillen Horse outside the former jail, *c*.1912.
12 6th Battalion, Inniskilling Dragoons, 1914.
13 Women's Branch, Florence Court Star of Victory, *c*.1920.
14 Orange Hall, Enniskillen.
15 3rd Battalion of UVF Enniskillen, 1914.
16 Royal Irish Constabulary officers with man at a checkpoint, *c*.1920.
17 Cumann na mBan pin badge.
18 Commemorative Belleek pottery vase.
19 Arthur Griffith.
20 Main Street, Roslea, Co. Fermanagh, after the burning of the village on the night of 21 February 1921 by the Black and Tans.
21 Frank Carney and Eoin O'Duffy.
22 Train derailed on the Great Northern Railway line from Dundalk to Enniskillen, 1922.
23 Seán and Mollie Nethercott, *c*.1920.
24 B Specials outside Coulter's grocery shop in Letterbreen, *c*.1920.
25 B Special patrol.
26 The *Lady of the Lake*, *c*.1900.
27 Boundary Commission first sitting, 9 December 1924.
28 Basil Brooke.

Credits
1, 11: kindly lent by Trimble family; 2, 3, 4, 28: National Portrait Gallery, London; 5, 6, 7, 10, 12, 13, 14, 15, 16, 17, 18, 23, 24, 25, 26: Museum Services, Fermanagh & Omagh District Council; 8, 9, 19, 20, 22, 27: National Library of Ireland; 21: kindly lent by Kate Tammemagi.

MAPS

1	Places mentioned in the text	xii
2	Roman Catholic population by district electoral division in 1911	3
3	Parliamentary constituencies	7
4	Local government divisions	8
5	IRA brigade areas	67
6	Distribution of Crown forces	71

Abbreviations

AOH	Ancient Order of Hibernians (Board of Erin)
ASU	Active Service Unit
BMH	Bureau of Military History
BN	*Belfast Newsletter*
CAB	Cabinet Office, TNA
Cd.	Command paper
CDB	Congested Districts Board
CI	County Inspector, Royal Irish Constabulary
CÓFLA	Cardinal Tomás Ó Fiaich Memorial Library and Archive
CSO	Chief Secretary's Office
DATI	Department of Agriculture & Technical Instruction
DED	District Electoral Division
DI	District Inspector, Royal Irish Constabulary
DIB	*Dictionary of Irish biography*
DJ	*Derry Journal*
FH	*Fermanagh Herald*
FJ	*Freeman's Journal*
FT	*Fermanagh Times*
IFS	Irish Free State
IG	Inspector General, Royal Irish Constabulary
II	*Irish Independent*
IMA	Irish Military Archives
INL	Irish Nation League
IPP	Irish Parliamentary Party
IR	*Impartial Reporter*
IRA	Irish Republican Army
IRB	Irish Republican Brotherhood
IT	*Irish Times*
ITGWU	Irish Transport and General Workers' Union
JP	Justice of the Peace
LGB	Local Government Board
LS	*Londonderry Sentinel*
MP	Member of Parliament
MSPC	Military Service Pensions Collection
NAI	National Archives of Ireland
NAUL	National Amalgamated Union of Labour
NEBB	North East Boundary Bureau
NLI	National Library of Ireland
PRONI	Public Records Office of Northern Ireland
RDC	Rural District Council
RIC	Royal Irish Constabulary

RUC	Royal Ulster Constabulary
SF	Sinn Féin
TD	Teachta Dála
TGWU	Transport and General Workers' Union
TNA	National Archives, London
UCDA	University College Dublin Archives
UDC	Urban District Council
UH	*Ulster Herald*
UIL	United Irish League
USC	Ulster Special Constabulary
UUC	Ulster Unionist Council
UWU	Ulster Workers' Union
UWUC	Ulster Women's Unionist Council
WS	Witness statement to Bureau of Military History

Acknowledgments

This book was first pitched to me in the summer of 2019 in the bright café of the National Library of Ireland. At the time I airily suggested that I could have a draft available in a year. Three years elapsed before a full draft reached the editors. While I do not fault the past version of myself for not foreseeing Covid-19, it is certainly true that researching and writing this book has been a long process. I have carried it with me through lockdown, starting a new career and marriage. In that time, I have come to appreciate the uniqueness of the Fermanagh story, and how privileged I am to be the one to tell it. As part of that long journey too I have reconsidered and revised my own thinking many times and have inevitably accumulated a vast array of people to whom I am indebted.

Most importantly, Dr Daithí Ó Corráin and Professor Mary Ann Lyons deserve unending thanks for their herculean work in editing this volume. Their detailed commentary on earlier drafts has been crucial in bringing it up to the high standard expected of the series. I have greatly enjoyed their engagement with my work; their suggestions and questions prompted me to think about my own research in ways I had never done before. Additionally, I would like to thank Dr Mike Brennan for his work creating some wonderful maps and Martin Fanning and the team at Four Courts Press for all their help in assembling this book. I also wish to make special mention of my doctoral supervisors Dr Anne Dolan and the late Professor David Fitzpatrick. Their early comments on my research on Fermanagh were crucial in shaping how I thought about Fermanagh and the border more generally.

I have been assisted by countless historians throughout the production of this book and in my earlier research on the topic. If I have forgotten anyone here or left them out, I can only apologize. I owe significant thanks to Dr Tim Wilson, Dr Jonathan Cherry, Dr Edward Burke, Dr Conor Morrissey, Dr Brian Hughes, Dr Fionnuala Walsh, Dr Ailbhe Rodgers, Dr Timothy Bowman, Lawrence White, Dr Mary McAuliffe, Professor Mary Daly, Dr Brendan Scott, Pamela McKane, Dr Patrick Maume, Dr Owen McGee and David Keys. I am extremely grateful to the staff at various libraries where I undertook research, particularly Theresa Loftus of Monaghan County Museum, Dr Dónal McAnallen of the Ó Fiaich Library, and Catherine Scott and Sinead Reilly of the Fermanagh County Museum. I am also grateful to the staff of the National Library of Ireland, the National Museum of Ireland, the Public Record Office of Northern Ireland, the National Archives of Ireland, UCD Archives, the Military Archives of Ireland and the National Archives in Kew.

I reserve my final thanks for my friends and family, especially to Owen Murphy and Stephen Bourke for being excellent sounding boards and editors. And last and most significantly to my wife Dr Nuria de Cos Lara to whom I owe far more than can be put in print.

The Irish Revolution, 1912–23 series

Since the turn of the century, a growing number of scholars have been actively researching this seminal period in modern Irish history. More recently, propelled by the increasing availability of new archival material, this endeavour has intensified. This series brings together for the first time the various strands of this exciting and fresh scholarship within a nuanced interpretative framework, making available concise, accessible, scholarly studies of the Irish Revolution experience at a local level to a wide audience.

The approach adopted is both thematic and chronological, addressing the key developments and major issues that occurred at a county level during the tumultuous 1912–23 period. Beginning with an overview of the social, economic and political milieu in the county in 1912, each volume assesses the strength of the home rule movement and unionism, as well as levels of labour and feminist activism. The genesis and organization of paramilitarism from 1913 are traced; responses to the outbreak of the First World War and its impact on politics at a county level are explored; and the significance of the 1916 Rising is assessed. The varying fortunes of constitutional and separatist nationalism are examined. The local experience of the War of Independence, reaction to the truce and Anglo-Irish Treaty and the course and consequences of the Civil War are subject to detailed examination and analysis. The result is a compelling account of life in Ireland in this formative era.

Mary Ann Lyons
Department of History
Maynooth University

Daithí Ó Corráin
School of History & Geography
Dublin City University

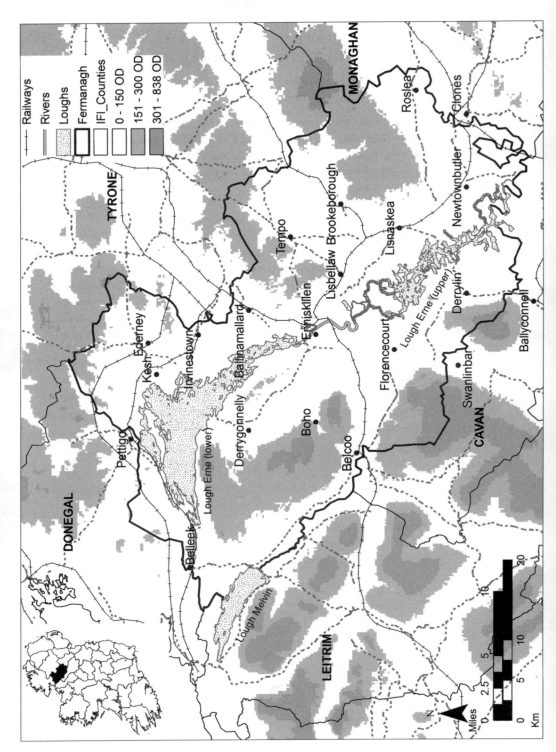

1 Places mentioned in the text

1 'Outpost of Ulster': Fermanagh in 1912

Fermanagh entered the 1910s in a position of hard-won, if fragile, stability. The county's relatively evenly divided nationalist and unionist population produced secure majorities for nationalist candidates in the South Fermanagh political constituency and unionist candidates in North Fermanagh. Only contests in local government offered any serious opportunity for political conflict. However, the turn of national events from 1912 meant that both nationalism and unionism underwent profound changes in a relatively short space of time. While the county's even population split led to both communities making strong efforts to manage their relationship with the other, the increasing likelihood of the partition of Ireland left both intensely aware that the political fate of Fermanagh was more uncertain than that of any other county. Fermanagh offers a fascinating example of how intercommunal tension was managed during the Irish Revolution and how long periods of peace and relative deadlock were punctuated by sudden outbursts of violence. It can be argued that Fermanagh was a laboratory for many features that would later characterize the Unionist government in Northern Ireland. The use of the Ulster Special Constabulary (USC), local electoral malpractice, and the suppression of the nationalist community had some of their earliest manifestations in Fermanagh precisely because of its large and difficult to control nationalist population.

At its widest points, Fermanagh spans forty-five miles by twenty-nine miles and comprises some 457,369 acres. As shown in map 1, it is dominated by Lough Erne and the landscape is marked by a contrast between the wetlands of the Erne and the limestone hills. This relief is most pronounced along the Cavan border around Cuilcagh. The best land has traditionally been in the east, around Ballinamallard, but there was considerable variability of farm sizes, types and prosperity across the county.[1] Lough Erne was the cause of frequent flooding and during the nineteenth century significant progress was made in controlling its water level.

In 1911 Fermanagh had one of the smallest populations in Ireland with 61,836 people. It was also the smallest Ulster county with over 10,000 fewer people than Monaghan, the next in size. Fermanagh accounted for just four per cent of the province's population.[2] Between 1901 and 1911, the county's population declined by 3,594 people or five per cent.[3] Surprisingly, one of the largest declines took place in Enniskillen which, despite its pre-eminent economic position, lost ten per cent of its population. The decline was borne relatively evenly by the different religious denominations. The religious divide in Fermanagh resulted in an approximate 55:45 split, with Catholics in the slight majority. Most of the Protestant population was Anglican. Presbyterians accounted for only two per cent of Fermanagh's population, the lowest in Ulster. Further distinguishing Fermanagh Protestantism was the presence of a large and prosperous Methodist community, proportionally the largest in Ulster. Methodists played a prominent role in the life of the county as shopkeepers, professionals and artisans and contributed men such as the MP Jeremiah Jordan to Fermanagh's public life. Although Fermanagh comprised only one per cent of the Irish population, it contained seven per cent of Irish Methodists.[4]

There was no clear settlement pattern in Fermanagh and the population was relatively evenly distributed. Enniskillen, by far the largest town, had a population of just 4,853 split across its eastern, northern and southern wards with a further 1,308 people living in the rural hinterland. The next largest town was Lisnaskea (2,047) followed by Irvinestown (1,577). Outside of the towns, Fermanagh's population was greater around the edges of the county. Rosslea (2,166), on the Monaghan border, was the largest district electoral division (DED) in the county due to its proximity to Clones. Crum (1,546) on the Cavan border and Inishmacsaint (2,036) next to Donegal also had substantial populations by Fermanagh standards.

While Fermanagh's Protestant population was relatively evenly distributed, the Catholic population was more clustered in the east and south-west as illustrated in map 2. Protestants were in the majority in the north and centre of the county while Catholics were dominant along the border with Monaghan, Cavan and Donegal. Although there were thirteen DEDs where Catholics made up four-fifths or more of the population (including major population centres like Inishmacsaint and Rosslea), there were only three DEDs where the same was true for non-Catholics (all three along the border with Tyrone). The county's towns tended to be either evenly split (such as Irvinestown and Lisnaskea) or strongly Protestant such as in Lisbellaw and Ballinamallard, which had a reputation for uncompromising unionist activity. Enniskillen Rural District Electoral Division (RDED) was split evenly between the two communities; Catholics held a majority in the town. The north ward was seventy per cent Catholic, the south ward, sixty-one per cent Protestant. The remaining eastern ward held a very slim Catholic majority of three per cent.

Fermanagh was a predominantly rural, agricultural county in 1911. Of its 457,369 acres, 106,439 were under tillage, 235,423 in pasture, 5,111 in plantations, 63,965 were unproductive bog or mountain and 46,431 were under water. The county had few strong native industries. Belleek had the only porcelain factory in Ireland and the Lough Erne Fishery Company. Forestry was well established around Lisnaskea, and Lisbellaw had a long-standing woollen factory.[5] By 1911 the *Belfast and Province of Ulster Directory* noted that linen manufacture in the county, which had waned since the nineteenth century, was 'of a coarse description chiefly for domestic use … [and] carried on to a small extent'.[6] Sixty-nine per cent of those registered in the 1911 census worked in

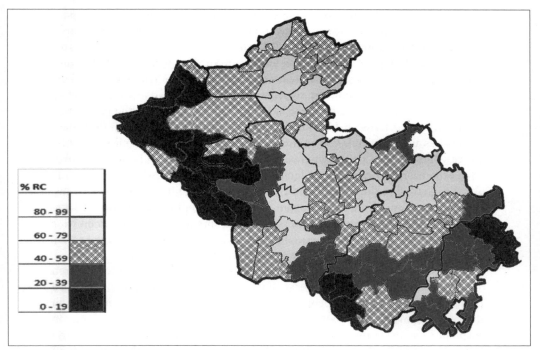

2 Roman Catholic population by district electoral division in 1911.

agriculture. This figure was twenty-four per cent above the national average. Meanwhile only one-fifth of the productive population worked in any industrial field, eleven per cent below the national average. Representation in the other occupational classes of professional, domestic and commercial workers was also below the national average, albeit by a smaller margin. Elsewhere in the county, the main non-farming economic activities were dependent on agriculture. The most important industrial employers in the county were creameries. Run on a co-operative model, they were a significant employer in almost every major town. Larger areas like Belleek could even sustain auxiliary creameries in nearby villages such as at Whealt and Garrison.[7] By 1900 twenty-seven creameries had been opened in the county, of which ten were large-scale churning centres.[8]

Various specialized markets held in the three main towns were important drivers of local trade. Enniskillen was the most significant with corn, pork and butter markets on Tuesdays and Thursdays as well as fairs on the tenth of every month. Lisnaskea held twice-weekly markets: on Wednesdays for pork and Saturdays for all other produce. There was also a flax market in the town during winter on the fourth Wednesday of the month. Lisnaskea boasted a permanent corn, butter, potato, egg and fowl market. Irvinestown had major monthly markets on Wednesdays as well as a monthly fair.[9]

The type of employment available was partially dependent on religious affiliation. The largest single employment sector for Catholic women, for example, was farm work while for non-Catholics it was domestic service. Flax manufacturing employed fourteen per cent of working Catholic women as compared with less than five per cent of working non-Catholic women. Only sixteen per cent of working Catholic women were domestic servants. The fact that thirty-one per cent of working non-Catholic women were in domestic service reflects the reality that those with the means to hire servants were traditionally wealthy Protestant landowners and merchants who preferred to employ their co-religionists. Existing power structures that perpetuated occupational discrimination against Catholics were even more pronounced in female employment. Protestants were heavily overrepresented in the fields of local government, banking and the professions. By contrast, Catholics were dominant in the trades and in agriculture. A large number of the poorly paid workers such as flax spinners and charwomen were predominantly Catholic. Catholics comprised seventy-two per cent of Fermanagh's general labourers and sixty-eight per cent of its agricultural labourers.

In terms of absolute poverty, Fermanagh was not noticeably different from other counties with a similarly rural economic profile. On the night of 2 April 1911, the county had 486 people in receipt of some form of relief: 272 in workhouses, 214 on outdoor relief, 185 deemed 'sick at home' and 142 in hospital. This was in line with levels of deprivation in neighbouring Tyrone and Monaghan. The quality of housing in the county in 1911 was also typical for a rural, relatively poor county and similar to Tyrone and Monaghan. The vast majority of houses (12,711) were either of the second or third class. Sixty-eight per cent of them were smaller than five rooms, with 523 being single room habitations, and a further 2,289 comprised only two rooms. There were 523 tenements in the county, of which 253 were home to more than one family. Fifty houses in the county were deemed fourth class, the lowest classification available.

Transport infrastructure in the county reflected Fermanagh's rurality and peripherality. As map 1 indicates, having an effective rail network was exceptionally important. It was the primary means of transporting goods from the major ports of Dundalk and Belfast as well as general travel. Three railway companies operated in Fermanagh during this period. The Great Northern Railway, which radiated out from Enniskillen in three directions, was the most important.[10] Running northwards, it travelled through Ballinamallard en route to Omagh and Derry and divided at Bundoran junction to provide a service to Belleek, Ballyshannon and Bundoran whose tourist trade relied significantly on this service.[11] Going eastwards, the route went via Lisbellaw, Maguiresbridge and Lisnaskea before coming to the important rail hub of Clones in Monaghan and on to Dundalk, a major port for the freight of goods to the north-west. The Clogher Valley Railway Company ran a route from Caledon in Tyrone to Maguiresbridge through Brookeborough and Colebrooke. A smaller south-western route was operated by the Sligo Leitrim and Northern Counties Railway Company through Belcoo and Florencecourt and into Leitrim. This rail infrastructure was supplemented by a number of steamers that ran service on the lakes, particularly Upper Lough Erne from Enniskillen to Belleek.[12] By far the most important of these transport connections was the railway route to Clones. It not only brought the majority of imported goods into the county but also connected them to the Belfast line.

Fermanagh's literacy rate of eighty-five per cent was the same as the national average and five per cent above the Ulster average. Among Catholics, the rate was only eighty-one per cent while it was eighty-nine per cent for Anglicans and ninety-six per cent for Presbyterians and Methodists. The county also recorded 1,563 gaeilgeoirí in 1911 – an increase of over 500 from the previous census.[13] This level of literacy was reflected in the strong reading culture in the county, which had three influential local newspapers. The *Impartial Reporter*, the third oldest newspaper in Ireland, was the largest and was edited by William Copeland Trimble, a major figure in Fermanagh unionism during the first half of the century. He had inherited the paper from his father William Trimble senior in 1883. The *Reporter* reflected the political development of its editor and moved from a liberal, pro-tenant stance in the 1890s to an arch-unionist position by 1910. Its biggest competitor was the *Fermanagh Times*, set up by landlords to counter Trimble's earlier liberal views. By 1912 the *Reporter* was viewed as the voice of the Enniskillen middle class and the *Times* the paper of the aristocracy and the Orange Order.[14] During this period the *Times* was owned and managed by William Ritchie. While Trimble was a Presbyterian, Ritchie was an Anglican and there was considerable personal animosity between them. For nationalists, the primary county paper was the *Fermanagh Herald*. It was established in 1902 by Louis Lynch, who had also founded the *Ulster Herald* a year earlier. For this reason, the *Reporter* dismissively referred to the *Herald* as an 'Omagh newspaper'. By 1912 the *Herald* was a strong supporter of John Redmond and the Irish Parliamentary Party (IPP), although it was critical of the influence of the Ancient Order of Hibernians (AOH).

A number of aristocratic families held most of the land in Fermanagh and played a leading role in the county's political and social life. The most important in order of seniority were the Coles (earls of Enniskillen), the Crichtons (earls of Erne) and the Lowry-Corrys (earls of Belmore).[15] The earls of Enniskillen had their seat at Florencecourt. The family dominated local politics. The heir designate of each generation was elected to the House of Commons before ascending to the House of Lords on their father's death.[16] In addition, successive generations of Coles served as grandmasters of the Orange Order in Fermanagh. The only family that could plausibly challenge the predominance of the Coles was the Crichtons whose family seat was at Crom Castle near the Monaghan border. The third and fourth earls of Erne served as Fermanagh's lord lieutenant, the ceremonial head of the county, from 1840 until 1914. John Crichton, the fourth earl, had served as a lord of the Treasury in Benjamin Disraeli's second government and was appointed to the Privy Council of Ireland in 1902.[17] The family seat of the Lowry-Corrys was at Castle Coole in Enniskillen. The family's attention was often divided between Fermanagh and Tyrone with previous earls representing the latter in parliament and the second and fourth earls serving as lord lieutenant of Tyrone.[18]

In theory, the three families were outranked by the Loftuses, marquesses of Ely. Although based in Wexford, they held the largest estates in Fermanagh, which they had inherited from the Hume baronets in the eighteenth century. However, for most of this period they were absentee lords, preferring to live in their original home of Loftus Hall. Their seat was located at Ely Castle, later Ely Lodge, on the southern shore of Lough Erne near Enniskillen. Consequently, while members of the family often served as justices of the peace or high sheriffs, the Loftus family never played a major role in local politics. A number of other significant landowners were influential politically and socially, among them the Brookes of Colebrook Park near Brookeborough, with Basil Brooke serving as prime minister of Northern Ireland in 1943. The Archdalls (later Archdales) of Castle Archdale near Irvinestown were equally prominent in local government. Three generations of the family held a single seat in the Fermanagh constituency from the Act of Union in 1801 to the reorganization of the constituency in 1885.[19] Another branch of the family at Riversdale were influential in the latter half of the nineteenth century with Edward Mervyn Archdale elected MP in North Fermanagh in 1898 and his brother John Porter-Archdale (later renamed John Porter-Porter to secure an inheritance) being a prominent local unionist.[20]

Politics in the county pre-1880 had been stagnant, dominated by its unique brand of unionism and its surprisingly underdeveloped nationalist movement. Brian Barton has characterized nineteenth-century Fermanagh as representing the final bulwark of conservative landlord-led unionism.[21] The 1884 Representation of the People Act and 1885 Redistribution of Seats Act widened the electorate significantly and crucially extended many provisions of the 1867 Reform Act to the countryside (particularly important in strongly rural Fermanagh). The impact of both was striking. In 1880 the constituency of Fermanagh had 4,778 registered electors but 13,542 in 1885. The older constituencies of Enniskillen and Fermanagh were reconfigured into North and South Fermanagh with each returning one MP (see map 3). In the general elections of 1885 and 1886 the IPP won both seats. This shocked the county's unionist leadership, which thereafter focused on mobilizing, uniting and registering unionist voters. The costs associated with registering new unionist voters were met by Fermanagh's aristocratic families.[22] Unionist efforts focused almost entirely on North Fermanagh as the nationalist majority in South

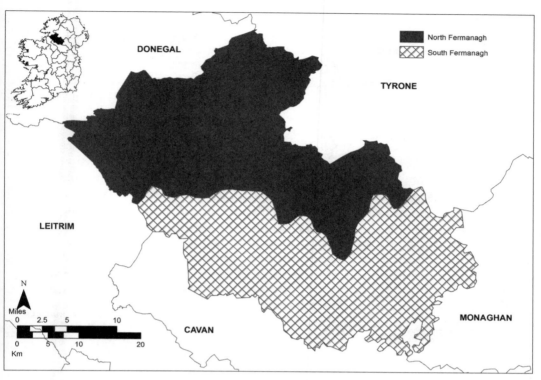

3 Parliamentary constituencies

Fermanagh was seen as too great to overturn. This, coupled with divisions within nationalism following the Parnellite split, allowed Richard Dane to retake North Fermanagh for the Unionist Party while Nationalist Patrick McGilligan was returned unopposed in the southern constituency. This status quo continued until 1918, despite occasional threats to unionist dominance in North Fermanagh from liberal unionists with nationalist support.

Local politics was the primary arena contested by Fermanagh nationalists and unionists. The 1898 Local Government Act created a hierarchical system of county, rural and urban councils (see map 4). Due to the population distribution within Fermanagh, the majority of these districts had very small nationalist or unionist majorities and could, therefore, be won by either side. The exceptions were Belleek and Clones No. 2 rural district councils (RDCs), which were consistently held by nationalists, and Enniskillen RDC which maintained a unionist majority. These councils were important as they allowed both the IPP and Unionist Party to influence local politics and were a conduit for spending public funds. In general, nationalists preferred higher rates and public spending on housing and road improvements, whereas unionists favoured limited

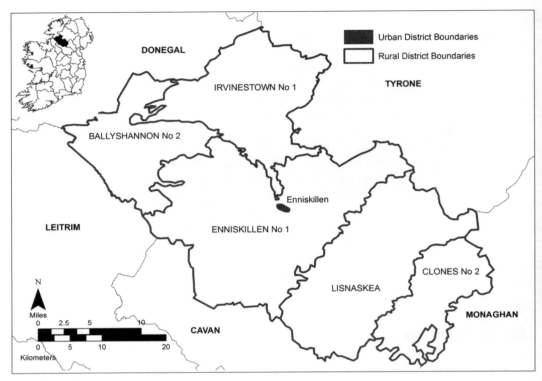

4 Local government divisions

spending and lower rates. This difference of approach became a significant point of contention.

By the early 1910s Fermanagh exhibited a fragile equilibrium. Unionism was controlled by an alliance of the traditional landed families and the burgeoning urban middle class. The earls of Erne and Enniskillen were regarded as the traditional leaders of unionism in the county. Of the two, John Crichton, earl of Erne, was the more active, serving as first chair of Fermanagh County Council until 1903. Lowry Cole, the earl of Enniskillen, was too elderly to play an active role in local politics and instead held political rallies on his estates. The lords Belmore were prominent as chairs of Enniskillen RDC. Unlike elsewhere in Ulster, the class of 'professional men' such as James Cooper (1882–1942) had been slow to supplant the traditional unionist leadership. Crucially, this class did not compete with the landed families for influence to the same extent as in Tyrone or Derry. The Orange Order was the strongest unionist organization in the county with one hundred lodges and approximately 3,200 members. Nationalists in Fermanagh were more united than in Tyrone or Derry. The competition between populist Dillonites and conservative Healyites that typified Tyrone nationalism was much less pronounced in Fermanagh.[23] Instead, the county was dominated by Jeremiah Jordan – a Methodist shopkeeper, a fierce enemy of the earls of Enniskillen and an anti-Parnellite who became a strong supporter of Redmond. Elected for South Fermanagh in 1895, he was re-elected at every subsequent election until 1910 with only nominal unionist opposition.[24] Jordan's Methodism allowed him to appeal to Fermanagh's liberal unionist tradition.

The United Irish League (UIL) was the strongest nationalist organization in the county and served as the local IPP apparatus. It raised funds, selected candidates, and held rallies and commemorations to energize the nationalist base. The UIL was partially opposed by the Ancient Order of Hibernians (AOH) – the Catholic fraternal organization closely allied with the IPP. The AOH grew after the Parnellite split and by 1910 was, in Kevin O'Shiel's words, 'exceedingly strong' in Fermanagh.[25] Despite Jordan's popularity, and his being backed by the Catholic Church, the AOH consistently opposed his nomination as the nationalist candidate for elections.[26] Many prominent nationalist members of the county and urban district councils (UDC) were members of both the IPP and the AOH. The growth of the AOH in Fermanagh during the 1910s exacerbated mounting political tensions in the county. The AOH's women's auxiliary was the only significant body of nationalist women in Fermanagh. Its political activities were limited to assisting the AOH with various rallies and social events.[27] The dominance of nationalism and unionism was not challenged by any serious third party. Labour was quiet in the county and industrial activity was generally limited to occasional strikes and pay disputes.[28] The Land and Labour League, which grew rapidly in the 1890s, had fallen into abeyance by 1900.

The nature of the Irish Revolution in Fermanagh was unique. The county's peripherality, its small population size and even religious divide combined in a manner not replicated elsewhere in Ulster. Although Tyrone had a similarly slim Catholic majority, it was located much closer to the Ulster unionist heartlands of Down and Antrim and had several large population centres. Cavan and Monaghan were equally peripheral but their large Catholic nationalist majorities ensured that they were not as central to the debate about partition as Fermanagh. The spectre of partition loomed large in the mind of both nationalist and unionist during the revolution. Profound uncertainties over whether some or all of Fermanagh would be excluded from the new Ulster haunted the dreams of all those engaged in shaping the future of the county. The desire to influence the partition settlement underscored all events in the county as both sides sought to articulate their specific visions of the nature of the county.

While the Irish Revolution was 'not carried successfully in any regard in the six counties that became Northern Ireland', the nature of the failure in Fermanagh is significant.[29] Fermanagh's revolution lacked many of the dramatic events of elsewhere in Ireland. Instead, it experienced a constant simmering tension as the two political communities sought to counter one another's ambitions. Fermanagh, as will be shown, was integral to the foundation of the Ulster Volunteer Force (UVF) and the USC. It contributed numerous prominent unionist and nationalist leaders such as Basil Brooke and Cahir Healy. Fermanagh also demonstrated the importance of local politics in influencing national events. More effectively than anywhere else in Ulster, the revolution in Fermanagh set the template for the future of nationalism and unionism in what would become Northern Ireland after 1921.

2 'Both sides may be said to be watching each other': the home rule crisis, 1912–14

By 1912 both nationalists and unionists had reason to be optimistic. Nationalists had witnessed a decade of growth and electoral success nationally and locally. They had established South Fermanagh as a secure IPP seat and their influence in North Fermanagh was increasing. They controlled the majority of local bodies in the county. Nationally, John Redmond had reunited the party after the Parnellite split. The IPP held considerable influence after the two general elections of 1910 when their support had allowed the Liberal Party to form a government with the promise of another home rule bill. Meanwhile, unionism in Fermanagh was also on an upward trend after the nadir of 1886. The rise of a new generation of young, active unionists had animated public opinion as never before. Between 1912 and 1914 unionism and nationalism mobilized in response to the third home rule bill, nationalists to defend it and unionists to oppose it. Both created militias to advance their aims. By the outbreak of the First World War, tension in Fermanagh was so high that some form of armed conflict looked probable. Under the direction of the Ulster Unionist Council (UUC), unionists were proactive in extending their local organization through the foundation of unionist clubs and branches of the Ulster Women's Unionist Council (UWUC) and by holding frequent public meetings. Fermanagh unionists played a leading role in the two key events of this period – the signing of the Ulster Covenant in September 1912 and the foundation of the UVF in January 1913. By contrast, the nationalist establishment in Fermanagh was curiously inactive, preferring to leave most political activity to the leadership in Dublin and Westminster. Fermanagh nationalists were slow to realize the threat posed by resurgent unionism. Even after the Irish Volunteers were established in November 1913, it took months before they had any significant presence in Fermanagh. However, once established, the organization grew rapidly and exceeded the UVF in membership but not arms. Only careful management of both groups by their leadership prevented serious violence before the onset of the First World War.

At first glance, it would appear that the two general elections in 1910 were a continuation of the electoral status quo of the 1900s. In both January and December 1910 (as well as in January 1906 before that) both Fermanagh constituencies demonstrated remarkably consistent electoral patterns. In North Fermanagh, the Unionist candidate held his seat against a challenge from Russellite and Liberal Unionists, while in South Fermanagh, the IPP candidate won with either massive majorities or unopposed. On both sides, however, changes were afoot that would later contribute to the radicalization of politics in the county and provide Fermanagh nationalism and unionism with many of its new leaders. The key departure from past politics came in 1905 with the foundation of the UUC to provide a central leadership for Ulster unionists both within and outside parliament. The foundation of the UUC was controversial because of its intention that Ulster unionists should split from their 'southern' unionist allies and organize along provincial lines. The profile of the UUC was boosted in 1910 when Walter Long was replaced as chair by Edward Carson. Although not an Ulsterman, Carson brought significant energy to the role and rapidly became the face of unionism in Ireland. His personal popularity was based on his fiery delivery of speeches that promised to spare Ulster from home rule by any means necessary. Carson was aided in his efforts by James Craig's organizational support. Organization and electoral strategy were perceived as key to political success. The electoral fate of North Fermanagh held particular symbolic significance for unionists. In January 1910 the *Irish Times* acclaimed the 'magnificent' unionist majority in the constituency, which was described as the 'Outpost of Ulster'.[1]

Fermanagh's most prominent member of the UUC was Edward Archdale (1853–1943), a former MP for North Fermanagh, who was elected chair of the standing committee at its inception in 1905. Archdale also sat on the council's executive committee. No other Fermanagh unionist sat on these committees before 1912.[2] Over time, Fermanagh's representation on the UUC standing committee grew to four with the earl of Erne joining in 1906 and remaining a member until his death in 1914, Godfrey Fetherstonhaugh in 1908 (by virtue of being a sitting MP) and John Porter-Porter, former high sheriff of the county, in 1912. Notably, the earls of Enniskillen and Belmore were unable to leverage their local pre-eminence into a national leadership role within unionism. This was despite Belmore's son serving as a delegate, and Belmore and Erne having been prominent in predecessor organizations such as the Irish Unionist Alliance.[3] The expansion of the UUC in 1911 allowed for more delegates from each county and in Fermanagh these were largely filled by professionals and middle-class farmers. The new delegates included future notables such as Archibald Cathcart (a grocer), William Copeland Trimble (a newspaper editor) and James Cooper (a solicitor). Indeed, of the seven new Fermanagh delegates in 1912, only Ffoliott Warren Barton of Clonelly could be said to come from the landed classes.

Efforts were also made to organize the unionist women of the county. In April 1911, the first branch of the UWUC in Fermanagh was established in Enniskillen. Despite changes in the composition of the male leadership of Fermanagh, the women's movement was dominated by the aristocracy and gentry. Lady Erne was elected first president of the UWUC and Elizabeth Archdale, wife of Edward, vice-president. The rest of the leadership comprised the wives of prominent unionists such as Josephine Porter-Porter (wife of John Porter-Porter) and Georgina Irvine (wife of Major J.G.C. Irvine of Rockfield).[4]

Despite the aristocratic composition of its leadership, the UWUC strove to make itself a mass movement. For Lady Erne, the primary purpose of the new organization was to 'join together as the times were so anxious'.[5] The call to action was framed in traditional terms of unionist womanhood. The main responsibilities of the UWUC were described as 'the distribution of Unionist literature amongst the electors and the personal canvass'.[6] It was also responsible for holding rallies and mass meetings for women in support of the UUC.

The UUC played a significant role in elections. Recognizing the importance of a safe seat on the fringes of Ulster, they directed significant resources to secure North Fermanagh for official unionism from 1905 onward. The changing face of Ulster unionism in Fermanagh was also reflected in its selection of candidate for the constituency. Godfrey Fetherstonhaugh was not a landlord, unlike Archdale, nor was he even from Fermanagh. The scion of a landed family in Mayo, he was a barrister based in Dublin. While Fetherstonhaugh's lack of a local connection may have disadvantaged him in his campaign during the 1906 general election, this was just about offset by the strength of local organization as well as UUC funding. He beat the Russellite Edward Mitchell by only eighty-eight votes.[7]

Fetherstonhaugh was a prominent and committed unionist with a national profile. Belonging to the dogmatic wing of the Unionist Party, he vigorously opposed any compromise on the home rule question. In November 1910 he characterized the choice between home rule or a federal solution for Ireland as being akin to a man on trial choosing between 'whether, if convicted, he would wish to be hanged or beheaded'.[8] Much like Carson, Fetherstonhaugh was keenly aware of his position as a non-Ulsterman leading Ulster in a time of profound crisis. In his speeches, he always took care to establish that, as he was not an Ulsterman, he could only speak for himself and not for Fermanagh as a whole.[9] The UUC also went to great lengths to support him and energize his base given the precarity of the seat in previous elections. Party grandees often lent their presence and vocal support to Fetherstonhaugh at local unionist rallies such as that in Ballinamallard on the anniversary of the siege of Derry in 1906 when James Craig attended and exhorted the crowd to return Fetherstonhaugh 'by a larger majority at the next election'.[10] These exhortations seem to have been successful. In January 1910 Fetherstonhaugh defeated the Liberal Samuel Kerr by 350 votes, a majority he mostly retained in December 1910, when he defeated another Liberal, Arthur Collum, by 347 votes. Both of these challenges to Fetherstonhaugh came from the Russellite Liberal unionist tradition, rather than the IPP. The new, centralized unionist administration in the county can be seen in the remarkable consistency of Fetherstonhaugh's vote. In the two elections in 1910 he polled 53.8 per cent and 53.9 per cent of the vote respectively.

Political violence in Fermanagh often erupted at moments of heightened tension and through the contesting of public spaces by both unionists and nationalists. For this reason, election campaigns pre-1912 (and especially those of 1909/1910) were often characterized by the bad temper and propensity for disorder that would later characterize the revolutionary period. While such disturbances happened in North Fermanagh, where both candidates were unionists (and indeed the Russellites were often excoriated as traitors to their own people), they were far more common and extreme in South Fermanagh, where divisions straddled religious and communal lines. Indeed, when such tensions did emerge in North Fermanagh it was often at events with a significant nationalist presence such as at a meeting in Enniskillen in January 1910 when the presence of Jeremiah Jordan on a platform with the Russelite candidate Samuel Kerr provoked jeers and chants directed against Kerr.[11]

It was into this newly dynamic political context that the British government threw a match. On 11 April 1912 the Liberal government under Herbert Henry Asquith introduced the third home rule bill in the House of Commons. While Unionist opposition to the previous two home rule measures in 1886 and 1893 had largely been a political, elite-led movement, in 1912 a variety of factors made the possibility of Irish self-government more real. First, the Liberal Party was more in favour of Irish home rule than was the case a generation before. Second, the prospect of home rule had become more palatable to the average British voter. Every general election since 1874 had seen Ireland vote in vast numbers for the IPP. For many in England, Ireland had demonstrated its desire for home rule so consistently and for so long as to lay bare the impracticality of British government over the whole island. Third and most importantly, the Parliament Act of 1911 curtailed the veto of the House of Lords – the greatest constitutional barrier against home rule – and replaced it with delaying powers of two years. As a result, home rule could only be delayed until 1914.

During the ensuing crisis, unionists were determined to defeat home rule and nationalists to defend it. The UUC stepped up its efforts to co-ordinate and strengthen resistance to home rule across Ulster by reviving Ulster clubs along with the pre-existing network of Orange lodges. Fermanagh is difficult to characterize in terms of its commitment to these various associative elements of Ulster unionism. It was not a bulwark of Ulster unionism like Tyrone, nor did its leaders display the same initiative and energy that Terence Dooley has identified in Monaghan.[12] Its pattern of behaviour is closest to that described by Pauric Travers in Donegal with unionist engagement driven by strong fraternal organization in place of relatively moribund unionist clubs.[13] David Fitzpatrick calculated that by 1919 just over one-third of the eligible population in Fermanagh were members of the Orange Order – the largest proportion of any Ulster county.[14] However, by contrast, he also noted that participation rates in the Ulster clubs stood at only 14.6 per cent, one of the lowest in the province. Despite a rapid initial growth, by June 1912 just twelve clubs were reported by the Royal Irish Constabulary (RIC). By the end of the year, only 1,404

Fermanagh unionists were said to be members of these clubs.[15] This slow growth was reflected in police reports. In February 1912 John McGuire, RIC County Inspector (CI), noted that the majority of clubs in Fermanagh 'are mostly inactive – there is no connection between them and secret societies and none of them is engaged in crime or disloyalty'.[16] However, the RIC consistently failed to grasp the threat posed by nationalist and unionist political organizations during this period. For the first time, drilling by unionist clubs was reported in July 1912 at Irvinestown, Lack, Drumad and Ardess.[17]

It seems that the strength of the lodges in Fermanagh may have stunted the growth and activity of the clubs, as Orangemen were reluctant to see their leading role in the county supplanted. By mid-1912 unionist newspapers were beginning to note sluggish recruitment for the clubs and the county's leadership had to assure local unionists that the Ulster clubs existed solely for propaganda purposes and not to compete with the Order. The RIC recorded weekly meetings by all clubs from May to September 1912. However, within two months nearly all drilling had ceased.[18] By May 1913 the number of clubs in the county had risen to seventeen but the actual number of members had declined slightly to 1,405.[19] At the same time, the unionist leadership in Fermanagh organized mass political rallies. These had multiple purposes. They not only afforded the party leadership such as Carson and Craig a chance to lend support to local leaders such as Edward Archdale, they also provided an opportunity to strengthen local unionist fervour. Brian Barton has noted that the only spurt in unionist club recruitment in Fermanagh during this period coincided with a visit by Carson to Enniskillen on 18 September 1912. Speakers at these meetings emphasized Protestant isolation in parts of Fermanagh and their subsequent vulnerability to persecution that would intensify were home rule to be granted. At a meeting in Enniskillen in October 1911, William Reid of Boho warned that in his area 'one could look ten miles as the crow flew and a Protestant household was not seen'.[20] The consequences of this isolation were also clear. Protestants in these remote areas were subjected to insults, assault and, most commonly, boycotting. Reid recounted the case of a Protestant farmer stoned to death in Belcoo for giving evidence in a malicious injury claim.[21] Religion and political identity were readily conflated.

These speeches were made with one eye on coverage in Britain. Mindful of appearing as sectarian bigots, tales of Catholic persecution were combined with claims of inter-denominational personal friendship. In most of this rhetoric, the ill-intentioned elements of the community were either faceless or represented by the Catholic clergy. At best, such stories were anecdotal such as the speech by James Dundas of Enniskillen who claimed to have been told by an unnamed nationalist friend of their plans to persecute the town's Protestant shopkeepers following home rule.[22] While many of these speeches served to energize the unionist base, they also had a broader propagandistic purpose. A meeting in Enniskillen town hall on 16 October 1911 attracted about 700 unionist farmers and businessmen. The guests of honour were a number of British election candidates in 1910 on a fact-finding mission to learn what Irish people really thought about home rule. The chair, Edward Archdale, expressed the hope that the visitors would return to England and become 'a fine thorn in the side of the Eighty Club [a London political club associated with the Liberals]'.[23] The meeting was conceived with an English audience in mind and speeches from prominent local unionists uniformly aimed to refute the claims of John Redmond that 'the only people against Home Rule in Ireland were the Orangemen of Ulster, the landlords and their agents in the rest of Ireland'. One visitor was shocked by the strength of feeling at increasingly strident unionist meetings, claiming 'there were knots of men able and determined to die in the last ditch'.[24]

As Fermanagh's unionists ramped up their political organization and engagement, nationalists in the county were surprisingly complacent, though not inactive. Throughout 1912 the UIL and AOH organized numerous rallies in support of the new home rule bill. Despite previous tensions over his nomination as a candidate, Patrick Crumley addressed an AOH meeting of 800 people at Derrylin in January 1912. A few days later another home rule gathering of 200 took place in Roslea.[25] On 31 December 1912 a large torchlight procession marched through Enniskillen to celebrate the victory of Liberal candidate David Cleghorn Hogg in the Derry City by-election.[26] However, the county leadership was content to let Redmond negotiate the passage of the bill with Asquith. In July 1912 the CI remarked with surprise, 'Up [to] the present, very little interest appears to be taken in the Home Rule Bill'.[27] The leadership of Fermanagh nationalism had been more concerned about the death of Jeremiah Jordan in December 1911. Despite defeating Thomas Battersby in January 1910, Jordan, who suffered a stroke in July, decided not to run in the December election.[28] The respect in which he was held was demonstrated by the scale of his funeral which was attended by three IPP MPs and was one of the largest and best attended to pass through Enniskillen.[29] Similarly, the unionist-dominated Enniskillen UDC adjourned for a week after his death.

Jordan left a massive gulf in IPP politics in Fermanagh, one that his successor as MP, Patrick Crumley, proved unable to fill convincingly. Like Jordan, Crumley was a prosperous Enniskillen merchant (a livestock trader and butcher) who had supported the Land League and had extensive local government experience. He had also served as vice-chair of Fermanagh County Council and the Enniskillen Board of Guardians.[30] Crumley did not represent a radical shift in the leadership of the IPP in Fermanagh. He shared Jordan's conservative stance on home rule and like his predecessor was not endorsed by the AOH.[31] Crumley's own term as leader of Fermanagh nationalism dealt little with growing militant unionism. Instead, he followed in the footsteps of his predecessor, eschewing most political issues and concentrating on local politics.

Indeed, Crumley's maiden speech in the House of Commons on 13 February 1911 focused on the poor quality of postal services in Fermanagh.[32] His contributions also reflected his own personal interests as a livestock dealer – in his first year he made speeches about tubercular pigs, swine fever and public health meat inspectors.

While in retrospect this might appear as indolent behaviour on the part of the IPP in Fermanagh, there was good reason to believe that a 'business as usual' policy was the most sensible course for nationalism in the county. After all, the previous twenty years had been extremely successful for the IPP in Fermanagh. They had secured a permanent majority in South Fermanagh, had taken control of many aspects of local government, and were in with a strong chance of reclaiming the county council at the next election. Indeed, in June 1914 they did just that when J.P. Gillin beat James Cooper in the Enniskillen urban division to give the nationalists a majority of one and to place John McHugh, a Belleek farmer, in the chair.

Militant nationalism had been very weak in Fermanagh for decades. The Irish Republican Brotherhood (IRB) became moribund after the retirement of its local leader Edward Madden around 1899. This was compounded by the purging of the old guard in 1908 by the new younger national leadership cohort. By 1914 only William Hegarty, manager of Lipton's shop in Enniskillen, was recorded as active.[33] Despite this, a number of important developments occurred after 1900 that set the stage for the sudden growth in republicanism in the county post-1916.

In November 1902 the first branch of the Gaelic League was founded in Enniskillen, chaired by Fr Patrick McKenna. Cahir Healy (1877–1970), the secretary, became the leading figure in cultural and republican circles in Fermanagh. By 1906 he was also chairman of Fermanagh GAA county board. Healy became the most influential Fermanagh nationalist of the twentieth century and one of the most important northern nationalist leaders during the struggle against partition. Initially a journalist and insurance agent, Healy was a poet and playwright by inclination and through this he became drawn into the burgeoning cultural nationalist movement. Éamon Phoenix has commented on the breadth of Healy's associations from Roger Casement to Alice Stopford Green, from William Butler Yeats to Francis Joseph Bigger. Most of those connections came through his publications in *Shan Van Vocht*, the nationalist literary magazine, and his membership of Bigger's informal literary circle – 'Ard Righ'.[34] Healy's role as leader of both the GAA and Gaelic League in Fermanagh further immersed him in the cadre of revivalists and nationalists who would later constitute the backbone of the republican movement. In 1906 Healy invited Patrick Pearse to address the Fermanagh feis.

Healy was a founder member of Arthur Griffith's Sinn Féin (SF) in 1905 but was unconvinced by Griffith's dual monarchy policy. He was particularly pleased to have found a national separatist cause to support that existed outside the aegis of the IPP, which he found objectionable due to the growing influence of the 'sectarian' AOH.[35] Michael Laffan has described how in most counties the initial growth of SF depended on the work of a leading organizer and Healy fulfilled this role for Fermanagh.[36] As with the Gaelic League and GAA before, Healy played a leading part in the organization of SF in Fermanagh and in Charles Dolan's election campaign for the party in North Leitrim in 1908. Healy's work led to the Enniskillen branch of the new party being one of the most vocal and radical in the country. By 1910 Healy held no significant political office in Fermanagh but had become a vocal critic of both unionism and the IPP establishment within the county. Despite this position, his connections to the world of advanced republicanism were, at this point, minimal. He did not appear to have been a member of the IRB (despite being investigated by the RIC after 1916), nor was he involved in any of the northern chapters of the Easter Rising (although he admired the 'martyrdom' of Pearse).[37] However, during the early years of the 1910s this threat still seemed relatively minor. Among the more mainstream political organizations, the CI reported that the primary activity of the UIL throughout 1912 was the collection of money for an anticipated future general election.[38] The growth in unionist clubs was not overly alarming relative to the strength of nationalist organizations in Fermanagh. Both the AOH and UIL had far larger membership pools than even the Orange Order. The Ulster clubs, with their documented recruitment struggles, were not an obvious threat.

While the home rule crisis was initially a struggle for the fate of the entirety of Ireland, sudden political shifts would propel to national importance the fates of Fermanagh and Tyrone specifically. When the partition of Ireland was first proposed in June 1912 by Thomas Agar-Robartes, a backbench Liberal MP from Cornwall, a four-county Ulster state was envisaged, comprising counties with a Protestant unionist majority. This was rejected out of hand by most politicians, although the only reservation Carson expressed was an unwillingness to leave behind Fermanagh and Tyrone. Cavan, Monaghan and Donegal were not considered.[39] However, in September 1912 the situation changed significantly with the signing of the Ulster Solemn League and Covenant. The Covenant transformed not only the militancy of unionist opposition to home rule but also the very basis for that opposition. A binding oath, it committed its signatories to resist the imposition of home rule in Ulster as a whole. The Covenant had been preceded by a week of rallies and speeches across the province – the so-called Ulster Campaign in which Fermanagh played a key role. The campaign was launched by Carson in Enniskillen on 18 September. The choice of Fermanagh reflected both the county's importance to the unionist cause as the 'Outpost of Ulster' and Carson's own commitment to resist home rule in as large a portion of Ulster as possible.

The event demonstrated the importance of unionist pageantry and symbolism. The Enniskillen Horse had been established specifically for the day to provide a guard of honour for Carson. Great effort was invested by the horsemen to make authentic riding formations and significant time was devoted to drilling exercises.[40] The company also included more ostentatious elements such as a standard-bearer and trumpeter. Enniskillen was festooned with Union Jacks, bunting and banners bearing unionist slogans. The route taken by the procession was circuitous and designed for maximum spectacle. Carson stayed in Crom Castle, near Newtownbutler, as the guest of the earl of Erne and the two men were taken by car to the outskirts of the town before getting into a horse-drawn carriage. From there they were met by the Horse, which escorted them into the town where the main body of the marchers joined.[41] The key speeches took place at Portora Hill on the outskirts of Enniskillen, where Carson was joined by Lord Hugh Cecil, Conservative MP for Oxford University, and James Craig, future prime minister of Northern Ireland.[42]

The public meeting had a far wider scope and audience than just Fermanagh unionism. Local loyalists were bolstered by a large influx from surrounding counties. Fourteen special trains were laid on. The marchers were organized on a county basis in the following order: Fermanagh, Cavan, Donegal, Leitrim, Monaghan, Sligo and Tyrone. This seemed to have been done to give prominence to unionists from peripheral areas. CI McGuire estimated that 20,000 attended, although his only further comment on the event was relief that it had 'passed off peacefully'.[43] North Fermanagh MP Godfrey Fetherstonhaugh passed the key resolution opposing home rule. Carson was cheered for over a minute before he could speak. His speech marked an intensification of unionist rhetoric and he envisaged 'no means too strong for the people of Ulster to take' to oppose home rule.[44]

The campaign initiated by this rally culminated on Ulster Day, 28 September 1912, when 8,219 men signed the Ulster Covenant and 6,884 women signed the accompanying women's Declaration in Fermanagh. Fermanagh unionists signed in great numbers with eighty-five per cent of the eligible male population and seventy-four per cent of the eligible female population doing so. Fermanagh had one of the highest participation rates in Ulster, only behind Armagh and Tyrone. Significantly, those counties with the most even Protestant-Catholic populations – Armagh, Tyrone, Fermanagh, Derry and Monaghan – participated in the largest numbers, with all participation rates above eighty per cent. The Ulster average was seventy-seven per cent.[45] By contrast, the average in the Ulster heartland of Antrim and Down was only sixty-five per cent. This suggests that the constant political struggle had led to internal organizational structures in Fermanagh that effectively compelled local unionists to sign.

The list of signing agents also demonstrates where much of the organizational impetus came from. Lords Erne, Cole and Belmore were noticeably absent. However, the lesser aristocracy and other unionist grandees made up a significant proportion of the agents. Edward Archdale, John Porter-

Porter, Basil Brooke and G.V. Irvine featured prominently, while the county secretary Charles Falls personally registered one-tenth of all signatories in Fermanagh. Godfrey Fetherstonhaugh was unable to sign as he was not an Ulsterman. Whether he felt aggrieved that Carson, who was from Dublin, could sign was not recorded.

This enthusiasm, however, did not carry over to the women's Declaration. Only three-quarters of Fermanagh women signed, a figure far below Armagh, Tyrone and Monaghan. This may reflect the strongly patriarchal nature of unionism in Fermanagh. The UWUC had a much weaker presence in Fermanagh than it did in surrounding counties. For the first twenty years of the organization's existence, no Fermanagh woman held office.[46] The first Fermanagh branch had been established only in April 1911.[47] In most counties where uptake of the women's Declaration was strong, prominent local organizers, generally aristocratic, shared in the campaign with men. Travers has identified the strong signing rate of Donegal women and noted the influence of a number of indefatigable local organizers as well as the attention given to them on the campaign trail.[48] Similarly, Adrian Grant has noted the prominence of the UWUC who escorted Carson through Derry city on his visit there.[49] No such privilege was accorded to the Fermanagh UWUC and anti-home rule rallies were dominated by male speakers. It is also possible that the UWUC's ambivalent position on key issues such as suffrage had damaged its standing among women in the county.

One might have expected North Fermanagh with its Unionist MP and more concentrated unionist population to have outperformed South Fermanagh but the difference was relatively slight. In North Fermanagh 8,448 men and women – about seventy-eight per cent of the eligible adult population – signed.[50] In South Fermanagh, the 6,245 signatories represented three-quarters of the eligible population. At least in broad strokes, areas with a larger nationalist population did not necessarily perform any better when it came to the Covenant and the Declaration. However, this can be broken down to a more granular level as each constituency was further subdivided into districts in which the actual signing events were organized. Fermanagh's border with Donegal and Cavan – the districts of Florencecourt, Belleek and Holywell – all saw less than half of the eligible population sign. The same was true for other districts with low participation rates such as Tempo and Maguiresbridge – neither was devoid of unionist communities but it seems that unionists in those areas signed in Enniskillen rather than locally. Roslea and Derrylin, near County Monaghan, saw higher participation rates probably due to a combination of unionists coming from Monaghan and the difficulty of travelling to Enniskillen.[51]

Overall, areas near the Tyrone border with the strongest unionist populations – Ederney, Clonelly, Brookeborough and Irvinestown (although the numbers in Irvinestown and Ederney were inflated by signatories from Donegal and Tyrone)

– witnessed the highest participation rate. Clearly, while Fermanagh unionists were willing to commit to the defence of Ulster, they were still conscious about being seen to have done so. Places of signing also reflected this. Sites of loyalist and Protestant power – Orange halls, Presbyterian churches and the estates of the landed gentry – were the primary sites of signing, as well as within people's own homes. Anglicans, Methodists and Presbyterians were all equally likely to sign. In terms of occupation, farmers were overrepresented in the Covenant while general labourers and domestic servants were underrepresented when compared with the census. Covenant signatories tended to be older with the average age being 43.7 for women and 44.3 for men.

Unlike Derry or Tyrone, Fermanagh unionists did not organize against the Covenant, nor are there any records of Fermanagh unionists speaking out against the Covenant.[52] This may reflect the strength of commitment among Fermanagh unionists to resist home rule, but it seems more likely this was a consequence of their isolated position. This new reformed unionist establishment would not risk the internal divisions of the previous century at a time when their minority status was most clearly in focus.

The scale of Ulster Day did not seem to perturb Fermanagh's nationalist leadership. No rally in response to Carson's meeting in Enniskillen was held and the following month the CI deemed the different nationalist societies 'inactive'. He commented on the passivity of the leadership which was 'watching closely the progress of the Home Rule Bill'.[53] The *Ulster Herald* denounced the Covenant as a 'blasphemous farce' and it focused on the use of a religious oath to oppose home rule rather than any perceived threat posed by the Covenant.[54]

The signing of the Covenant sparked a significant surge in unionist activity in the county. In October 1912 the RIC reported only one instance of twenty people drilling (compared with twenty-nine instances in Tyrone and eighteen in Cavan). On 26 December 330 members of the Enniskillen Horse paraded through the town.[55] By February 1913 regular drilling was conducted by all unionist clubs in Fermanagh.[56] Drilling had an important symbolic and performative purpose – to demonstrate Ulster (and Fermanagh's) willingness to oppose home rule militarily. On the third reading of the home rule bill in late January 1913, all unionist clubs were ordered to drill at full strength.[57]

The symbolic commitment to military resistance in Ulster became more real with the foundation of the UVF. While it was officially established by Carson and the UUC in January 1913, the UVF was built on pre-existing local militia that had been organized and drilled on the initiative of local Orange lodges and Ulster clubs. Ulster and Fermanagh, in particular, had a long-standing 'Protestant volunteering tradition' that manifested itself in response to political tensions, such as during the Land War in the 1880s.[58] Even the relatively peaceful 1890s had seen sporadic drilling across Fermanagh organized by G.J. Irvine, a local landlord.[59] As early as 1911, there were reports of some lodges aiming to arm for mass demonstrations, putting themselves in a halfway house between traditional mass rallies and paramilitary drilling.[60] However, as Alvin Jackson argues, the true significance of the UVF did not lie exclusively in its military aspirations and the danger it posed to peace on the island. Rather, the true power of the UVF lay 'in terms of popular culture and mass politicization'.[61]

In Fermanagh three battalions were duly established in Crom (the estate of the earl of Erne), Enniskillen and Irvinestown. The UUC planned for the UVF to number 100,000 men who had signed the Covenant with each county contributing proportionally to that total. For Fermanagh this meant that their county battalions were expected to have 3,000 men. But recruitment was slow. By mid-1913 only about 1,200 of the roughly 6,000 eligible men in Fermanagh had enlisted in the UVF.[62] By the start of 1914 Fermanagh was performing respectably, if not exceptionally, with approximately thirty per cent of the eligible male population signing up. This compared to forty-six per cent in Tyrone and exceeded the participation rates of twenty-five per cent in Down and Antrim.[63]

Barton has suggested that the landed unionist leadership's initial failure to support the organization of the UVF and Ulster clubs may have contributed to their relative weakness when compared to the Orange Order. At first, the Coles, Ernes and Crichtons all refused to help.[64] The *Fermanagh Times*, the organ of establishment unionism, was also vocal in opposing UVF drilling.[65] This was partially informed by doubt over the efficacy of military opposition to the British army but, more generally, it was driven by the desire of Fermanagh's landed grandees to delay their public opposition to the British government until it was absolutely necessary. Crichton, Cole and Erne may all have declined to assume an early role in the UVF but they permitted drilling on their estates from early 1913. The main impetus for promoting the UVF in Fermanagh came from what Barton termed 'the upper squierarchy' – the Archdales, Irvines, Porter-Porters and Brookes. It was only in late 1913, when the movement was too large to be ignored any longer, that the county's earls were drawn in.[66]

This hesitancy in certain parts of Fermanagh is partly explained by the relatively even religious distribution and the ever present need for the community to manage the potential reaction of their nationalist neighbours. The CI noted in April 1913 'a tendency to hold back until it is seen how far the movement is a success elsewhere', but believed the UVF would be successful given its popularity with the Orange lodges.[67] In neighbouring Cavan, local UVF chief Colonel Oliver Nugent actively attempted to downplay the military aspects of the UVF to assuage nationalist suspicions.[68] Similarly, in Fermanagh drilling and unionist organization tended to take place in areas with significant Protestant population such as Enniskillen or in localities with a Protestant majority such as the Crom estate. There was a disconnect between the sluggish initial recruitment to the UVF in Fermanagh and the marked enthusiasm for other militia units elsewhere in the county. Both Enniskillen and Crom saw some of the earliest organized militias in the province in 1912. At the same time, however, the *Times* correspondent following Carson in 1912 noted a marked difference in enthusiasm between the working men of Lisburn and the rural labourers of Enniskillen, with the former impressing him more.[69]

The Enniskillen Horse became one of the largest and most active pre-UVF unionist militias. Although initially an independent entity under its own local leaders, the Horse was subsumed into the UVF along with various other groups in January 1913. The Enniskillen Horse easily predated the first recorded mention of the term UVF at a meeting of the Bangor unionist club in December 1912.[70] In September 1912 it already had a strong local core of members and after the foundation of the UVF it constituted the largest single unit within the force.[71] The pageantry of its formation meant that from the outset, loyalist organization in Ulster was as much about 'the marketing of unionism' as it was about its military defence.[72] Even after Carson's initial visit, its founder, William Copeland Trimble, was extremely aware of how the Horse was portrayed in the press and often demanded full turnout at drills when he suspected journalists would be present.[73] That the Horse had been founded initially for propaganda rather than military purposes can be seen in the readiness to promote anyone with a service record to leadership positions. Robert Abraham, who served in the Royal Dragoons, and Robert Wylie, William Bracken and Humphrey Boyd, who had been in the Northern Irish Horse, were all appointed commanders. The commander of the Glenawley Troop, Francis Carson, was a pensioner from the South African Constabulary. George Achingham, a Household Cavalry Life Guards veteran, was paid a salary by the UUC to drill the unit.

Despite these efforts, the fundamental military weakness of the unit was obvious. At a rally in Enniskillen on 10 October 1913, CI McGuire noted that only eighteen attendees out of 205 had guns. Nearly twice this number (primarily the band and various orderlies) were unarmed. The majority of the group (141) held lances, which had greater symbolic than military power. As with other branches of the UVF, the Enniskillen Horse's military pretentions invited scrutiny by the RIC, although this manifested itself as passive observation. At the same October rally, McGuire estimated 205 attendees, of which 170 were either farmers or the sons of farmers.[74] Membership of the Horse was a mix of small and large farmers and labourers. Notably, there were no Archdales, Coles, Brookes or Irvines on the membership lists. The Horse, in common with the profile of the UVF elsewhere, was an endeavour led by the middle class. The average age of members was around thirty; about half were younger. The youngest was 15-year-old James Moore of Mullaghmeen, another fourteen members were also teenagers while 60-year-old William Trimble was the oldest.

The UVF, therefore, was surprisingly limited in its early days in Fermanagh but gained momentum owing to a number of related factors. As 1913 progressed, the need for a military response to home rule became ever more pronounced.

This encouraged recruitment as well as participation of the local grandees. Lord Cole, for example, established his own training camps at Florencecourt and began to attend parades of the Enniskillen Horse. Cole's engagement aided recruitment generally but also prompted other members of the 'better class of the unionist persuasion' to take part.[75] In October 1913 the CI noted a marked increase in the level of unionist drilling.[76] Between November 1913 and March 1914, UVF membership rose from 2,159 to 2,920. This proportional increase of 35 per cent was the largest in the province.[77] Throughout this period the various battalions and the Enniskillen Horse continued to drill and parade. In July 1913 it was estimated that 1,246 unionists had been drilling but, to the relief of the CI, most were unarmed.[78]

In August 1913 the UUC assigned Jack Sears, a retired NCO, to be the county inspector of the Fermanagh UVF. An estimated 5,000 people and thirty-nine bands attended a demonstration in Enniskillen on 18 August to welcome him. Fetherstonhaugh and Trimble both made speeches before the party decamped to Drumard where the assembled county UVF battalions were put through a series of drill and signalling exercises.[79] Sears immediately began a tour of each club and company in the county 'to get the Protestant men of the county to take a greater interest in drill now that the dark season is drawing near'.[80]

Despite the presence of a county inspector, the corps struggled with its training. Drilling was 'more for demonstration work than actual warfare', especially for the benefit of political allies from England.[81] The Enniskillen Battalion was still not officered by October 1913. In response to these issues, a military camp was held at Crom Castle in early November 1913 for the training of officers; another was organized for February at Knockballymore, a vacant house of the earl of Erne.[82] Sears also sought to adapt the organization to Fermanagh's agricultural life. Traditionally, attendance at unionist drilling dropped off in spring when there was more farm work to do. In an effort to test proficiency, Sears began to visit each company. Those deemed satisfactory received a certificate of proficiency that exempted them from attending drills during spring farming season.[83]

Despite recognition of their 'keen interest in the Ulster movement', women were not directly involved in the UVF itself.[84] There were no attempts to mobilize female unionists into something like Cumann na mBan, although they were occasionally employed as dispatch riders on horseback.[85] Rather, unionist women were primarily employed in support services. In July 1914 Henry Brown Morrell, the new RCI, noted that nursing and ambulance classes for women had been held across the county with the intention of converting a vacant residence near Lisbellaw into a UVF hospital.[86] Constance Bloomfield, originally from Castle Caldwell near Enniskillen, was central to the founding of the Ulster Aid Ambulance Corps in England. This corps was designed to support the UVF should hostilities break out in Ulster. Bloomfield turned the corps over to Lady Londonderry, chair of the Ulster Women's Association, in March 1914. In her speech of thanks, Lady Londonderry noted 'there was hardly one unionist woman in Ulster who was not connected with a base hospital, a clearance hospital or a detachment'.[87]

By mid-1914, the three Fermanagh battalions had reached their maximum membership of 3,000. However, the weakness of Fermanagh within the broader UVF movement was reflected in the number of arms allocated to the county just before the Larne gun-running of April 1914. Fermanagh had only 183 rifles or one for every fourteen volunteers. This was by far the lowest across the province.[88] In contrast, counties with smaller unionist populations such as Cavan, Monaghan and Donegal held 2,676, 2,070 and 3,099 arms respectively.[89] Travers and Dooley have demonstrated how Donegal and Monaghan benefitted from a systematic campaign by the UVF to arm loyalists on the fringes of Ulster. Such efforts were absent in Fermanagh.[90] Most of the UVF weapons in the county had been smuggled in by Revd William Stack via Bundoran and taken to Irvinestown and Kesh by small boats.[91] Despite their lack of arms, the size of the UVF in Fermanagh made it a major threat. On Easter Monday 1914, 1,800 members of the UVF from Enniskillen, Crom Castle, Kesh and the Enniskillen Horse paraded at Enniskillen and in Ballinamallard. While they had no weapons, the men proudly displayed their new haversacks, belts, bandoliers and water bottles. The Enniskillen Horse also bore new blue capes.[92] The previous month, a similar UVF gathering had marched en masse through Tempo to divine service. They too were growing more proficient. By March 1914 the county leadership was able to call up Volunteers at two days' notice and post them on duty to Belfast. For this they were given 30s. a week and travelling expenses.[93]

The establishment of the UVF in Fermanagh placed the nationalist community at a severe disadvantage. They would be unable to defend themselves in the event of conflict over home rule. They also feared that their voices would carry less weight in Westminster if they remained unarmed. Despite this, nationalists in Fermanagh and across Ireland were remarkably slow to react to the new questions posed by the UVF. In April 1913 the CI suggested that most nationalists 'profess to regard it all as a mere bluff and have no apprehension of any future danger'.[94]

A belated nationalist response came in November 1913 with the establishment of the Irish Volunteers in Dublin. The IPP leadership was reluctant to antagonize British opinion in the manner that the Ulster unionists were willing to. This was partly in the hope that the Ulster unionist movement would discredit itself through its armed opposition to the government and partly due to suspicion that any armed nationalist militia in Ireland would inevitably be dominated by advanced, physical-force nationalists such as the IRB. On the first point, the IPP leadership was misguided but on the second it was surprisingly prescient. In fact, the IRB had been laying the groundwork for a nationalist counterpoint to the UVF for a long time. As early as 1912, Cathal Kickham and Bulmer Hobson had been agitating for the IRB to establish its own army.[95] While they could not do this openly themselves, it was hoped that the rising tensions in Ireland would provide them with a respectable front that they could organize behind. An opportunity arose in November 1913 when Eoin MacNeill, a UCD professor of early and medieval history, published an article 'The North began' in the Gaelic League paper *An Claidheamh Soluis*. MacNeill called for a nationalist response to the UVF. On 11 November 1913 a conference in Wynn's Hotel, Dublin, established the Irish Volunteers as a body 'to secure and maintain the common rights and liberties of Irishmen'.[96]

A branch of the Irish Volunteers was quickly established in Fermanagh. In January 1914 a large nationalist rally was held at which a county committee was organized with Joe Gillin appointed secretary. The county was divided into eight battalions: (1) Enniskillen, Boho, Carrigans, Cavanacross and Coa; (2) Newtownbutler, Currin and Lisnaskea; (3) Coonian, Brookeborough, Maguiresbridge and Tempo; (4) Aghadrumsee and Roslea; (5) Roslea; (6) Cleenish, Kinawley and Killesher; (7) Garrison, Belleek, Monea and Derrygonnelly; (8) Kesh, Ederney, Irvinestown and Pettigo.[97] The most active of these battalions in the early days was Belleek which the RIC had observed drilling in February. The CI also noted that enrolment was strongest in the north-west of the county, along the border with Donegal and Leitrim.[98]

The Enniskillen Battalion had approximately 300 members, the majority of whom could be reliably called upon for surprise drills and other marches. The battalion was subdivided into three companies, A, B and C. Despite the role of the IRB in organizing the Volunteers on a national scale, in Fermanagh the movement was strongly under the thumb of establishment nationalism. The influence of the IPP was demonstrated in the choice of adjutant for the Enniskillen Battalion – John Wray, a solicitor's apprentice and son of John Francis Wray, one of Fermanagh's prominent party members.[99] The battalion was eventually equipped with 100 rifles and bayonets but no ammunition. The weapons were kept in the furniture store of secretary J.P. Gillin, a prominent publican and later chair of Enniskillen UDC. Gillin was also a member of the IPP and one of the leading figures in the local AOH. In Lisnaskea, Thomas Gavin JP and a member of Fermanagh County Council was the leading figure. In Enniskillen, the men were drilled by Bernard Keenan, a former infantry sergeant, who was regarded as a competent leader. Drilling focused on field training, officer instruction and marching.[100]

Despite initial misgivings among some nationalists that the Irish Volunteers would only 'embitter the present situation in Ulster', recruitment was strong in Fermanagh. It was spurred on by the combination of a sizable Catholic population and an immediate and active UVF enemy.[101] By September 1914 twenty-eight companies existed with 3,933 members. The membership was larger than the Fermanagh UVF although this was partially because the UVF had stopped recruiting after reaching its 'quota' of 3,000 members.[102] In terms of the proportion of Catholic males volunteering, Fermanagh was among the most enthusiastic counties in Ireland. In Ulster, only Derry had a higher proportional participation in the Irish Volunteers.[103] The Irish Volunteers appealed to the same type of person as the UVF: 'in the country labourers and sons of farmers, and in town shop assistants and men of the labouring class'.[104] Despite this, the RIC noted that organization was relatively chaotic compared to the UVF. As late as July 1914, while the UVF were described as being 'well if not completely supplied with arms' and were beginning long-range rifle training, the Irish Volunteers were said to be 'deficient in organization and have no arms beyond what is owned privately ... they have no prominent leaders in this county'.[105]

For many who joined the Volunteers, the presence and size of the UVF was their primary concern. Francis O'Duffy (Proinnsias Ó Dubhthaigh), a Volunteer captain and teacher in St Michael's Intermediate School in Enniskillen, noted that 'large numbers joined who had no aim or motive beyond opposition to the Ulster Volunteers'.[106] Nicolas Smyth, who lived over the Tyrone border in Rakeerinbeg, recalled 'the object of the Volunteers in 1914 was to oppose and, if necessary, fight Carson's Ulster Volunteers'.[107] John Connolly of Roslea remembered being pressured by his father to join, despite being only fourteen.[108] For their part, the RIC believed that the Irish Volunteers would not have seen much uptake in the county if the UVF had not armed itself.[109] This observation came in May 1914, one month after the Larne gun-running when the UVF had smuggled about 25,000 rifles into Ulster. That event sparked a crisis in nationalism in Ireland generally but particularly in Fermanagh where nationalists now found themselves facing an enemy, equal in size and far better armed.

In summer 1914 Fermanagh had two large militia groups in direct opposition to one another. In May the CI described the tense situation as 'one of preparation and expectancy ... both sides may be said to be watching each other'.[110] When nationalists took control of Fermanagh County Council in June, serious violence erupted between nationalists and unionists and the police had to be called in. Within the militias, however, discipline held. Leaders of both groups had no interest in the immediate outbreak of violence and took steps to avoid antagonizing the other. To avoid provocation, neither party organized demonstrations after the passage of the third home rule bill through the House of Lords. On 27 May the captains of the Enniskillen battalions of the UVF and the Irish Volunteers met with the RIC to ensure that their planned drilling that night did not coincide.[111]

The IRB did not have a strong presence in Fermanagh at the time. The most prominent member of the society from Fermanagh was George Irvine who sat on the Leinster Council and was the centre of the Clarence Mangan circle.

However, Irvine did not play a part in the organization in Fermanagh itself and
had joined in Dublin after moving there to study at Trinity College.[112] For many
involved in advanced nationalist politics in Fermanagh before 1916, the Gaelic
League provided the initial gateway into that world. Francis O'Duffy, who later
commanded an IRA company in the War of Independence, noted that he became
a member of SF due to the influence of a young Gaelic Leaguer named Fintan
Ó Faoláin.[113] Similarly, Irvine was approached to join the IRB through the Gaelic
League.[114] However, by 1914 none of the men who would become prominent
leaders of the Fermanagh IRA were in the IRB.

As the battle over the home rule bill in Westminster dragged on and the
possibility of armed conflict in Ireland became more likely, John Redmond was
put under increasing pressure to give some form of concession to Ulster
unionists. By the close of 1913 it was apparent that the only way to ensure a
peaceful implementation of home rule was the exclusion of some part of Ulster
from it. David Lloyd George, then chancellor of the exchequer, proposed a
number of compromises to Carson and Redmond. Of these, one quickly gained
prominence and would form the basis for most negotiations between the two
factions from February 1914 onwards. Under the proposal, individual Ulster
counties would be able to vote to exclude themselves temporarily from home
rule. Asquith's government deliberately kept the terms of such an arrangement
vague as regards the nature of the temporary exclusion or how such plebiscites
would be arranged. This would have profound consequences for Ulster in
general and Fermanagh in particular. These terms guaranteed a four-county
unionist exclusion but the fate of Fermanagh and Tyrone was more ambiguous.
The proposals prompted internal unionist discussion about the feasibility of a
six versus a nine-county Ulster unionism. From this point forward, the UUC
distanced itself from Cavan, Monaghan and Donegal while simultaneously
strongly committing to Tyrone and Fermanagh.

Despite the Fermanagh nationalist establishment's faith in Redmond to
deliver an all-Ireland home rule, he was under considerable pressure to accept
Lloyd George's compromise. In March Redmond indicated that he would agree
to the scheme if the UUC consented to it and gave a further concession by
accepting an exclusion term of six years instead of three. However, details of the
plan leaked and it was dismissed out of hand by the opposition in the House of
Commons. While this news precipitated mass outrage on both sides in
Monaghan and Donegal, in Fermanagh the news was received more placidly.[115]
Neither side organized significant demonstrations in protest and the local
nationalist leadership appeared content to continue to keep the faith in
Redmond.

On 25 May 1914, with no agreement between Redmond and Carson, the
home rule bill was read in the House of Commons for the third time and carried.
In June a version of the bill was introduced in the House of Lords that allowed

for a nine-county Ulster to opt out of home rule temporarily. This provision was utterly unacceptable to Redmond and was modified by the Lords to exclude Ulster permanently instead. In response, the government allowed it to lapse. With both sides seemingly unable to reach a compromise, King George V called a conference in the hope that nationalists and unionists would hammer out a solution. Redmond remained wedded to the principle of county plebiscites while Carson insisted on a six-county exclusion. In essence, Fermanagh and Tyrone had become the key sticking point. Neither Redmond nor Carson were willing to abandon the counties. After three days with no solution in sight, the conference broke down.

At this point it appeared as if Ireland was destined to succumb to armed conflict. Both nationalists and unionists had developed highly motivated, militia groups determined to either enforce or resist home rule. National political leaders seemed unable to reach a compromise but the government was obliged to introduce a home rule bill that year. Ultimately, however, the assassination of an Austrian in Sarajevo and the outbreak of the First World War rendered these considerations moot.

Fermanagh unionism and nationalism in 1914 were greatly changed from the relatively amiable and staid entities they had been as late as 1910. On the nationalist side, the inactivity and relative complacency shown by the county's leadership were not atypical of the period. However, the slow reaction to unionist mobilization was replicated a few years later in a similarly slow response to the rise of Sinn Féin. The IPP's failure to grasp the strength of people's fear of and antipathy towards Ulster unionism would damage their electoral prospects for years to come. Fermanagh's engagement with the new, more militant Ulster unionism was mostly typical of what occurred elsewhere in Ulster. Yet, the precarity of the county's place in any future partition settlement had strengthened the resolve of those within Fermanagh unionism to resist. The county made some important contributions to the cause of Ulster unionism, notably through the Enniskillen Horse. Significantly, Edward Carson's decision to launch Ulster Day from Enniskillen bound Fermanagh and Tyrone irrevocably to the cause of Ulster unionism. If there was to be a partition settlement, it would at least be a six-county one.

3 'Bury the hatchet and take up the rifle': the First World War, 1914–16

Ironically, the outbreak of the First World War led to some of the most peaceable conditions in Fermanagh in decades. Taken exclusively in the county context, the years 1914–16 appear as a short respite between two periods of extreme political tension. The war immediately removed the threatened outbreak of violence as both nationalists and unionists committed themselves to the war effort. Indeed, the conflict nearly killed both unionist and nationalist forms of Volunteers as political organizing in Fermanagh fell into almost complete abeyance. Recruitment presented both communities with an opportunity to share a podium, something not subsequently repeated for decades. Despite unionist whispers about the commitment of nationalists to the British war effort, both communities performed creditably in terms of enlistment and home front activities, many of which were organized by women. Significantly, the war also led to the growth of a small, advanced nationalist contingent in the county.

Almost immediately after the British declaration of war on 4 August 1914, political tensions in Fermanagh abated. CI Brown Morrell observed that 'from the outbreak of war a better condition of affairs prevailed during the remainder of the year'.[1] This was primarily due to the decision of John Redmond and the IPP leadership to rally behind the British cause and encouragement of all eligible Irish Volunteers to enlist. From Redmond's perspective, supporting the war effort was crucial to securing the rapid and partition-free implementation of home rule. He feared that if the nationalists showed anything less than fulsome support for the war, they would be outmanoeuvred by Ulster unionists when it came to negotiating with the British government. Home rule was placed on the statute book on 18 September 1914 but was immediately suspended for the duration of the war and accompanied by an unspecified provision for the special treatment of Ulster. Redmond's support for the war split the Irish Volunteers. A minority retained the name and seceded, whereas the pro-Redmondite majority became known as the National Volunteers.

On the unionist side, active operations against home rule ceased and members of the UVF were encouraged to enlist.[2] Carson and Craig had met with the secretary of state for war, Lord Kitchener, shortly after the outbreak of war to place the UVF at the service of the British army. They promised Kitchener 35,000 recruits. In October 1914 the 36th Ulster Division was established and based on the organizational structure of the UVF.[3] Timothy Bowman has highlighted the fact that the most fervent UVF members who enlisted in August and September were consequently never deployed to the Ulster Division. Many served instead with the Royal Irish Rifles. This was also the case for army reservists who had supplied many UVF officers and drill instructors.[4]

Fermanagh was within the 27th (Omagh) regimental recruiting area – that of the Royal Inniskilling Fusiliers.[5] Fermanagh men were to comprise the 11th Battalion.[6] Initial enthusiasm seemed high, especially among the UVF. For example, in September it was reported that almost all eligible members (excluding those too young or old) of the Enniskillen company volunteered for unconditional service.[7] Also that month 140 men from the 3rd Battalion enlisted.[8] On 9 September 1914, 120 UVF recruits became the first section from Fermanagh to depart for Finner camp in Donegal – the regional recruitment centre of the Royal Inniskilling Fusiliers. Before their departure they were addressed at Enniskillen barracks by Canon Webb, the local Anglican curate, who gave advice on life in an army camp. They were given a guard of honour and accompanied by the Mullaghy Orange Band as they left the town.[9] An effort was made to transfer UVF command structures intact. The 11th Inniskillings, for example, were commanded by Charles Falls and contained all the men who had served under him in the UVF.[10] Similarly, Copeland Trimble and the Enniskillen Horse looked to associate themselves with the 6th Inniskilling Dragoons, which drew over half its membership from Fermanagh. A number of members of the Horse joined the Dragoons itself. Denied military rank within the Dragoons, an infuriated Trimble complained directly to Carson.[11] Bowman has highlighted that Falls was only commissioned as a second lieutenant despite being a battalion commanding officer in the UVF. Prominence in the UVF did not directly translate into high military rank.[12]

War recruitment offered the aristocracy a chance to return to their position as leaders of unionism in Fermanagh. Archdale, whose four sons had enlisted, was particularly prominent in hosting recruiting events. Numerous 'recruiting marches' were organized across the county. In these, enlistees would march, accompanied by their band (normally with instruments loaned by local Orange lodges), through the towns in the county where they would be entertained and establish hiring fairs for the duration of their visit. The men would stay either in local parochial and Orange halls or with friends.[13] In Fermanagh, the most prominent of these was the 11th Inniskillings. Under Falls, 210 men left Finner camp on 7 November 1914 and visited Irvinestown, Enniskillen, Lisbellaw, Lisnaskea, Tempo, and Maguiresbridge before finishing in Clones ten days later. The march yielded nearly 100 recruits.[14] They were hosted by Lord and Lady Erne at Crom Castle. In Lisbellaw they were greeted by Archdale as well as Brigadier-General T.E. Hickman, commander of the 109th Brigade of the 36th (Ulster) Division.[15]

By contrast, the nationalist leadership was again slow to react to changing circumstances. In August 1914 the CI believed they stood aloof due to uncertainty about home rule.[16] He also noted that most prominent nationalist leaders in Fermanagh were reluctant to come out publicly in favour of the war. Addressing a meeting on 4 October, Crumley encouraged nationalists to 'bury the hatchet and take up the rifle' but that was his only engagement with the campaign for the entire month.[17] By this time, the *Impartial Reporter* and *Fermanagh Times* had begun to comment on nationalist reluctance to enlist. Throughout this period, various Volunteer branches continued to drill.[18] David Fitzpatrick has highlighted that in Ulster recruitment among nationalists did not peak until 1915 when the local IPP swung behind it.[19]

The tight grip of the IPP leadership on the nationalist community in Fermanagh can be seen in the strength of support for Redmond. Nearly all branches of the Volunteers voted to become National Volunteers, although for many this decision was not finalized until nearly 1915. The Boho company voted by twenty-five votes to ten to stay neutral in the conflict. When this proved impossible, they dissolved themselves.[20] Francis O'Duffy attributed the slowness of the Fermanagh Volunteers to choose a side in the split to local jealousies between the AOH and UIL.[21] The strongest opposition came in Enniskillen where a quarter of the town's battalion resigned, as well as the company at Carrigans.[22] Following the split, James Rogers of Mullinawina near Blacklion was nominated by Colonel Maurice Moore, inspector general, to organize the National Volunteers in Fermanagh.[23]

The most prominent nationalist supporter of the war in Fermanagh was John Francis Wray, an Enniskillen solicitor and member of the UDC. At O'Neill GAA club in Enniskillen on 30 August 1914, he warned of the threat of German invasion.[24] At Monea in September, Wray declared it 'the duty of every young man to shoulder his rifle and join the Volunteers' as 'the National Army of Ireland'.[25] Wray's son John P., Enniskillen Battalion adjutant, was granted a commission in the Connaught Rangers. It was later alleged that he had 'bought it' with recruits to the army, which the CI put at sixty-seven.[26] The troop left Enniskillen on 18 November to join the Connaught Rangers in Fermoy, the training centre of the 16th (Irish) Division.[27] By the end of the year, the RIC reported that nationalists and unionists were enlisting in roughly even numbers.[28] The National Volunteers were primarily linked to the 7th and 8th battalions of the Royal Inniskilling Fusiliers which were part of the 16th Division. In some cases, men who had been assigned elsewhere, such as Wray's troops in the Connaught Rangers, sought a transfer to the Inniskillings.[29]

Initial reports of recruiting in Fermanagh emphasized an enthusiastic local response. At a grand jury session in Enniskillen in April 1915, Judge Johnston expressed his gratitude to the men of the county who had 'been doing such a noble part in connection with the Great War'.[30] On 10 March 1915 it was reported that since the war began, Fermanagh had contributed 838 men to the army (excluding those who had enlisted in the English sportsmen's battalions and the sports battalion of the Royal Dublin Fusiliers). The majority joined the

36th Division and approximately 250 joined the 16th Division. The *Belfast Telegraph* praised the county's record, noting that its total population was only 61,000.[31]

However, even by early 1915 the initial surge of enthusiasm had died down. In May 1915 the RIC noted only twenty National Volunteers and thirty-nine Ulster Volunteers had enlisted over the previous month. The CI remarked that most of the population have 'to a large extent held back and are likely to do so, so long as enlistment remains voluntary'.[32] The 11th Inniskillings suffered from understaffing and was only brought up to full strength with the addition of 'C' company, drawn from the British League for the Support of Ulster and the Union.[33] Recruiters in Fermanagh were further pressurized by the announcement of a new battalion: the 12th Inniskillings under Colonel John Leslie. The new unit was to be established and quartered in Enniskillen from April 1915. It was hoped that it would reach a strength of 2,000 men but by mid-June, Leslie had only 800.[34]

To counteract this decline in recruitment, both nationalists and unionists organized joint recruitment events with John McHugh, chair of the county council, and Edward Archdale taking the lead. They downplayed the tensions that only a few months previously had threatened to erupt in all out civil war. McHugh, whose accession to the chairmanship had sparked a riot in Enniskillen, presided over a large mixed recruitment drive in Enniskillen town hall in June 1915.[35] Those in attendance included Edward Archdale, J.P. Gillin (IPP vice-chair of Enniskillen UDC), Wray and James Porter-Porter.[36] Both sides were keenly aware of the unusual circumstances that united them. At a recruitment meeting in staunchly unionist Ballinamallard, Edward Archdale joked that this was 'the first time in history that a nationalist addressed a meeting in Ballinamallard'.[37] At another meeting a few days later, Archdale expressed his happiness that 'unionists and nationalists were joining together to smash the Kaiser!'[38]

On 15 June 1915, at the behest of the Central Recruiting Committee, Fermanagh County Council established the Fermanagh Recruiting Committee. John Collum, a prominent local unionist, was appointed president and McHugh chairman. Aiming to be representative, the committee included both Crumley and Fetherstonhaugh, the earls of Belmore and Enniskillen, and the chairs and vice-chairs of the urban and rural district councils. However, it was clear that this ecumenical spirit was essentially a matter of practicality. In June 1915 the committee passed a resolution that the Ulster Division be opened to men of all creeds. This move was not motivated by any renewed esprit de corps in the face of war. Rather, Colonel John Leslie worried that he would not fulfil the quota if recruitment was based on religion.[39] Ultimately, the rigid religious and cultural associations that had grown around Fermanagh politics now served to limit recruitment. At the same meeting, John Collum pointed out that whereas

Catholics who had wished to join the Enniskillen Horse had been refused on the grounds of their religion, their Catholicism no longer appeared to be a problem now that it affected recruitment.[40]

While nationalist women did not feature prominently in the campaign to encourage recruitment, their unionist counterparts did. In early October 1914 the Fermanagh Women Unionists Committee (a branch of the UWUC) passed a motion, proposed by the countess of Erne, calling on all unionist women to further the cause of recruiting in Fermanagh in every way they could 'as was desired by Edward Carson'.[41] The Fermanagh Ladies' Recruiting Committee was established in June 1915 at the same time as the male counterpart. It comprised the wives of the men on the county committee and members of the UWUC. Elizabeth Archdale, Catherine Wray and Mary D'Arcy Irvine were all prominent members. The committee performed a number of open and clandestine roles. Publicly, it was involved in organizing recruitment drives and entertainments. However, more importantly, it was used as an informal source of local knowledge. The women were expected to provide the names of potential recruits to recruiting sergeants (as well as lists of those who had refused to sign up). They were expected to shame un-enlisted men and exhort them to enlist.[42] Shop assistants were a particular target.

Outside of recruiting, women, both unionist and nationalist, were involved in setting up ambulance corps and in fundraisers for the front. Frequently, they were required to host important guests. The women's nursing corps entertained Wray's battalion of National Volunteers with a night of 'speeches and a cinema show' on the eve of their departure for Fermoy camp.[43] Over 100 Fermanagh women, mostly Protestant, joined the British Red Cross throughout the war. The work assigned to them was varied, including the collection of moss (which was used to dress wounds), needlework, knitting and general war work. Margaret Lowry-Corry, Lady Belmore, enlisted as a general service member with St John's Ambulance where her duties primarily involved housework in the wards. Phyllis Richardson of Rossfad served as quartermaster at Lady Murray's hospital in France.[44] However, the tradition of women's war work was not as established in Fermanagh as it was elsewhere. Fionnuala Walsh has noted, for example, that it was one of only five counties that had not established a sub-depot for the Irish War Hospital Supply Depot by 1918.[45]

The new committees quickly threw themselves into work. Recruiting drives organized to coincide with fair days targeted the large number of farmers' sons and labourers who would enter the county towns: 'young men eligible in every respect for the Army'. These drives involved open air meetings often accompanied by fife and drum parades through the town centre. Frequently, local enlisted men were dispatched from Finner camp to canvass potential recruits in the town.[46] Tom Kettle, the Tyrone IPP MP who had enlisted on the outbreak of war, conducted a speaking tour of the county in a bid to drum up recruits. A massive recruitment drive was organized for Enniskillen on 10 November 1915 to coincide with one of the largest fairs of the year. A detachment of the 12th Inniskilling had been deployed to canvass personally. Speakers from both sides of the political aisle included McHugh, Crumley, Porter-Porter and Archdale. They were complemented by their guest speaker – Private McNamee, an Australian soldier who had been wounded at the front and who was now undertaking a recruitment tour of the United Kingdom. McNamee was greeted with a roar of approval as was each speaker. However, the event failed to yield a single recruit.[47]

As voluntary recruitment continued to decline, demands for conscription became more pronounced in the unionist community. This echoed similar calls elsewhere in the United Kingdom, and in January 1916 conscription was introduced in Britain. At a special meeting of the Fermanagh ladies recruiting committee in July 1915, a resolution was passed that urged the government to apply conscription to Ireland.[48] In part this resolution was motivated by women's frustration arising from their recruiting efforts. At the meeting, numerous committee members reported difficulties in finding any more willing recruits and claimed that the majority of those in Fermanagh responded to efforts to recruit them with a simple 'we will go if called upon'.[49] Nationalist speakers were less enthusiastic about conscription, portraying it as the inevitable consequence of poor recruitment. Tom Kettle declared himself 'not a conscriptionist' but one who was 'sick and tired of the sight of faces of young men who come to recruiting meetings, who applaud, and slink away and never turn up at the recruiting office'.[50] This speech caused bickering between nationalist and unionist as Kettle refuted the previous unionist speaker's claim that conscription was inevitable, and instead asserted that it would only be inevitable if Fermanagh men failed to volunteer.

Despite the official support among mainstream Fermanagh nationalism and the relative lack of cohesive opposition, recruitment remained sluggish. This was partly a cross-community phenomenon as both nationalist and unionist were motivated by two common concerns – the uncertain fate of Fermanagh under the Home Rule Act of 1914 and growing awareness that the war represented a great economic opportunity for Fermanagh agriculture. As the war progressed, prices for the food required to feed soldiers at the front grew higher and higher. Irish butter in December 1915 was more expensive than in the previous month by 6s. 6d. per hundredweight.[51] By November 1915 Enniskillen UDC was obliged to raise the wages of its labourers after concluding that rising prices had increased the cost of living 'by something like one third'.[52] This issue appeared almost immediately in public discourse on the war. The *Fermanagh Times* expressed its fear that an influx of patriotic unionists into the British army would leave the UVF, and therefore Fermanagh unionism, dangerously under-powered.[53] Both nationalist and unionist farmers recognized the benefits of war.

Recruiters deplored the number of men of enlistment age who preferred to stay at home and work the fields for better pay. At a recruitment speech on 26 July 1915, Kettle critized such an attitude, declaring 'the farmers would be undone and lost if Germany won'.[54] The CI identified the two most reticent groups to enlist in August 1915 as 'the farming and shop assistant classes'.[55]

There was a consensus, particularly among unionists, that the county was failing to contribute as it should to the war effort. This view was shared by new RIC CI John Hughes who claimed that while the 'Ulster Volunteers have done very fairly', the rest of the county had lagged behind.[56] However, this outlook does not stand up to scrutiny, certainly for the first half of the war, when Fermanagh's recruitment figures are placed in context. Between 15 December 1914 and 15 December 1915, 215 National Volunteers, 167 Ulster Volunteers and 155 non-aligned men enlisted: a total of 537 for the county. As a proportion of the strength of each organization, about six and a half per cent of National Volunteers in Fermanagh enlisted during that timeframe and five and a half per cent of UVF.[57] Between the start of the war and December 1915, membership of the National Volunteers had dropped from 3,963 to 2,514 and that of the UVF from 2,637 to 2,300.[58]

Strikingly, sixty per cent of Fermanagh recruits were Catholic. This was not the case for Tyrone, Armagh and Derry, which had a comparable religious split. In Derry, the stronger undercurrent of advanced nationalism blunted recruitment efforts among Catholics while in Tyrone a more coherent unionist machine delivered strong levels of Protestant recruitment.[59] Proportionally, Fermanagh under contributed. In 1911 it comprised roughly four per cent of the population of Ulster but only returned two per cent of its enlistment total by the end of 1915.[60] However, this was true of all Ulster counties bar Antrim (and Belfast). Indeed, Fermanagh's shortfall was much less than that of Tyrone (its closest neighbour) which made up roughly nine per cent of the population of Ulster in 1911 but contributed four per cent of its recruits.[61] As a percentage of the eligible population, recruitment in Fermanagh was much stronger than it appeared, particularly in comparison with other Ulster counties. By December 1915, roughly 116 Catholics had enlisted for every 1,000 eligible. For Protestants, this figure was 96. Only Antrim (including Belfast) outperformed Fermanagh in this regard, with 135 Catholics and 110 Protestants pre 1,000 eligible men. For the remaining counties, the median was 56 eligible Catholics enlisting per 1,000 and 70 for Protestants. Fermanagh was also noteworthy as its Catholic population proportionally outperformed its Protestant counterpart. Again, only Antrim saw more Catholics enlist then Protestants. This was especially striking as the neighbouring counties of Cavan, Monaghan, Tyrone and Donegal all saw the most significant discrepancies between Catholic and Protestant enlistment.[62]

In January 1915 the CI noted that while 'there is a minority not in favour of recruiting there is no active hostility to the policy of the Irish Parliamentary

Party and there are no branches of the McNeill [*sic*] section'.[63] Although not entirely accurate regarding the 'MacNeill' section, the report's assertion that anti-recruiting activity was very limited in Fermanagh before the 1916 Rising is correct. In September 1915 anti-war pamphlets entitled: 'Ireland, Germany and the Freedom of the Seas' were mailed to Enniskillen addresses in envelopes purporting to be from reputable firms.[64] That November, a 'so-called demonstration' was held in Irvinestown against recruiting but was only attended by a small number. In the same month, several anonymous posters were put up around the town.[65] However, that appeared to be the extent of anti-recruitment in the county.

The republican movement in Fermanagh was largely dormant during the period between the Volunteer split in 1914 and the 1916 Rising. It failed to attract even those future die-hards such as John Connolly, who became a captain of the Roslea company of the IRA during the War of Independence. Connolly noted that after 1914 the Volunteers in his area 'ceased to exist' and that he took little interest until efforts were made to revive them in 1918.[66] After the Volunteer split, only two companies in Fermanagh continued to support MacNeill. The largest, based in Enniskillen, drew most of its membership from the Mullylogan and Ashwoods districts to the west of the town.[67] That company was led by Francis O'Duffy.[68] Although inactive in the immediate aftermath of the split, O'Duffy maintained contacts with the advanced nationalists in the locality and was able to reform the group early in 1915. The other company operated in Derrylin near the Cavan border.[69] This was in contrast to neighbours such as Monaghan where the Volunteer split was considerably more acrimonious.[70]

O'Duffy was an example of the more radical undercurrents within the Fermanagh Volunteer movement that had been obscured by the predominance of the IPP. A Monaghan native, he had taught from 1902 to 1906 in the Christian Brothers School in Carlow where he also served as secretary of the Carlow branch of the Gaelic League. In this position he became acquainted with Patrick Pearse whom he later invited to speak at the Enniskillen branch of the Gaelic League. At the time of the home rule crisis, O'Duffy was teaching in St Michael's Intermediate School in Enniskillen, a position he held until 1918. Like Cahir Healy, O'Duffy was a founder member of SF and had moved from cultural to political nationalism through the influence of friends in the League who were members of the IRB. However, despite his strong ties to advanced nationalism, O'Duffy did not join the IRB until after the Volunteer split and was sworn in by Ernest Blythe in late 1914.[71]

O'Duffy later recalled that the IRB was not very well developed in Fermanagh, a relic of Blythe's earlier purges. He recalled that William Hegarty was the only other member in Enniskillen. They later admitted a further three or four other individuals. Seamus Dobbyn, a leading Belfast republican, also spent significant time in Enniskillen as an IRB organizer. However, Hegarty and

O'Duffy declined to expand the membership too much so as not to draw attention. Promoting SF and 'sound national propaganda', rather than the IRB or the Volunteers, was O'Duffy's main concern before 1916.[72]

In early 1915 SF and other radical organizations in Fermanagh were estimated to have less than 150 members.[73] O'Duffy recalled that despite major hostility from the IPP and AOH in Enniskillen, neither body openly opposed the Irish Volunteers or SF which were considered 'too unimportant and insignificant to bother with'.[74] O'Duffy never fully embraced the IRB. Gradually, he formed the view that it did not need to exist within the Volunteers and that the overlap in membership might lead to confusion. While he remained an active member of the Volunteers and SF, his association with the IRB lapsed.[75] Despite this, by 1916 the Irish Volunteers were the most active nationalist force in Fermanagh. The National Volunteers, notwithstanding their larger numbers, had begun to fall apart almost as soon as the war began. Efforts to continue drilling throughout 1914 and 1915 were made difficult by the loss of members who enlisted. Many drill instructors were army reservists who had been among the first to be called up. In addition, it was reported that the majority of Volunteers were unwilling to be seen publicly drilling in case they were identified by the police and subject to conscription if that policy were ever applied to Ireland.[76] The secretary of the National Volunteers in Fermanagh outlined the reasons for the organization's collapse: 'want of instructors, want of arms ... [and] an erroneous idea regarding enlisting for the Army'.[77]

By April 1915 the position of the National Volunteers had deteriorated to the point that two mass gatherings were scheduled for Enniskillen for the purpose of reviving the organization. These meetings were poorly attended and by May three branches in the Ennsikillen rural district had been dissolved. That month the RIC reported a drop in membership of 866, of which only twenty were as a result of recruitment.[78] However, as Joost Augusteijn has noted, at this stage the organization had become tantamount to the IRB and this connection to a much more active nationalist organization would have significant consequences after 1916.[79] Other nationalist organizations had also fallen into inactivity during the war. For example, in April 1915 the UIL considered reducing its membership fee to boost membership. In July Joseph Devlin ordered the AOH to assist the UIL in setting up a series of conferences aimed at reviving the organization in the county. The annual convention of the Fermanagh UIL, held in November, was poorly attended, especially by those from the north of the county. After a speech by Crumley, the UIL decided to soldier on in its efforts to collect for the IPP fund and organize election campaigns.[80]

By April 1916 Fermanagh had settled into a relatively comfortable pattern of cross-community war work. Both nationalist and unionist leaders shared platforms calling for more army recruits. Nationalist and unionist women volunteered together. Only a small minority of nationalists were committed republicans but increasing their number proved difficult despite the continuation of the First World War. While there were signs of probable conflict to come over the introduction of conscription to Ireland, in general it seemed possible to someone living in Fermanagh in 1916 that the war had served to unite nationalists and unionists in common cause and had permanently ameliorated many of the intercommunal tensions of July 1914. However, both Fermanagh nationalism and unionism would soon receive a sharp shock and be sent careening off on entirely different historical trajectories.

4 'Rebels, traitors and pro-Germans': the rise of Sinn Féin and the unionist response, 1916–18

The period from the Easter Rising in April 1916 to the December 1918 general election when SF usurped the IPP as the dominant nationalist party in Ireland was one of tremendous change. While this has traditionally been framed as a series of fallouts from the Rising, it is better viewed as a series of crises that the IPP failed to respond to satisfactorily. The Rising, the Belfast convention of June 1916 and the conscription crisis all represent different moments when the IPP establishment in Ireland generally and in Fermanagh failed to provide sufficient leadership and as a result lost their support base. The trend towards republicanism in Fermanagh was surprisingly unaffected by Fermanagh's large unionist population, which denounced the growing influence of SF but otherwise were mainly occupied with war work. The reorientation of nationalism in this period saw a number of important developments – the growth in influence of the Roman Catholic clergy, the rise in membership of the Irish Volunteers, and the re-affirmation for unionists that nationalism was both untrustworthy and hostile. The period ended with arguably the most significant election of the period – the 1918 general election – which broke the IPP's hold over South Fermanagh while also precipitating one of the most influential and dramatic contests of the whole election in North Fermanagh.

In common with most counties in Ireland, Fermanagh's Irish Volunteers were not heavily involved in the Rising. This reflected the relatively moribund state of advanced nationalism in the county as well as the domineering influence of Redmond and the IPP. Enniskillen town was fortified by the Enniskillen Dragoons with soldiers posted on both sides of the bridge through the town. In 1966 Séamus G. O'Kelly, son of Enniskillen draper James O'Kelly, recalled the Dragoons pulling an artillery gun through the town to the bridge.[1] Francis O'Duffy took no part in the Rising, having received no orders. The Fermanagh IRB's involvement was limited to ensuring that orders coming from Dublin were passed on to Fr James O'Daly of Clogher. These orders related to the intentions of the Tyrone and Belfast Volunteers to congregate around Coalisland and push through Belcoo in the direction of Galway.[2] However, neither O'Duffy nor his company were invited to take part and ultimately the plans were abandoned when the leaders realized that any such march would take them through strongly hostile areas. Notably, it was against this threat that the Dragoons had fortified Enniskillen rather than any from within the county itself.

For his part, O'Duffy had made plans to go to Dublin on Easter Monday, not to join the fighting but to collect a small parcel of five revolvers for the Derrylin company. Aware that his movements were being watch by the RIC, O'Duffy first went to his home in Ballybay before setting off in the evening for Dublin. He was only able to get as far as Dundalk that night and had to stay there before returning home. Despite his failure to accomplish anything of note, O'Duffy's aborted trip earned him the distinction of being one of the few people in Fermanagh interrogated in relation to the Rising when he was arrested by the RIC shortly after his arrival in Enniskillen. He was released within a few hours after insisting to the sceptical CI that his business in Dublin had been to obtain laboratory equipment that he needed for teaching. Aside from the interrogation of O'Duffy and other notable Volunteers in the county, there were no arrests in Fermanagh following the Rising.[3] On 27 April the leadership of the Fermanagh UVF met and decided to contact the military authorities in Dublin to offer UVF units if needed, but otherwise to take no independent action.[4]

While the Fermanagh Volunteers had no real engagement with the Rising, at least ten men from the county took part: eight Irish Volunteers, one member of the Irish Citizen Army and one member of the Hibernian Rifles.[5] The majority joined the Volunteers after leaving Fermanagh. These were Philip Cassidy, Joseph Duffy, Owen Greene, George Irvine, Michael Love, Patrick McGuire, Michael Conway McGinn, Patrick Romauld McGinn, John Joe Scollan and William Scott. The McGinns and Scollan were born to Fermanagh parents outside of the county. The most notable participant was George Irvine, not only for his background as a Fermanagh Protestant but also for the prominent role he played in Fermanagh republicanism after the Rising. At the time of his birth in Enniskillen in 1877, Irvine's parents owned a book and stationery store at 19 East Bridge Street. He was educated at the Enniskillen Model School and Portora before attending Trinity College Dublin. From a narrowly Fermanagh-based perspective, this is where his involvement with the county ended for a number of years. After graduating, he remained in Dublin and taught in several Anglican schools.[6]

Like Healy and O'Duffy, Irvine came to radical republicanism through cultural nationalism. He joined the Gaelic League in 1905 and quickly entered into Irish nationalist social circles. He was friendly with Bulmer Hobson, Ernest Blythe, Seán O'Casey and Sinéad Ní Fhlannagáin (who married Éamon de Valera). In 1907 Irvine joined the IRB initially as part of the Teeling circle but he soon became the centre of the offshoot Clarence Mangan circle. He rose rapidly within the organization and in 1913 was appointed secretary to the Dublin Centres' Board and a member of the Leinster Council. In this role he served as a deputy to Bulmer Hobson.[7] Irvine was involved in the initial foundation of the Irish Volunteers and was one of the first to enrol. He was appointed captain of B company, 4th Battalion, Dublin Brigade, under Éamonn Ceannt. After the Volunteer split in 1914, Irvine sided with the MacNeillite Volunteers along with most of the company.[8]

During the 1916 Rising, B company was ordered to hold the back gate of the South Dublin Union and prevent any military progression along the South Circular Road. Irvine had only nine men to carry out this order (as most of his own company had simply joined whichever unit they met on their way to muster on Easter Monday). The company was poorly prepared to defend their position. They relied on huts inside the workhouse gates for cover. These were made of flimsy corrugated iron and the British military was able to shoot directly through them, trapping the company in a deadly crossfire. Irvine later recalled the death of 17-year-old John Traynor, whose birthday it was that day. He was shot through the eye before gasping out his last words to Irvine: 'may Jesus have mercy on my soul'.[9] In the face of insurmountable odds as the British forces took the hospital grounds and set up a machine gun to fire directly on the hut, Irvine consulted with his men and surrendered. Interrogated at Kilmainham police station as to the extent of the Volunteers' plan, he refused to divulge the number of Volunteers in the South Dublin Union. Irvine was court-martialled and sentenced to death but this was commuted.[10]

Irvine was not the only Fermanagh Protestant to take part in the Rising. William Scott was born into an Anglican family in Derrycormick in 1872 and later converted to the Plymouth Brethren. He was unique among the Fermanagh men involved in the Rising as he was a member of the Irish Citizen Army. Together with James Connolly, Scott was a founder member of the Irish Socialist Republican Party in Belfast in 1896 and moved to Dublin in 1900 to work as a bricklayer. He was involved in the 1913 Lockout and subsequently joined the Citizen Army. During the Rising Scott served in St Stephen's Green under Michael Mallin and Countess Markievicz. Although injured during the fighting, he avoided immediate arrest and was able to join the Volunteers the following year. Like so many of the men named here, he never returned to his native county.[11] Peadar Livingstone identified a third Fermanagh Protestant named Wilson who also fought in the Rising but few records exist to confirm this.[12]

While no other Fermanagh men were as prominent as Irvine, many of them followed similar trajectories on their path to Easter 1916. James Philip 'Phil' Cassidy from Letterbreen moved to Cavan in 1914 where he became involved with the Volunteers and later relocated to Dublin where he joined B company, 1st Battalion. During Easter Week he was assigned first aid duties by Thomas Clarke and fought in the GPO until ordered to evacuate. Cassidy remained active in the struggle for Irish independence after the Rising but this was primarily in Dublin and he did not return to Fermanagh for any length of time until 1922 when he was promptly arrested.[13]

Similarly, Owen Greene of Gortatole moved to Dublin after leaving school to train as a draper's apprentice. A member of C company, 3rd Battalion, he served with de Valera at Boland's Mills before being shot in the knee and permanently crippled while attempting to dislodge a unit of snipers on Mount

Street. Unlike Cassidy, however, Greene returned to Fermanagh in 1917 and was central to the establishment of the IRA in Mullaghdun. He later served as quartermaster, 3rd Battalion, Fermanagh Brigade.[14] Michael Love of Enniskillen had also moved to Dublin in his teens to work for a shipping company. Unlike Irvine or Greene, he came to the IRB not through adjacent forms of nationalism but through his uncle Michael McGinn who was a long-time IRB member. He inducted Love into F company, 2nd Battalion. Love fought in Jacob's Factory under Thomas MacDonagh and evaded capture. He rarely returned to his home county, especially after partition as he risked arrest. Love continued to serve in the IRA throughout the War of Independence and was involved in the attack on the Custom House in May 1921 for which he was arrested. He was released after the truce.[15]

Outside of the Volunteer movement, many in Fermanagh were not even aware the Rising had taken place for days and weeks afterwards. Francis Tummon of Newtownbutler recalled the parish priest, at Mass on Sunday, 30 April, reading a pre-written statement from the local RIC sergeant announcing Pearse's surrender. This was his first intimation that anything was even going on.[16] Séamus O'Kelly remembered there were rumours and counter-rumours as darkness fell on Easter Monday: 'all Ireland went to bed wondering what morning would bring'. O'Kelly also noted that many in Enniskillen itself became aware that something was amiss when the mail train failed to arrive from Dublin.[17] News was even slower to spread in the immediate aftermath of the Rising as many of the inhabitants of the town and Enniskillen hinterland stayed at home due to the presence of soldiers in the locality. The market days on Tuesday and Thursday were not attended. The CI noted how 'some rather wild rumours of the involvements of arms and so forth were put about by Ulster Unionists'.[18] Papers, even those a week old, that contained information about the Rising were exchanged on Sundays while any locals who received and read the daily papers were badgered for information. The *Impartial Reporter* was the first newspaper, local or national, to report on the Rising because Egbert Trimble, son of editor William Copeland Trimble, was in Dublin and sent reports immediately to his father. In Tummon's recollection, 'The war news faded into insignificance when this real hot topical stuff came in'.[19] Stories that originated in English papers, such as Countess Markievicz's farewell kiss to her revolver as she was arrested, were reprinted across the local press.[20]

The *Fermanagh Herald* covered the Rising in detail during the weeks that followed. In common with most regional papers, it worked hard to find a local slant to the news. In the absence of any revolutionary activity in the county, it reported on Fermanagh men who had experienced the Rising as civilians. Any references to Fermanagh men who had actually fought in the Rising were not included, even as details emerged in the weeks and months after. Jack McPhail, of the *Freeman's Journal*, wrote a dispatch for the *Herald* where he made a half-hearted attempt to frame the event in terms his readers would understand: 'To get a true picture of what happened in Dublin, you have to picture the town of Enniskillen on fire.'[21] The *Herald* expressed fear for the safety of Patrick Crumley who was known to have been in Dublin for Easter and who had not been seen since the Rising. The paper made no attempt to follow up on this investigation and Crumley resurfaced in parliament on 25 May, enquiring about naval pensions.[22]

The *Herald* itself reflected mainstream nationalist opinion in Fermanagh. It initially condemned the Rising, focusing on the devastation caused. In particular, it mourned the deaths of two members of the Inniskilling Fusiliers: Private Francis William Knox was killed on 27 April when a grenade he was holding exploded and Lance Corporal Charles Love Crockett was shot the day after by a sentry on Fitzwilliam Street.[23] Neither was from Fermanagh. Crockett hailed from Derry and Knox was from Kilmannock, County Wicklow, but was buried in Breandrum cemetery in Enniskillen as at the time his next of kin could not be traced.[24] The only attested Fermanagh-born soldier to have died in the Rising appears to have been 19-year-old John Alexander Thompson of Florencecourt. A first-year engineering student in Trinity who had enlisted in the 10th Battalion, Royal Dublin Fusiliers, he was part of a small group of soldiers fired on from City Hall as they attempted to reach Dublin Castle. He was shot and brought to the Adelaide hospital.[25]

Tummon recalled how initial reaction in Newtownbutler to the Rising was mixed. When it was announced at Mass, many 'older men shook their heads and expressed the opinion that the use of arms was a misguided action and doomed to failure from the start'.[26] However, while at first there was little sympathy with leaders of the Rising, their executions turned opinion strongly against the British. Nicholas Smyth recalled that the executions 'caused sympathy amongst nationalists generally' but also a broader romanticization of the leaders. First hand accounts of the Rising, many from British soldiers, 'described the great fight the rebels put up'. Additionally, Smyth mentioned the great number of new songs and ballads about the Rising that imbued people 'with a very high spirit of patriotism'.[27] As early as May, the CI noted a 'sharp divide between nationalists and unionists, not as regards the rebellion itself or its suppression but as to the military measures after the surrender'.[28] Patrick Crumley became a vocal advocate of the rights of the prisoners in the months after the Rising. He fought against detaining internees in solitary confinement for up to twenty-two hours a day, demanding that they be given six hours in the open air with liberty to socialize and smoke. Crumley also pressed the case of Peter Fox, an American citizen, who had been arrested in Tyrone following the Rising and held without charge at Wandsworth.[29]

Arguably, the Belfast conference of June 1916 had more long-term consequences for Fermanagh than the Rising because six-county partition emerged as the favoured solution to the home rule question. The prospect of partition occasioned deep divisions among Fermanagh's previously unified nationalist front. Ultimately, the conference fatally undermined the confidence of Fermanagh nationalists in the IPP. The conference was convened on 23 June 1916 in St Mary's Hall to vote on the proposals on the settlement of Ireland that emerged from the efforts of Lloyd George who had been charged by the prime minister to resolve the 'Irish difficulty' through negotiations with Nationalists and Unionists. It was hoped this would enable all groups to focus more fully on the war.[30] At the time Lloyd George was minister of munitions but he succeeded Asquith as prime minister at the end of 1916. He saw an Irish settlement as a means to boost his own profile in the short term and this was evident in his approach to the negotiations.

Lloyd George met with the IPP and Unionist leaderships separately and aimed to persuade both to accept the implementation of the 1914 Home Rule Act with the specific exclusion of Antrim, Armagh, Down, Fermanagh, Londonderry and Tyrone which would continue to be ruled from London. This was the first time that an official, six-county formulation for resolving the Ulster crisis had emerged. The Ulster unionist movement had embraced the nine counties of Ulster, as had the Covenant. Terence Dooley has highlighted that the first time unionists on the margins of Ulster had to engage with their potential abandonment was after Lloyd George's 'county-option' proposal in March 1914, whereby counties could chose to vote themselves temporarily out of a home rule settlement.[31] Monaghan, Cavan and Donegal, with their pronounced Catholic majorities, would have been effectively abandoned by this principle with the futures of Tyrone and Fermanagh more ambiguous. Redmond rejected this proposal outright and it was also resisted by the UUC. The council's compromise was to insist that the option to withdraw should operate on an Ulster-wide and not county-by-county basis. The Covenant became an important article of faith among the marginal loyalist population – an oath to continue negotiations only on an Ulster-wide basis.

It is significant that in summer 1916 Lloyd George settled on six counties as the most viable solution to the Ulster crisis, even to the extent of overlooking the democratic wills of Fermanagh and Tyrone. Future discussion about, and opposition to, partition assumed a six-county partition as the default position. This placed Fermanagh and Tyrone on the edge of two potential settlements. A more nationalist-inclined settlement would see them in a home rule Ireland. The sense that the fate of the county was vulnerable to far-reaching change dominated political discourse among Fermanagh nationalists and republicans, unionists and loyalists. Lloyd George's key strategy was to leave the wording of the proposals deliberately vague. He was, therefore, able to promise Carson that the settlement would be permanent, while simultaneously assuring Redmond that the exclusion would only last for the duration of the war. Due to a lack of face-to-face meetings, both camps believed they had secured their goals. Carson called a meeting of the UUC on 6 June 1916 where the proposals were unanimously accepted (although protests later emerged from Cavan, Monaghan and Donegal delegates that they had been coerced into accepting it). Likewise, the IPP convened the St Mary's Hall, Belfast meeting of delegates from the six counties.

The IPP conference was strongly divided on the issue. Joseph Devlin delivered a 45-minute speech in favour of the proposals and put the full weight of his considerable east Ulster powerbase behind it. The proposals ultimately passed by 475 votes to 270 against. Some 183 opposing votes were from Fermanagh, Tyrone and Derry city (the three most nationalist areas to be excluded). This represented sixty-eight per cent of all delegates from those counties.[32] Fermanagh delegates, in particular, were bound by their own local convention to vote against the proposal. As the voting figures suggest, a number were pressured into supporting the proposals by the party leadership.[33]

The opposition of most of Fermanagh was strongly supported by nationalists in the county itself. A large rally was held in Enniskillen during August 1916 to rebuke the IPP leadership. This also extended to Crumley who was seen as a strong ally of Redmond and the nationalist establishment. This discontent, importantly, was not expressed by SF but by the local IPP. John McHugh and John Crozier, a Protestant member of the IPP, led the calls for Fermanagh nationalists to demand inclusion under a Dublin parliament.[34] Notably, the local Catholic clergy played a leading role in opposing the Lloyd George proposals.[35] Mass protest meetings took place in Enniskillen on 12 June and 20 July, and in Derrylin on 9 July. A number of UIL branches passed motions against the proposals and a new branch in Derrygonnelly was established to protest the convention.[36]

At the same time, something of an internal civil war took place among the Fermanagh AOH. Devlin had asserted his influence to ensure that all AOH delegates to the conference supported the proposals. In response, numerous AOH branches in Fermanagh passed motions of censure against their delegates. In return, they were censured by their central executive. By October, eleven of the thirty-two branches in the county were in open revolt against the executive. Six branches had been suspended while another five had seceded. The branches that withdrew met in Enniskillen on 17 October 1916 to discuss establishing a new organization. The failure of the convention's proposals defused the tension. In December Boho branch was reinstated and the others followed shortly after.[37]

Ultimately, the proposals collapsed for a number of reasons unrelated to the opposition of Fermanagh delegates. When Lloyd George's duplicity emerged, it alienated both sides. Additionally, the presence of several Unionists in prominent coalition positions allowed them to exert significant pressure on the government. Two amendments were proposed in parliament – advocating permanent exclusion and a reduction in the number of Irish MPs. These were unacceptable to Redmond and the IPP and forced them to reject the proposals.[38] The whole affair damaged Redmond's position and that of the IPP in Ireland. In Fermanagh and Tyrone, the St Mary's Hall vote was seen as a betrayal; SF exploited those resentments. Lloyd George, for his part, was relatively unscathed and continued to sail through wartime politics until he took power from Asquith in December 1916 with the backing of the Conservatives.

The 1916 Rising and the St Mary's conference shocked all factions of nationalism in Fermanagh and in the months afterwards they began to shake off their torpor. On Sunday 22 May a large meeting was held in Ederney to revive the UIL in the county and prevent any further risings. J.P. Convery, the organizer, denounced the Rising as 'an act of madness' that would 'pass into history'.[39] Perhaps anticipating the movement of nationalist opinion in another direction, he was keen to emphasize that all progress on the national question over the past century had come through 'the Revolution under the leadership of Parnell, Davitt, Dillon and Redmond'.[40] The *Fermanagh Herald* suggested that 'good may yet come out of bad' and noted that the Rising seemed to have swayed many English voices as to the necessity of moderate home rule.[41]

However, other expressions of anti-Redmond nationalist feeling were evident even before SF established itself as the dominant outlet for these currents. This was especially evident in the second half of 1916. The Irish Nation League (INL) grew in popularity in Fermanagh during this period, attracting hundreds of members, mostly younger men. In August 1916 four branches of the INL were established in the county and a central organizing committee was set up in Omagh. The RIC viewed the emergence of the INL as a direct response to the handling of the exclusion crisis.[42] A large number of prominent leaders of Fermanagh nationalism such as Frank Wray (chairman of Enniskillen UDC) and John Crozier (JP and chair of Enniskillen guardians) also joined. Wray had been an election agent for the IPP in the county and had organized Fermanagh's recruiting campaign at the start of the war. By August 1916 he actively opposed Redmond and learned Irish in his spare time.[43] While the purpose of the INL was primarily to oppose partition, it began to represent a much broader anti-Redmond sentiment. This manifested itself most clearly when the INL organized a mass rally on 4 November 1916 in Enniskillen to rival an IPP rally there on the same day. The growth of the INL also demonstrated that Fermanagh's Catholic clergy were going to stay politically engaged even after the collapse of the Belfast convention. The CI noted that many of the INL branches were close to collapse and the league itself was 'largely dependent on the influence of the local RC clergy'.[44]

As elsewhere in Ireland, this discontent eventually solidified into support for SF. With characteristic naivety, in February 1917 Samuel Hanna, the new CI, wrote: 'the MacNeill faction are now looking with favour upon the extreme movement in the belief that the constitutional movement has failed … this will hardly develop into a danger'.[45] The first new SF club was founded in Belcoo on 20 May 1917 by Fr Terence Caulfield, the Catholic curate. It immediately garnered sixty members.[46] On 17 June Fr Michael McCarvill founded the Enniskillen SF club. Within a few months, SF was well organized in Fermanagh with a cumann in nearly every parish overseen by a comhairle ceantair. While many of these branches were small, they were energetic and organized numerous public meetings and aeridheachta (festivals) attended by younger people, including several priests and teachers. The most prominent organizers in Fermanagh were Francis O'Duffy and Frs McCarvill and Caulfield.[47]

In October 1917 Hanna reported that 'the majority of RC priests' supported SF.[48] In this they were implicitly supported by Bishop Patrick McKenna of Clogher.[49] Caulfield was at the centre of most of the early SF organization work in Fermanagh. In January 1917, along with McCarvill, he hosted a 'rebel social' at which photos of the leaders of the Rising and the proclamation were displayed on the walls.[50] The following month, Fr McQuaid of Boho was noted by the RIC as 'using disloyal, seditious language' from the altar.[51] Caulfield tirelessly lectured across the county on the SF movement, sharing platforms with Griffith, MacNeill and Seán MacEntee.[52] He also began to involve himself in local land agitation, writing to two landlords in March 1918 that some land ought to be let to small tenants for tillage at a reasonable rate.[53] The clergy were the ideal proselytizers for the republican movement due to their influence at parish level. One motivated priest could convert a district almost on his own. As Hanna observed in March 1918, 'where the priest tends in this direction clubs are formed and every effort is made to get not only the men but the girls and women into the movement'.[54] However, clerical involvement in SF was hampered after Cardinal Michael Logue's pastoral letter of 25 November 1917, which denounced the organization. This appeared to have curtailed the activity of clergy in Fermanagh in December and January.[55]

It was at this point that O'Duffy's earlier decision to focus his energies before the Rising on SF instead of the IRB began to pay dividends. The lack of a strong IRB presence in the county meant that few Fermanagh Volunteers were arrested in the aftermath of the Rising and were able to commit themselves to the political organization. These Volunteers functioned as dispatch carriers between the various cumainn, making up an uneven but effective postal service within the county.[56] Additionally, many of the institutions of establishment nationalism did not recognize the threat posed by SF until it was far too late. Livingstone notes, for example, that the AOH, who had a very strong presence in the county, viewed the SF clubs as 'too insignificant and unworthy of notice'.[57]

Cumann na mBan was also established in Fermanagh throughout 1917, often through the initiative of organizers from outside the county. Ellen J. McGrath of the Ballyshannon branch organized new branches in Belleek, Mulleek,

Garrison and Devenish during 1917. This was part of a wider campaign along the Donegal–Fermanagh border.[58] Alice Cashel was appointed primary organizer for Fermanagh by Nancy Wyse Power and served in that capacity until 1919.[59] In autumn 1917 she founded the Enniskillen branch of Cumann na mBan which was placed under the command of Cissie Maxwell. The branch only comprised about twenty members but became important during the War of Independence for the support it provided the Fermanagh Brigade IRA.[60] In March 1918 Cashel was observed by the RIC travelling between Enniskillen, Belcoo and Derrygonnelly. In the latter it was reported that she had established 'an ambulance corps of women Sinn Féiners'.[61] By December 1917 the *Fermanagh Herald* was reporting on the opening of a new branch in Cashelnadrea and by early 1918 another branch had been established at Toura.[62] The Belturbet branch of Cumann na mBan was so large that it also served the women of Blacklion across the border. This branch was particularly active in supporting Arthur Griffith's by-election campaign in June 1918.[63] This stood in significant contrast to the role played by the UWUC and other unionist women's organizations. Members of Cumann na mBan enjoyed a more active role in political republicanism in the county. They generally shared a platform with male leaders at public meetings and rallies and had a great deal of autonomy in growing their own organization. It is likely this was a result of both the good relationship between male and female leaders within the county but also due to the energy and capabilities of women like Cashel and McGrath. Importantly, this active role set them apart from not only unionist women in the county but also women who supported constitutional nationalism.

The changing attitude of Fermanagh nationalists to the Rising and the IPP can be seen in the reception given to George Irvine when he was released from Lewis Jail in June 1917. Invited as the guest of honour of the Fermanagh feis, Irvine, in his Irish Volunteer uniform, was chaired through the town at the head of a large parade of people. This stood in stark contrast to his experience in 1916 when he was heckled and abused by Dubliners after his capture.[64] In his speech, Irvine modestly declared that he had 'only done what was his duty'. Notably, he promoted donations to and membership of the Gaelic League as the best way for Fermanagh people to gain 'the privilege of taking part in the work'.[65] Tempo GAA club was renamed in his honour in 1917.[66] Much of Irvine's time in Fermanagh was spent either delivering speeches or undertaking valuable SF propaganda work such as when he attended service at St Macartan's Anglican church in full Volunteer uniform and refused to stand for 'God Save The King', thereby providing an explicitly Protestant model of Irish republicanism that he hoped others would follow.[67]

Evidence of growing support for SF could be seen elsewhere in the county throughout 1916 and 1917. A large SF rally was held in Lisnaskea in August 1917 and an even larger one was planned for Enniskillen in October to rival Carson's march on Ulster Day in 1912. The Enniskillen meeting was banned but thousands showed up.[68] The police were forced to allow the rally to take place in the GAA ground while blocking the primary bridge to access it. Consequently, the speakers – Eoin MacNeill, Arthur Griffith, Herbert Pim and Darrel Figgis – were forced to reach the field by boat.[69] By December 1917 the RIC estimated that there were twenty-two SF branches with 1,665 members in Fermanagh. This was less than half of the UIL's 4,188 membership. However, the CI noted that while the UIL was dormant, SF was 'active and well organized and have support far greater than their apparent strength'.[70]

On a number of key occasions, factional tensions spilled out into the public arena. Following the victory of Joseph McGuinness in the South Longford by-election in May 1917, celebrations across Fermanagh were met with an organized RIC response as crowds were ordered to disperse. SF attempted to use these acts of repression as part of their ongoing propaganda efforts by bringing cases against the RIC to court through friendly solicitors. For example, in Belcoo during May two charges of assault were brought against RIC Constable Hughes who, it was alleged, had attacked Patrick Leonard and Thomas Gilmurray without warning while clearing the town of Sinn Féiners.[71] The case was rejected with considerable rancour from both sides. The solicitor for Leonard and Gilmurray, Moloney, openly accused the IPP magistrates of bias for which he was rebuked and was threatened with being reported to the Incorporated Law Society.[72] The RIC district inspector for Belcoo, Patrick Marrinan, called Moloney a 'young pup' and the case was dismissed. Similar scenes took place after a number of Sinn Féiners were arrested for harassing an IPP celebration following their victory in the South Armagh by-election. The defendants were accused of hurling stones and abuse at those gathered to celebrate as well as at the RIC. All accused were openly disdainful of the court, smoking and refusing to remove their caps until ordered to do so.[73] These new divisions were not limited to such overtly political incidents but created fractures in families and social groups. In November 1917 the eighteen members of the Ballinamoan A.M. Sullivan flute band ended up in court divided along political lines. The SF members, it was alleged, were attempting to appropriate the instruments to use at SF rallies.[74]

Typically, these new hostilities and personal animosities manifested themselves within local politics. At a meeting of Belturbet UDC on 15 January 1917, a discussion on the allocation of plots of land from the Congested Districts Board was broken up by an argument between nationalist members in which the chair was decried as 'only a Hibernian, and a betrayer of the country'.[75] Despite the sea change in sentiment in Fermanagh, the constitutional nationalist establishment was either unwilling or unable to acknowledge that the political scene had changed. At the annual meeting of the Enniskillen AOH in February 1917, a toast was proposed by William Maguire, a local solicitor, to Redmond and the 'impregnable position of the Irish cause'. Maguire asserted that the future of the party was very bright due to 'the constitution of the Party and the absolutely democratic principles all of which had won the entire confidence of the people'.[76] In this he was supported by Patrick Crumley who declared he 'could not see why any section of the people should have any reason to lose confidence in Mr Redmond'.[77]

Elsewhere, local IPP members tried to adopt positions they thought would be amenable to the new republican sentiments they found in their communities. In May 1917 Thomas Maxwell, an IPP member of Enniskillen UDC who declared he 'was no Sinn Féiner', proposed a motion protesting the treatment of Countess Markievicz in prison. The IPP members supported the motion in sufficiently republican terms that the *Impartial Reporter* informed its readers 'Mr Maxwell made some disloyal remarks which we are forbidden by the Censor to publish'.[78] James McGovern, another IPP member, declared that the only person who should have been jailed for the Rising was Edward Carson. Similar scenes occurred in Enniskillen guardians when the same motion was passed with John Crozier, the IPP chair, declaring that 'nothing had ever been wrung from England except by bloodshed'.[79] In November 1917 McGovern again caused a stir in Enniskillen UDC when he proposed banning the British army from using recreational facilities owned by the council after soldiers had broken up a dance in the town's minor hall. A common thread here was the desire to associate these actions with the IPP specifically. McGovern was careful to declare he 'had no sympathy with Sinn Féin' and instead framed the proposal as the IPP 'protecting their citizens'.[80] From November 1917 the RIC detected that many nationalist magistrates in the county were 'becoming reluctant to discharge their duty fairly either from fear or unpopularity of Sinn Féin sympathy'.[81]

Most unionist political activity during this period involved opposing the radical drift in Fermanagh nationalism. On local bodies where they held a majority, they could exert considerable influence. A resolution protesting the treatment of Countess Markievicz, which passed easily elsewhere, was successfully voted down in Clogher RDC in an ill-tempered debate that saw its proposer, Patrick Bailey, insulted for 'making a fool of himself' and 'bleathering'.[82] Unionists accused Nationalists of gerrymandering, especially in Enniskillen. There were complaints about what Kevin O'Shiel termed 'swallow voters' or men to whom property was let in a constituency solely for the purpose of voting in local elections.[83] O'Shiel noted that this was how Omagh Council in Tyrone was eventually captured by Nationalists.[84] In October 1919 Richard Mogaghey of Ballinamallard, the Unionist agent for Trillick, wrote a letter to the Local Government Board (LGB) complaining about the subletting of smaller cottages in the area to multiple Catholics at any one time and noting that 'if this were allowed to continue there would soon be 75 votes out of 25 cottages in the Trillick district'.[85] A particularly egregious example of this was alleged by the

Impartial Reporter in Enniskillen in 1922 which claimed that 92 nationalist votes in the contested district of Enniskillen East bypassed the occupancy threshold on the basis that they held grave plots in the district and were, therefore, occupiers and entitled to vote in that district.[86]

These complaints were not paranoia. Under a plan devised by Archdeacon John Tierney in 1914, nationalists used such methods to wrest Enniskillen UDC from unionist control.[87] However, this reasoning was used primarily to delegitimize the nationalist vote. We have seen earlier that the idea of the landed permanence of the unionist vote as contrasted with the itinerant Catholic vote was crucial to unionist justifications that Fermanagh was Protestant. Such stories allowed groups like the *Reporter* to frame certain newspaper articles as 'how Nationalists make votes' and undermine their numerical supremacy.[88] Despite this, it should be noted that the rise of SF often provided the IPP and Unionists with opportunities to ally together. For example, in April 1918 they combined on the county council to defeat SF's resolution denouncing Lloyd George and the prospect of partition.[89]

The final great radicalizer of nationalist opinion in Ireland after the Rising was the conscription crisis of late spring and summer 1918. While this is often treated as separate to the Rising, just another in a succession of British errors in Ireland, in actuality the Rising was critical in exacerbating the severity of the crisis. It had served to harden opinions on the question of conscription on both sides. With the growing numbers of republicans constituting a strong anti-war, anti-conscription lobby, the remaining constitutional nationalists found themselves also required to oppose its implementation strongly lest they concede yet more ground to SF. For unionists the position was more ambiguous. Nationalist opponents noted with relish that Fermanagh unionists' recent recruiting record suggested they were as reluctant to be sent to the front as nationalists. In Enniskillen UDC, three Unionists supported the Nationalists in opposing the implementation of conscription.[90]

However, among unionism's public representatives in Fermanagh the exclusion of Ireland from conscription was both an ongoing injustice and a way for Ireland to regain its honour after the stain of the Rising. In January 1918 Edward Archdale unsuccessfully proposed an amendment to the national service bill, declaring that 'no further demands should be made upon the manpower of Great Britain without an assurance from the government of its intention to bring forward a concurrent measure for compulsory military in Ireland'.[91] Unionists soon had their wish when in April 1918 Lloyd George's government announced plans to extend conscription to most men aged up to fifty-one years and, crucially, to Ireland. These came after the German Spring Offensive had broken through British and French lines and seemed likely to break the deadlock in Germany's favour. While unionists strongly favoured the measure, nationalists strongly opposed it. Indeed, Lloyd George recorded in his war diaries that while he and Bonar Law had some misgivings about the proposal, the strength of support among the other Conservatives in government was too strong for him to resist.[92] On the nationalist side, the IPP had consistently resisted the application of conscription to Ireland, both out of conviction and from the fear that SF would make political capital out of any prevarication on the issue. At national level, the IPP was further outraged by Lloyd George's new 'dual policy' in which the introduction of a new home rule bill was linked to the implementation of conscription. When the new conscription bill was passed in the House of Common on 6 April 1918, John Dillon (who succeeded Redmond as party leader in March) led his MPs out of the chamber in protest.

Kevin O'Shiel described the bill as a 'veritable miracle' owing to its successful unification of all quarrelling strands of Irish nationalism.[93] On 18 April the Irish Anti-Conscription Committee was established with representation from the leaderships of SF, the IPP, the All-for-Ireland League and Labour. On the same day, the Catholic hierarchy released a statement condemning the scheme. The committee planned a series of rallies after Sunday Mass on 21 April 1918 to enable people to sign a pledge opposing conscription. At the same time, Labour committed to a strike on 23 April to protest against conscription. Dillon and de Valera even shared a platform at one such rally in Roscommon. Nevertheless, SF was perceived as the primary force behind the campaign. In Fermanagh, the clergy were again at the forefront. On 21 April priests read out the hierarchy's statement against conscription and exhorted their parishioners to sign the pledge which they did in their thousands. A week later, collections were held after Mass for a 'National Defence Fund'.[94] At an anti-conscription rally in Derrygonnelly on 9 May, all but two speakers were Catholic priests.[95] Caulfield, by now described in police reports as 'notorious', had four anti-conscription notices removed from the walls of his house on 11 April. When he subsequently placed posters inside his window, the police forced their way into the priest's house to remove them and Caulfield was given an official warning for 'threatening the police'.[96] Priests also allegedly urged parishioners to receive the sacraments because if conscription were implemented, they would almost certainly be killed in France.[97]

As part of this campaign, a mass rally was organized for the county hall in Enniskillen on 25 April with representation from SF, the UIL, the AOH, the Irish National Foresters, the Enniskillen Labour Union and even some unionists. The meeting was chaired by Archdeacon Keown, parish priest of St Michael's church, Enniskillen, while Francis O'Duffy and John Keenan, secretary of the Enniskillen UIL branch, were appointed secretaries. The attendance was reported as 'vast' and far exceeded the capacity of the hall. J.P. Gillin welcomed attendees of all faiths, specifically welcoming 'Protestants' to loud cheers. Similarly, William Clarke of the Enniskillen Labour Union declared he 'knew the feelings of the Protestant section of the workers just as well as the feelings of the Catholic section and he could say that there was not a single one of them in favour of conscription'. Nevertheless, the tone of Keown's keynote was stridently nationalist. To raucous cheers, the priest declared 'it was against every law, human and divine, for one nation to tell another: "come out and shed your blood for us". No nation was bound to it.'[98] Similar meetings were held around the county on the same day at Mullaghdun, Holywell, Coonian and Irvinestown. Newspapers that opposed conscription were keen to highlight the cross-community appeal of the campaign, although such reports should be viewed with some suspicion. For example, the *Anglo-Celt* happily declared that the 'vast majority of the Unionists of Fermanagh are as strongly opposed to conscription as the Nationalists and several of them declare that a Unionist member will never again be returned for North Fermanagh'. However, the evidence for this was not a unionist anti-conscription pledge or resolution but rather the anti-conscription proposals adopted by the unionists and nationalists of the Enniskillen branch of the National Amalgamated Union of Labour (NAUL), which denounced the continuation of a 'Capitalist War'.[99]

The fight against conscription was the first major action undertaken by the Enniskillen branch of NAUL, which had only been founded in January 1918. The NAUL was a British union which had a stronger presence in Fermanagh and Ulster more broadly than the Irish Transport and General Workers' Union (ITGWU). This was primarily due to the suspicion harboured by Protestant workers of the nationalist links of Dublin-based unions, as well as the NAUL's pre-existing bases in Belfast, Omagh and Derry. Despite its newness it grew rapidly, boasting 181 members by the autumn.[100] Jim Quinn has identified the uniquely tense position the NAUL faced in Fermanagh. Labour in the south had been strong in both its criticism of conscription and in the strike action it undertook as part of this opposition. Meanwhile, labour in Belfast had tended to side with official Unionist policy and support conscription. In Fermanagh the labour movement was forced to navigate a fairly even division over conscription between the two communities. As Quinn put it: 'To ignore the anti-conscription campaign would alienate the Nationalists; too much action might alienate Unionists'.[101] The union openly denounced the scheme but did not commit to a full strike like the ITGWU.

The conscription crisis represented an opportunity for the nationalist community to unite in common cause. As O'Duffy stated at a rally in Enniskillen, 'this was not a time for argument or discussion as to past mistakes or past blunders ... [but] what was going to happen in the future'.[102] Nationalist-controlled local bodies passed resolutions criticizing the scheme and the hypocrisy of the British government that refused to deliver any form of self-government while also demanding a 'blood tax' from Ireland. In Enniskillen UDC, a debate lasting two hours descended into acrimony with SF and the IPP members taunting the ancestry and honesty of Unionist member William

Copeland Trimble. This culminated in Trimble storming out and refusing to return for the vote. Ultimately, the nationalist members were able to pass a motion protesting conscription. J.P. Gillin, the leader of the AOH on the council, declared that 'the AOH were ready to fall into line to take whatever steps they were advised to do to resist compulsion'.[103] This was followed up by a resolution of the Enniskillen lodge of the AOH to commit to a policy of 'passive resistance'. If conscription were introduced, the AOH would send all men of an eligible age into the mountains and provide a monetary fund for sustenance.[104] The CI noted, however, that this co-operation may have been less than enthusiastic, 'the official Nationalist party have a distrust of the Sinn Féin party but they are too afraid of the priests'.[105] He suggested that many IPP members regretted contributing to the defence fund as they feared SF would simply claim the money for themselves as nearly all parish treasurers were either members of SF or priests.[106]

Despite their stated commitment to this united front, the Fermanagh IPP lost credibility in the eyes of the nationalist community when they united with Unionists on Fermanagh County Council to defeat a SF resolution condemning conscription in April 1918. There were a number of reasons why they did this but primarily they did not wish to see SF successfully propose such a resolution. The IPP put forward an amendment with milder wording. When that was defeated, they then switched to opposing it. Some members expressed opposition to it based on the war effort and their unwillingness to pass 'sedition' while it was ongoing.[107] This view, sincerely held or not, was frequently cited afterwards by SF to highlight the IPP's disconnection from the common man who cared little for how seditious the county council appeared. By contrast, SF was able to play up the commitment of its members such as Cahir Healy who was prosecuted in September 1918 for putting up anti-recruiting posters around Enniskillen.[108] By May 1918 the *Fermanagh Herald* (proudly republican since March 1918) was denouncing the IPP as a 'Dangerous Party' and John Dillon as 'High Chief Factionist ... [who has] raised the banner of revolt against the Sovereign Independence of Ireland'.[109]

The incident further underlines the confused IPP response to the rise of SF in Fermanagh. Councillors and local leaders were pulling in numerous opposing directions. Some doubled down on the language of compromise and loyalty that had been at the core of Redmondism. Others sought to radicalize and occupy the space that SF was claiming as its political case. However, there was no effort to outline a consistent strategy that allowed SF propaganda to portray the party in whatever manner they needed. In many ways, the IPP was hamstrung because its previous support for recruiting was incompatible with the more generally anti-war rhetoric of much of the anti-conscription movement. While nationalist councillors like Felix Leonard and J.P. Gillin should have won great credit in nationalist circles for their opposition to the establishment of the recruitment committee in Fermanagh, their efforts were hampered by their need to assert continually their support for the war itself and their general support for army enlistments once the crisis had passed.[110]

Yet, it should be emphasized that the degree to which public opinion had changed since April 1916 was still not obvious. CI Hanna was convinced that the movement in Fermanagh was primarily being driven by the clergy and that the majority of people's personal opinions had not changed radically. He was convinced that the IPP's traditional farming base was still strongly in favour of Redmond and believed that most Sinn Feéiners would accept home rule.[111] In March 1918 he suggested that 'the vast majority of the people would welcome the suppression of this disloyal and mischievous body'.[112] Despite SF's growth, the UIL and AOH both had membership twice as strong.

SF was proactive in its efforts to capitalize on the crisis. Old Volunteer companies were revived and included both National and Irish Volunteers. These companies met twice or three times a week to march.[113] Such reorganization should not necessarily be viewed as a growth in militancy. These companies had little, if any, arms and marched with hurleys or wooden guns. Insofar as a wider structure existed, it was provided by Hugh McManus, who had succeeded Francis O'Duffy as the head of the Volunteers in the county, and Frank Carney who was drill master.[114] The real significance of the Volunteer reorganization was as an expression of increasing and widespread discontent. Francis Tummon, a prominent Newtownbutler Sinn Féiner, recalled of the Wattlebridge company: 'Almost every able-bodied man or boy in my locality joined this force'.[115] Many men who would later become prominent in the War of Independence joined the Volunteers in this period, such as Patrick McNulty, who took part in the attacks on Ballytrain barracks and on unionist houses after the burning of Roslea.[116] By early 1918, however, most of these units still lacked training. For the CI, 'the rank and file need hardly be considered as a fighting body and the local leaders in this county are hardly men in the ordinary sense of it'.[117]

Growing public support for SF was further enhanced by the arrest of their leadership in May 1918 for an alleged conspiracy with Germany to betray the British war effort. The flimsy evidence provided by the British authorities for a so-called 'German Plot' only enhanced the impression that this was an extra-legal move by the British authorities to quieten separatist sentiment in the country.[118] Among those arrested was Seán O'Mahony who, although not a Fermanagh native, sat as MP for the county from 1918 to 1921. The *Fermanagh Herald* denounced the evidence against the arrested men as a 'forgery' and claimed the scheme 'no doubt aims at weakening Ireland's opposition to Conscription and menacing the demand for full National Independence'.[119] Repressive measures in Fermanagh served further to radicalize the population. Whereas Volunteer marches had previously been warily tolerated in most parts of the county, from July 1918 the RIC actively broke up anything designated as an illegal assembly. To make a mockery of this effort, in August 1918 football matches were organized all over Fermanagh. In Wattlebridge, the RIC arrived to stop the game as both teams took the field. In response, the Volunteers took the goalposts and sailed them across Lough Erne to an island, leaving the police stuck on the opposite bank. As Tummon put it, 'the game was played and the law thus broken'.[120] Importantly, he estimated that there were only a handful of Volunteers in the crowd at the game and that the majority of those defying the law were regular civilians.

Official Unionism threw the full weight of its support behind the conscription proposals. In practice, this frequently involved opposing anti-conscription resolutions at county council and UDC meetings. In most cases these speeches placed the blame for Ireland's poor recruiting record and the need for conscription squarely at the feet of nationalists. As William Coote, MP for South Tyrone, declared to a cross-border Orange gathering at Fintona in May 1918: 'Ulster had few available sons to give now. Her sons did not require conscription.'[121] The reluctance of Ireland to accept conscription was evidence of the nationalist population's moral failings, which increased unionist opposition to home rule. As John Porter-Porter declared at Lisbellaw in July 1918, 'the clerical and lay leaders of the Nationalist Parties have openly engaged in preventing Irishmen from taking their fair share in the dangers of the present war. Under these circumstances we assert with confidence that a Parliamentary Union is necessary for the preservation of the liberties of Ireland'.[122]

The single largest outpouring of support for conscription came during the Twelfth (of July) gatherings in 1918 with numerous speeches across Fermanagh in favour of Lloyd George's proposals. At the joint Twelfth for Enniskillen, Lisbellaw, Maguiresbridge, Tempo and Glenawley, Porter-Porter proposed 'a justly and impartially administered system of compulsory service for the whole of Ireland'.[123] At the joint Lisnaskea and Newtownbutler Twelfth, meanwhile, Revd F. St Clair Caithness of Ballyhullagh declared to applause that 'Up til now the greater proportion of Irish soldiers were Protestants. But they demanded compulsory service not for Protestants only for certain parts of the country but all equally.'[124] At the Ballinamallard Twelfth, Edward Archdale declared to cheers that conscription was bound to be implemented soon.[125] Archdale remained one of the most vocal proponents of conscription in Ireland. Even as late as October 1918 with peace in sight, he maintained it was a 'damned good job that voluntary recruiting was nearly over as it was all rot'.[126]

In another less visible act of support, unionist grandees took over the bulk of the organizational responsibilities for recruiting drives as many IPP counterparts withdrew from active involvement in the recruitment and enlistment committees. As attempts to implement conscription faltered, many unionists threw themselves into supporting the efforts of the newly established Irish Recruiting Council. At a meeting of Fermanagh County Council on 18 July

1918, a recruiting committee for Fermanagh was established, despite the Irish Recruiting Council's focus on urban areas. The motion was carried due to unanimous unionist support; the nationalists on the council uniformly opposed it but were missing some of their number. Felix Leonard, an IPP councillor, formally submitted a rescinding motion which he did not withdraw until September under intense pressure from both his own party and the Unionists on the council.[127] Eventually, John McHugh was able to frustrate attempts to create a recruiting committee by simply declining to act.[128] The committee was entirely composed of unionists and while they were open to appointing nationalist members, no councillor was willing to join, aware of its political impracticability in the midst of the conscription crisis. Even Joseph Gillin, the former 'arch-recruiter', demurred when asked to join, stating 'England was fighting for the rights of small nationalities and she should put her own house in order first'.[129] The conscription crisis rumbled on in a sort of administrative stasis until the signing of the armistice in November 1918. The end of the First World War in Enniskillen was greeted with significant public participation, but the celebrations belonged more to one community than the other. The town was 'beflagged by the Protestant people and just a few of their Roman Catholic neighbours', while celebrations carried on into the night.[130] In Maguiresbridge a torchlight procession marched twice around the town.[131]

Given the number of significant political changes in such a short period, the December 1918 general election was unknown territory for many of its participants. Notably and unexpectedly, Godfrey Fetherstonhaugh, MP for North Fermanagh, had resigned in October 1916. An *Irish Times* report suggested that this was due to failing health but a subsequent report in the same newspaper claimed Fetherstonhaugh wished to focus more on his legal practice.[132] Fermanagh unionists had clearly learned from their tribulations in previous decades and quickly announced a by-election; this was held on 28 October and won unopposed by Edward Archdale.[133] Despite the growing political tensions both within and across party lines, there had been no major outbreaks of violence in Fermanagh between 1916 and 1918 but there had been few opportunities for the new political alignments within nationalism and unionism to be tested until December 1918. While SF was clearly in the ascendancy, the level of influence still retained by the AOH and IPP institutions in Fermanagh was unclear. For unionists, the election was an important moment to signal that a newly fervent nationalism would be met by an equally zealous unionist response. Further complicating this was the fact that this was the first election since the Representation of the People Act 1918 had vastly expanded the franchise and which all parties hoped to benefit from by registering the greatest number of voters.

Nationally, the 1918 election provided a *de facto* mandate for SF to pursue its republican agenda. It signalled the electoral eclipse of the IPP and, in the northern six counties, recommitted Ulster Unionism to opposing Irish independence. Few local contests in the election were as important as those in Fermanagh. In the South Fermanagh constituency, the ballot paper showed both a SF and IPP candidate, although the IPP candidate had officially withdrawn. Despite unionist hopes that this confusion would allow them to sneak in, Sinn Féiner Seán O'Mahony was returned with a huge majority. He was a commercial traveller, who owned Fleming's Hotel in Dublin and who had been imprisoned in Lincoln Jail after the Rising. O'Mahony had also served as chairman of the board of directors of the SF newspaper and had spent several months promoting SF across Fermanagh.

Initially, the Unionist Central Council of South Fermanagh had selected William J. Brown JP as their candidate.[134] However, Brown, a respected Derrylester farmer, was in his late seventies at the time of the nomination and a downturn in his health forced him to withdraw just before the finalization of nominations on 4 December. With Unionist electoral plans in disarray, Enniskillen solicitor James Cooper agreed to stand in Brown's place.[135] Brown's decision also caused a shift in nationalist strategy. Conscious of the dangers of splitting the nationalist vote in constituencies that were so tightly contested, SF and the IPP agreed to divide seats in Fermanagh South, Londonderry city, Down South, Tyrone North West, Tyrone North East, Donegal East, Armagh South and Down East. The pact was brokered by Cardinal Logue, who chose to assign South Fermanagh to SF.[136] SF then nominated Seán O'Mahony.

Patrick Crumley, the sitting IPP MP, was the unanimous choice of the IPP before being sidelined by Logue's electoral compromise. However, after Brown withdrew, perhaps envisaging that no other unionist would come forward, Crumley decided to accept the nomination and to run against O'Mahony. Unionists failing to contest South Fermanagh elections was not unheard of. Indeed, Crumley had been previously elected unopposed. Despite this decision and Crumley's own personal optimism, the IPP campaign recognized the difficulties he would face to win over an alienated nationalist community. The *Impartial Reporter* reported that Crumley was looking to canvass among the Protestant community – to present himself as a compromise candidate between two extremes.[137] However, Crumley's campaign proved short-lived due to the emergence of Cooper as the Unionist nominee. On 10 December 1918 James O'Mara, SF director of elections, telegrammed Logue threatening that if Crumley did not withdraw then SF would reinstate their own candidate in South Down. Crumley withdrew that day and his 'patriotic action' earned him considerable praise in the local press, the *Freeman's Journal* and from senior Catholic clerics such as the bishop of Clogher.[138] Despite his prompt exit, Crumley's name remained on the ballot paper. O'Mahony won convincingly with 6,673 votes to 4,524 for Cooper. Crumley garnered 132 votes despite his withdrawal.

In North Fermanagh the nationalist community could not afford to run two candidates and so Kevin O'Shiel was brought in as a last-minute compromise. He narrowly lost to the incumbent Unionist MP Edward Archdale. North Fermanagh was possibly the most influential contest on the island. South Fermanagh would return a nationalist MP of one type or another. North Fermanagh, however, had always been decided by tight margins. While the Unionists had consistently won the seat, infighting had enabled nationalists to edge the contest in the past. A loss to either SF or the IPP in 1918 would have left the entire county under nationalist MPs and would have made it very difficult to justify the establishment of a six-county Ulster state. Archdale won North Fermanagh by 532 votes, one of the tightest Unionist margins in the North with only Londonderry city providing a closer race. It was by far the most nationalist constituency to elect a Unionist MP and North Fermanagh was of great symbolic importance for unionists in Fermanagh as a whole.

While SF and the IPP had agreed to run a compromise candidate, the selection of that candidate led to some controversy. SF proposed George Irvine, who was now immensely popular among Fermanagh republicans. His nomination was described by the *Impartial Reporter* as 'too grotesque for words!'[139] However, Irvine was deemed unacceptable by the Enniskillen AOH which proposed J.P. Gillin instead. Realizing that only one candidate could possibly win, a local plebiscite was held outside Catholic churches after Mass to determine the candidate. Irvine won comfortably. In response, local Hibernians made it known that they would not support him in the election with his parents 'proselytising Protestantism' given as a primary reason.[140] SF agreed to withdraw Irvine. When Francis O'Duffy refused the nomination, the party put forward O'Shiel.

This election was a minor episode in O'Shiel's long and varied career. He had served as a barrister before joining the Volunteers. He was Arthur Griffith's election agent in the East Cavan by-election in 1918, which won him some prominence and was assigned to run as the SF candidate in heavily unionist South Antrim in the general election. O'Shiel was nervous but accepted. When asked if the central organization could do anything to help him, he replied that he would only expect a republican funeral.[141] O'Shiel was reluctant to take on another campaign and was disdainful of whatever 'chicanery' had seen Irvine dropped. Ultimately, Irvine convinced him to run. While Irvine resented the 'bigotry' of the Hibernian contingent that forced his withdrawal, he was keen to secure a candidate 'who stood for the principles of 1916 and Sinn Féin'.[142] O'Shiel was conciliatory and agreed to meet with Gillin and the rest of the county's Hibernian leadership before accepting the nomination. His speech was appeasing. It praised the achievements of the organization in the county and avoided references to SF policy. The Hibernians agreed to support O'Shiel.[143] This election wrangling was an error on the part of the AOH which had no chance of electing its own candidate. Irvine seems to have been an excellent choice as candidate, described by Eda Sagarra, O'Shiel's daughter, as 'ideal' for such a mixed area.[144] However, O'Shiel's attentions were now divided between two constituencies and he had lost valuable time for campaigning. Furthermore, unlike Irvine, he had no particular connection to Fermanagh – something used against him by Edward Archdale.

Previous elections had witnessed electoral violence, especially when results were announced such as the clashes in Maguiresbridge after Jeremiah Jordan's victory in 1910. However, O'Shiel's campaign struck a nerve with local unionists and proved far more hostile than his campaign in the unionist stronghold of South Antrim. This was partially due to SF's strategy of canvassing in as many areas as they could, irrespective of their political leanings. This was in contrast to the IPP which had been content to contest only winnable localities. In North Fermanagh, O'Shiel was strictly informed to 'on no account, ignore the Protestant and Unionist districts' nor did he have any illusions as to why this was done, noting: 'we were fundamentally a propagandist movement'.[145] This led to a number of tense encounters on the campaign trail. O'Shiel recalled one incident in strongly Protestant Ballinamallard. Recognizing the risks, the visit took place in the afternoon in the hope that increased visibility and the absence of men at work would offer protection. O'Shiel found himself addressing a crowd of 200 women and children. Initially, he was only interrupted with traditional unionist chants such as 'to hell wi' the Pope's man'. Having heard of the impudent national speaker, three drummers began playing loudly which excited the crowd. According to O'Shiel, the women took 'long hat-pins from their hair and made wicked stabs with them at us'. This was enough to cause Dick Herbert, O'Shiel's campaign manager, and O'Shiel to flee the town 'amidst a shower of stones and clods and a salvo of curses'.[146]

Archdale lost no opportunity to depict O'Shiel as an outsider. In a speech in Ballinamallard, he asked the crowd how many men his opponent had ever employed. He pointed out his own sterling record as an employer as well as emphasizing his own credentials as a 'Fermanagh man born and bred'.[147] His language during the campaign was typical of a Unionist candidate – Sinn Féin and O'Shiel were 'more invidious than the Kaiser'.[148] This was a traditional argument about those who owned property in a county being the most invested in seeing it prosper. Comparing candidates in the 1918 election, the *Fermanagh Times* also employed this rhetoric. It characterized the Unionist candidates James Cooper and Edward Archdale as having 'large financial stakes in the county' and used this as evidence that both men wanted the county to flourish. O'Shiel and O'Mahony were portrayed as

> Two perfect strangers who only come to Fermanagh at all in order to see if they can fool the people sufficiently to make them return them … if

they fail ... they will shake the dust of this county off their shoes and will not care two straws what becomes of it or its people.[149]

The day of the count, New Year's Eve 1918, passed off peacefully. While there was a slim unionist majority on the electoral register, nationalists held out hopes of upsetting that with a stronger turnout (although it was noted that the Spanish flu had spread to Fermanagh and had mostly confined itself to the Catholic community). Despite this, initial counts pointed towards a nationalist victory. To O'Shiel, Archdale seemed 'a mildly spoken, gentle old chap' whose anxiety about the election result prompted O'Shiel to attempt to comfort him, telling him that the solid Unionist votes were yet to come in and that he had time to make a comeback.[150] So it proved as the votes from Lisbellaw, Kesh and other unionist areas came in to secure victory for Archdale. Despite O'Shiel's compassion for his political opponent and Archdale's own seemingly mild nature, Archdale's victory speech enflamed the crowd as he congratulated his 'fellow Orangemen and fellow Loyalists' for clearing the 'rebels, traitors and pro-Germans out of loyal North Fermanagh'.[151] The local Anglican church was broken into, the curate overpowered and the bells rung in celebration (it would later emerge the men who broke in were not even Anglican themselves but Presbyterian).[152] When Canon Webb complained about his treatment and the religious identity of those who rang the bells, the *Fermanagh Times* jocularly asserted that it was an Ulster Protestant victory and, therefore, could be celebrated as such.[153] O'Shiel himself was surprised: 'Were that voice and those words, the voice and words of the nervous, mild little man in whose mellow company I had spent the day? It was a violent, rabble rousing, bitter speech, such as would be made by the average semi–educated Orange mob orator.' He feared for his life but was eventually rescued by a large crowd of sympathetic soldiers who began brawling with the Unionist supporters and escorted O'Shiel to his hotel.[154]

While the strength of this reaction from Fermanagh unionists to their victory might seem surprising in retrospect, O'Shiel understood it. Had he won the seat, 'the entire parliamentary representation of the County Fermanagh would have been held by Sinn Féin – in other words, by anti-partitionists of the most uncompromising type'.[155] The reaction to Archdale's win was primarily one of relief at an extremely important and tight victory. The vociferousness of this reaction, and the campaign in general, reflected the severe anxiety felt in Fermanagh about its future and the crucial role played by the 1918 election in determining this. The *Fermanagh Times* put it succinctly: 'will Fermanagh come within the definition of Ulster when the time comes?'[156] Unlike in Tyrone where the more concentrated distribution of unionists allowed William Coote to win the South Tyrone election with a majority of over 5,000, in Fermanagh unionists were more evenly distributed and, consequently, did not hold an outright majority in either parliamentary constituency. South Fermanagh was 62 per cent Catholic and North Fermanagh 51 per cent. The fear of ending up with no real parliamentary representation and, therefore, being grouped with Cavan, Monaghan and Donegal and put at risk of exclusion from a northern state was real and keenly felt in the 1918 election, the first under a greatly expanded franchise.

For the *Fermanagh Times* especially, the idea of voter engagement was crucial. The organization and motivation of the SF machine was held as an example of the need for Fermanagh unionists to turn out in large numbers. The election was portrayed as the community's greatest opportunity to be vindicated as an 'integral part of that "Ulster" against which the government has on successive occasions announced that it has no intention of applying methods of coercion'.[157] Even failure to get elected, as happened in the case of James Cooper in South Fermanagh, was a valuable reminder that 'there are at least 4,524 men and women in South Fermanagh who will have no truck with Home Rule or Sinn Féin'.[158] The political campaign provided common goals for disparate unionist groups to unite behind. As the new rector of Enniskillen parish, Canon Arthur Webb, was testily informed on his refusal to hold a combined Protestant memorial service: 'Enniskillen Protestants agree in all things political ... whenever opportunity offers such as some manifestation of public rejoicing, of national thanksgiving ... they should mingle their voices together in common prayer'.[159] Indeed, the political vote was often the ultimate expression of unionism; the failure to exercise it rendered all other displays meaningless.

5 'There was little sign to be seen of the war': the War of Independence, 1919–20

The face of nationalism and unionism in Fermanagh was transformed in the two years following SF's electoral victory in 1918. Before the election, Fermanagh on the surface appeared as it had in 1900. Politically, all positions were held by either the Ulster Unionist Party or the IPP. Despite the near civil war in 1914, militant unionism was dormant and militant nationalism was still marginal. By 1920 SF was the rising nationalist power in the county. Ulster unionist militias were not only resurgent but had taken on a new form, one that would persist for almost half a century – the Ulster Special Constabulary (USC). Both nationalism and unionism were more irreconcilable than at any point in the previous few decades and a new unionist-dominated Northern state was rapidly appearing on the horizon. Fermanagh's experience during the War of Independence was unique for a number of reasons. First, it was characterized by an unusually weak IRA movement. While the Fermanagh IRA was able to undertake a number of operations, it never reached the scale of activity achieved in neighbouring Tyrone, Monaghan or Donegal.[1] Second and relatedly, in Fermanagh the organized unionist military response to the IRA was proportionally stronger than elsewhere in Ulster. Fermanagh's even population divide and relative lack of religious clustering meant that unionists across the county felt surrounded by hostile republican forces and vowed to arm themselves. The example of Fermanagh's unionist militias was influential across Ulster. It inspired others to do likewise, but more significantly it provided much of the initial structure and impetus for the USC. The image of unionist soldiers defending the frontier of Ulster became central to the ethos of the USC. Third, local government in most of Ireland was dominated by SF but not in Fermanagh, which remained highly contested. Unionists struggled for control in Fermanagh against a fractious alliance of the IPP, SF and the labour movement. Indeed, the 1920 local elections were remarkable for the manner in which the IPP clawed back a modicum of political relevance.

In the 1918 general election, SF won seventy-three seats to the IPP's six. While this represented a seismic shift in Irish politics, it was underscored by two further events in January 1919 that profoundly changed Ireland. On 21 January the newly elected SF MPs followed through on their election manifesto by refusing to take their seats in Westminster. Instead, they met in the Mansion House in Dublin to establish Dáil Éireann. Fermanagh's representative, Seán O'Mahony, was unable to attend as he was in Lincoln Jail following the 'German Plot' arrests of 1918. When his name was read out on the roll, he was simply registered as 'faoi ghlas ag Gallaibh' – imprisoned by the foreigners. After his release, O'Mahony attended most of the First Dáil's proceedings. He also undertook a pro-Dáil speaking tour in Fermanagh over six weeks beginning in Belcoo in early March.[2]

While the establishment of the Dáil was guaranteed to exacerbate tensions with Britain and unionists, it was not in itself a declaration of war. However, on the same day, without official sanction, a group of Volunteers (hereafter generally called the IRA) ambushed and killed two members of the RIC at Soloheadbeg in County Tipperary. On 31 January *An tÓglach*, the organ of the Irish Volunteers/IRA, declared that 'all legitimate methods of warfare' were permissible in the struggle against the RIC and British army.[3] These events are conventionally regarded as the beginning of the War of Independence and led to a gradual upsurge in revolutionary violence across the country over the next two years. Fermanagh proved an exception to this general trend, with a markedly lower incidence of 'outrages'. In March 1919 the Fermanagh judges of assizes boasted that the county was the quietest in the country.[4] This was echoed by the republican side when Joseph Lawless, Dublin Brigade engineering officer, travelled from Virginia to Pettigo and noted that 'there was little sign to be seen of the war which the daily press reports showed to be widespread'.[5]

The impact of the new Dáil was initially manifested in Fermanagh through the establishment of the Dáil courts and the raising of the Dáil loan. The courts were slower to establish themselves fully in Fermanagh than elsewhere. While James J. Smyth of Lisnaskea would later describe enforcing the decrees of Dáil courts as one of the primary duties of the new IRA companies, Livingstone has characterized the efforts to establish a parallel legal system as only partially effective and mainly limited to the county's southern borders.[6] The activities of these courts were largely restricted to raids on illegal poteen-makers. Cahir Healy served as county registrar for the Dáil courts in Fermanagh. In that role he forged a strong friendship with Fr Lorcán Ó Ciaráin of Maghermeenagh Castle near Belleek whose parochial house was commonly used as a courtroom.[7]

More successful was the Dáil loan, instituted in June 1919 by the Dáil to raise money to fund itself and the new state it was trying to establish. Michael Collins instructed all SF TDs and candidates to return to their constituencies to promote the loan. The loan was primarily organized in South Fermanagh by Seán O'Mahony and Terence Caulfield with Fr Patrick Cullinan of Belcoo serving as the treasurer.[8] Kevin O'Shiel also returned to North Fermanagh for the same purpose, although, as he freely admitted, the 'Trojan work' was done by 'that splendid patriot, Cahir Healy'. Two other key organizers were Fr Peter Connolly of Garrison and Seán Carty of Devenish West.[9] O'Shiel, for his part, travelled the county with local leaders delivering impromptu speeches to exhort people to buy republican bonds. Junior clergy were especially active in promoting the loan.[10] Names of contributors were listed in a notebook but no amounts were recorded. This allowed O'Shiel to tell the RIC the list merely contained names of people he intended to canvass for the next general election. This caution proved well founded as O'Shiel was frequently searched by the police who never found anything incriminating on him.

A total of £3,226 was raised in Fermanagh: £1,768 in the north and £1,458 in the south respectively. While one of the smaller totals collected in Ulster, which was itself less successful in raising money for the loan than elsewhere, proportionally Fermanagh contributed more per head than any other Ulster county apart from Cavan, Monaghan and Donegal.[11] O'Shiel declared it 'not a bad total' before noting: 'North Fermanagh was not a typical constituency. It was a doubly divided constituency, divided almost 50–50 between Catholics and Protestants, with the Catholics again divided sharply between the Hibernian and Sinn Féiners.'[12] He also remarked that contributions came from both republicans and Hibernians and even some unionists who he understood were later mocked by their neighbours for having given away money they would never see again. In contrast to his election campaign, O'Shiel reported good relations with the unionists whom he encountered. On one occasion he was able to escape an RIC raid on Boa Island due to a timely tip-off from local Catholics and Protestants.[13]

As Michael Hopkinson has noted, despite the establishment of a General Headquarters (GHQ) in March 1918 with the aim of formalizing Collins's and Mulcahy's influence over the IRA, many counties displayed highly variable levels of central control.[14] This was especially pronounced in Fermanagh, where a number of highly motivated battalions and companies worked under their own initiative; however, most were inert until prodded into life by Dublin. The IRA in Fermanagh, as elsewhere, was structured as brigades composed of battalions which in turn comprised companies as the basic unit of organization. After March 1921 these brigades were organized into divisions. Parts of Fermanagh came under the jurisdiction of a number of divisions (see map 5). The 4th South Donegal Brigade included the area around the north shore of Lower Lough Erne. The brigade O/C was Seán Fitzgerald and its adjutant was Seán MacCool of Stranorlar. The 2nd Battalion was commanded by Liam Carty and contained the Belleek and Mulleek companies. The 3rd Battalion was commanded by Daniel Gallagher and included the Pettigo, Ederney and Lettercran companies, all either within Fermanagh or along the border. After March 1921 these battalions became part of the 1st Northern Division under Frank Carney and later Joseph Sweeney.[15]

The 2nd Tyrone Brigade covered much of the central part of north Fermanagh, including Irvinestown and Ballinamallard but not Enniskillen. The brigade O/C was Michael Gallagher of Dromore and his adjutant was Patrick Donnelly. The 2nd (Dromore) Battalion under James Gallagher included the Irvinestown and Sheemuldoon companies. After March 1921 these companies were part of the 2nd Northern Division under Mick Gallagher. Two battalions

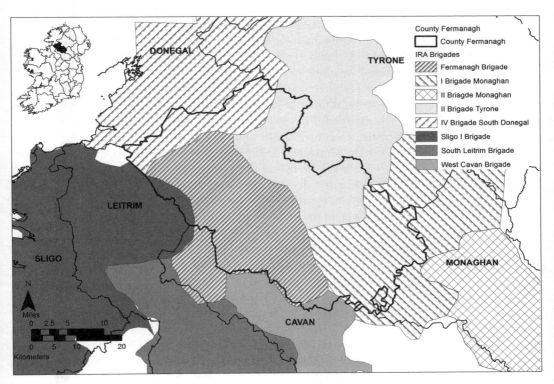

5 IRA brigade areas

of the 1st Monaghan Brigade (commanded by James McKenna) covered much of east Fermanagh, including Roslea, Lisnaskea and Newtownbutler. The Clones Battalion was led by Matt Fitzpatrick. It contained the Wattlebridge company while the Scotstown Battalion under James Smyth included the Roslea company (and after March 1921 the Lisnaskea, Moen's Cross, Killyrover and Knocknagun companies). These battalions became part of the 5th Northern Division commanded by Eoin O'Duffy and later by Dan Hogan.[16]

Part of the 1st Midland Division, the Fermanagh Brigade itself covered the southern half of the county and extended into Cavan and Leitrim. This division was under the command of Seán Mac Eoin. After the divisional reorganization, the Lisnaskea Battalion was transferred to the 5th Northern Division. This brigade was based in Enniskillen and was commanded by Frank Carney, a former soldier who had been employed previously to drill the Irish Volunteers. Seán Sheehan, who worked in the Enniskillen tax office, was adjutant.[17] The Fermanagh Brigade had five battalions. The Enniskillen Battalion under Frank Duffy comprised Boho, Derrygonnnelly, Eniskillen, Monea and Rosinuremore companies. Peter Maguire commanded Belcoo Battalion which included Belcoo, Woobally, Glan Lower, Glan Upper, Killinagh and Mullaghdun companies. Derrylin Battalion, under Felix McMullen, had Arney, Kinawley, Kingarrow (Derrylin), Mountain Road, Kiflosher and Wheathill companies. Edward Gray led Temp Battalion which drew together Breagho, Cavanacross, Coa, Temp, Toneyglaskin, Trillick and Whitechurch companies. Lastly, Francis Courtney was commandant of Lisnaskea Battalion, which comprised Lisnaskea, Killyrover, Moen's Cross and Knocknagun companies.[18]

Frank Carney was the most significant figure in the Enniskillen IRA from late 1918, when he took over command of the Fermanagh Brigade from Patrick Nulty, until March 1921 when he was appointed head of the 1st Northern Division. Born in Abbey Street, Enniskillen, in 1896, Carney enlisted in the Royal Inniskilling Fusiliers on the outbreak of the First World War. His brother James was killed in Gallipoli, after which Carney was assigned to home service in England where he was eventually discharged on medical grounds in January 1916.[19] At that point he was not affiliated with the Irish Volunteers. A traditional account holds that Carney joined the Volunteers immediately after the Easter Rising in full military uniform. However, Lawrence White has described this story as apocryphal.[20] He joined the Volunteers in 1917 and offered his services as a drill sergeant. James Smyth recalled that Carney had 'companies throughout the county under proper discipline and doing rifle and open formation drill'.[21] As a brigade commander, Carney was extremely active, undertaking activities across Fermanagh, Tyrone and southern Donegal. Seán Sheehan later described him as 'one of the ablest Volunteer officers in the North'.[22] He was noted for having created a loyal cadre of 'helpers' who often held no rank in the IRA but who were always in the presence of Carney and critically involved in the planning of actions.[23] Carney situated the brigade headquarters in the Brooke Hotel in Enniskillen, the home of the secretary of the town's branch of Cumann na mBan, Cissie McGovern.[24] Carney was arrested in early 1920 and held for a number of months in Belfast Jail. He was eventually released after he and a number of other prisoners went on an extended hunger strike.[25]

This hunger strike and Carney's later internment in Ballykinlar damaged his health. Sheehan recalled how Carney's chronic asthma and bronchitis (the cause of his discharge from the British army) grew steadily worse over the course of the War of Independence. He remembered undertaking numerous all-night bicycle and boat rides across the county with Carney in the middle of winter and often through rain. According to Sheehan, Carney's health began to decline almost immediately in 1919 due to 'the loss of sleep, constant changing of abode, exposure to night air and dampness etc'.[26] In 1920 Carney intended to take charge of the Fermanagh Active Service Unit (ASU) but only lasted a fortnight before he had to be replaced on health grounds. He rarely allowed himself sufficient time to recover after an attack of bronchitis and was frequently on

Volunteer duty in 'an entirely unfit state of health for such duty'.[27] Carney died in 1932 at the age of just thirty-six.

In Charles Townshend's three-stage model of the War of Independence, initial IRA activity was characterized by small-scale arms raids that transitioned over the winter of 1919–20 into direct attacks on RIC barracks.[28] Fermanagh roughly fits this pattern although with a time lag when compared to the national pattern. Both Travers and Grant have noted similar delays in Donegal and Derry respectively.[29] The Fermanagh IRA also demonstratd a proclivity for arms raids that would last well into 1920, long after the county should have transitioned to the next stage of the war. Such raids were intended to enhance the capabilities of local IRA companies and to intimidate their victims. Livingstone refused to assign any sectarian character to them, claiming that some captains only raided nationalists, while others exclusively focused on unionists and that this pattern was entirely local.[30] However, bodies of unionist opinion such as the *Impartial Reporter* asserted that these raids were strongly, if not entirely, sectarian in character. Most arms raids were motivated by the desperation of the Fermanagh IRA. Companies were operating under extremely reduced circumstances in terms of arms and men. Tummon recalled the significant difficulties the Wattlebridge company faced in terms of securing arms:

> A couple of revolvers of an old obsolete type were received from supporters. Such weapons had little practical value, being useless for instruction and dangerous to use ... There were few modern shotguns in our area. The old muzzle loading type were still being used for wild fowl use. Cartridges for these weapons were also controlled during the war and even more rigidly after the 1916 Rebellion.[31]

In these circumstances former members of the UVF presented a natural target for raids as it was believed they still held their Mauser rifles. On this assumption the Wattlebridge company raided Castlesaunderson, along the Cavan border, in the winter of 1919. The raid lasted for almost two hours. Most of the operation involved searching the property for the Mausers the IRA believed were stored within. In the end, five single-shot Martini–Henry rifles, a small cache of ammunition and miscellaneous military equipment such as helmets and haversacks were all that was seized.[32] Accounts of arms raids in the county in the Bureau of Military History tend to emphasize the quantity of weapons and ammunition located. John Connolly recounted a raid on loyalists in the Roslea area that encapsulated the opportunity and difficulties of this approach. The first house raided, the Warringtons were taken completely by surprise, mid-prayer, and relieved of three rifles and two revolvers. On its own, this was a significant addition. A search of the out offices yielded even more ammunition. 'Elated', the party moved on to the next loyalist family, the Andersons, only to find they had already been alerted and were too well prepared and armed for the house to be taken.[33]

The Fermanagh IRA was also slow to transition into attacking barracks. In the early phase of the War of Independence most Fermanagh companies were more active outside the county. On 15 February 1920 the Wattlebridge, Coranny and Roslea companies took part in the burning of Ballytrain RIC barracks. Under Matt Fitzpatrick the Wattlebridge company, in particular, distinguished itself by capturing and storing the gelignite used in the operation.[34] In response to this attack, the RIC arrested Matt Fitzpatrick, Frank Fitzpatrick, Frank Sheridan and Tommie Houston of the Wattlebridge company and moved 200 soldiers to Newtownbutler to protect the barracks there.[35] This may be a consequence of Fermanagh's general slow start to join the War of Independence. As Townshend has noted, 'the performance of IRA units in 1920–1 depended on their initial impetus in 1918–19: thereafter no amount of prodding from above could spur on slow starters to make up lost ground'.[36] It was only as the RIC began to withdraw from isolated stations and rural barracks that such attacks began in Fermanagh (see map 6). On 3 and 4 April 1920 the abandoned barracks in Letterbreen, Trillick and Arney were burned down by the IRA. Lisbellaw courthouse was also burned to the ground. In June Derrylin courthouse and tax office were both burned. Not all such operations were successful, however. Two attempts to burn Carngreen barracks were resisted by the RIC.[37] Another vacant barracks in Roslea was spared as it adjoined the house of the local Catholic curate who was ill and confined to bed at the time.[38]

Reflecting pre-existing rivalries in the county, AOH halls were also occasionally attacked. The hall in Dernawilt was targeted in March 1920 while the hall in Aghadrumsee had been partially demolished the previous month due to local tensions over its construction.[39] SF and other republicans in the district argued that the pre-existing SF hall in the area was the proper gathering point for nationalists in the district.[40] Unlike the situation in Tyrone and Monaghan, tensions between SF and the AOH did not spill over into street violence.[41] Both sides endeavoured to maintain relations as best they could. Even after the AOH's contentious vetoing of George Irvine in 1918, O'Shiel and SF were careful to pass a resolution at the post-election rally thanking the AOH for their conduct in the election and the enthusiastic support shown for O'Shiel.[42]

The Hibernians for their part avoided frequent large-scale marches or rallies that had been a source of conflict with SF in neighbouring counties. When such demonstrations did take place, they were on a large scale in areas where the AOH was pre-eminent. The largest of these was held at Newtownbutler in August 1919 when two trains were hired to bring members from Enniskillen to the district.[43] Within these events the local Hibernian rhetoric was confident and assertive, indeed it bordered on the deluded and belligerent. At that same rally in Newtownbutler, Patrick Crumley, the ousted MP for South Fermanagh,

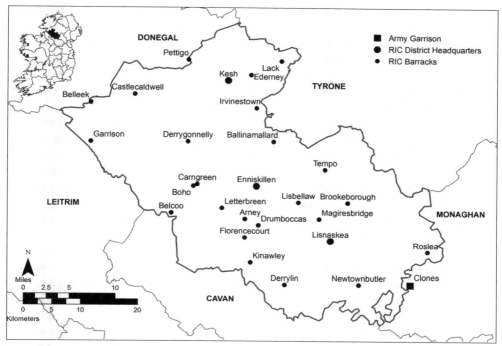

6 Distribution of Crown forces

declared that the country 'had woken up to the fact that it had been grossly misled at the election'. P.J. Donnelly, IPP MP for South Armagh, declared that Crumley would 'sweep Fermanagh at the next election'.[44]

Raids by the IRA did not always go smoothly. In April 1920 a general order was issued to burn all income tax offices. This was not carried out in the Fermanagh Brigade area due to the 'action or inaction of one Volunteer officer'.[45] Consequently, these attacks were undertaken on 14 May 1920. Seven collector's offices scattered across the brigade area as well as the central office in Enniskillen were targeted. The raids were more difficult than they had been for other brigades as now the RIC and the collectors were expecting some attack to be made. Fortunately, Sheehan was an employee of the tax office as was another Volunteer, Robert Burns. They were able to bring in two cans of petrol the week before the attack and conceal them within the office. Sheehan then arranged to work overtime on the day of the raid and was able to let the Volunteers in when the RIC guard was changing. Sheehan left the office before the fire started. The tax office was only partially destroyed as the IRA was reluctant to start too large a fire lest it spread to the pharmacy on the ground floor and adjacent homes. Elsewhere in the county, six of the seven collector's offices were destroyed. One was spared as the collector made a direct appeal to Sheehan.[46]

The two most significant raids in the county took place towards the end of 1920. On the morning of 5 September 1920, the Enniskillen company, led by Carney, attacked Belleek barracks while most of the police were at Mass. It was arranged that the local curate, Lorcán Ó Ciaráin, would deliver an especially long sermon to delay the police as long as possible. The raiding party, dressed as British soldiers and led by Joseph Smyth who had a pronounced cockney accent, approached the barracks pretending to have a document to deliver. When the guard opened the door, he was overpowered and locked in an outhouse with the other policemen in the barracks. Although they had hoped to be able to undertake the entire raid while Mass was being said, the IRA had been delayed and were forced to barricade the chapel door. Carney and the Enniskillen company then departed while a separate company from Belleek removed ten light machine-guns, ten rifles, ten revolvers, a number of bombs, and ammunition. The party set fire to the barracks and drove off. The police in the chapel escaped in time to put out the blaze.[47]

A raid on Tempo barracks on 25 October 1920 proved less straightforward. James Smyth later described it as 'a fight to get in and a fight to get out!'[48] A number of the RIC had been tipped off about the raid, two had taken leave and another had arranged to be captured and detained while out on patrol. The IRA party selected for the raid was drawn primarily from the Enniskillen company but with certain men from Wattlebridge, Belcoo and Lisnaskea.[49] Members of the Bundoran company were also called to be ready but were not summoned.[50] The raid took place at 8 p.m. when three Volunteers entered the barracks through the back door. Only Sergeant Samuel Lucas and Constable O'Brien were inside. The IRA men startled a dog, which prompted Lucas to investigate. He wounded Joseph Slavin before being disarmed and ordered into the yard. There, he again struggled with his captors and wounded a second Volunteer, Joseph Trainor, before running through the rear gate. Lucas was fatally wounded as he reached the street and died on 4 November. The shooting alerted local UVF members who opened fire on the raiders.[51] The operation verged on disaster when the car carrying the petrol to burn the barracks was unable to stop due to fire from the UVF. Without petrol and transport the IRA could not burn the barracks or carry away any captured arms. James Smyth ordered four of the party to cover their retreat while the rest carried the seized weapons to Doon cross where they were able to find a second car. Despite being under fire, the IRA suffered no casualties during this retreat. Eight rifles, three carbines, three revolvers and two boxes of ammunition were obtained.

While these raids were undoubtedly major undertakings, they also demonstrated that the Fermanagh IRA lagged behind the rest of the country. Townshend has characterized mid-1920 as the beginning of the second major phase of the War of Independence with the creation of Active Service Units (ASU), or flying columns, to undertake major operations such as ambushes.

However, Frank Carney only established one in Fermanagh in September. It was not intended as a means to ramp up operations but to give men on the run somewhere to go. Both raids on Tempo and Belleek, with men drawn from regular IRA companies instead of ASUs, were more characteristic of the IRA in early rather than late 1920. On his release from prison, Carney ordered most companies to focus on nightly raids for arms. Nevertheless, some units were more effective than others in this period, especially along the Monaghan border where Eoin O'Duffy oversaw operations.

In particular, the Wattlebridge company was active at this time and was involved in the most significant ambush in Fermanagh during the War of Independence. In September a Sligo, Leitrim and Northern Counties train was successfully held up by the Mullaghdoon company and a county-wide arms raid was undertaken. On 1 October 1920 near a bridge crossing the Ulster Canal in Edergole, the company successfully surrounded a military tender travelling from Cavan to Enniskillen. The soldiers surrendered without a fight and the company were able to seize four rifles, the first rifles it possessed. The tender was then burned.[52] The Wattlebridge company was also responsible for the destruction of a boat used by the RIC in Newtownbutler to travel along the Erne. The vessel was taken from its moorings at night to a deep part of the Erne between Goladuff and Galoon, loaded with a large number of heavy stones, and then had its hull punctured with a crowbar. It sank in five minutes. Francis Tummon claimed that the boat was never replaced. Actions like this severely hindered the police in a county so heavily dominated by waterways.

In all of these actions the IRA were strongly supported by Cumann na mBan. Cissie McGovern identified a number of key tasks carried out by Cumann na mBan throughout 1919 and 1920. Its members carried dispatches throughout the county. This duty fell especially heavily on McGovern herself as the IRA were headquartered in her home. Consequently, she was often handed orders directly by Carney. Cumann na mBan were also used as one of the main means of moving arms around the county. McGovern estimated that she had moved arms personally three or four times. Twice she led an operation to smuggle cases of revolvers and grenades via the railway into the county. Cumann na mBan was also responsible for holding arms that were dropped off by Volunteers until they returned. Consequently, McGovern's home was raided by the police several times. But she listed her most regular contribution to the revolutionary cause as catering. In addition to hosting the brigade headquarters and occasional divisional meetings, she provided food and supplies to men on the run. Seán Sheehan 'could not speak too highly' of the work of McGovern and Cumann na mBan.[53]

The IRA clearly struggled to assert itself consistently in Fermanagh during the War of Independence but it faced significant operational difficulties. Indeed, the war in Fermanagh is distinguished by the presence of an aggressive and organized unionist opposition to the IRA. In June 1920 a mixed IRA force, under Carney, Sheehan and Philip Breen attempted to burn down the recently vacated RIC barracks at Lisbellaw. With advance warning, local unionists prepared to ambush the IRA.[54] They demonstrated a level of tactical discipline in their response, refusing to fire on sight at the IRA scouts, instead drawing their main force into the town proper and using church bells as a means of co-ordinating and summoning help from the countryside.[55] In the subsequent firefight, two unionists named Eadie and O'Donnell were wounded along with two IRA men before the IRA retreated.[56]

That this should happen in Lisbellaw was unsurprising as it had always been a centre of unionism in Fermanagh and was known by the IRA to be '99% hostile'.[57] The Lisbellaw militia had only been founded in the weeks immediately before the IRA attack. George Edwin Liddle, later county commandant, had received a tipp-off in Bangor about the attack and took it upon himself to warn figures in the town who had been prominent in the UVF – Billy Clendinning (elsewhere Glendenning) and Samuel McCreery of Derrybrusk and Frederick Nawn of Lisbellaw.[58] These men organized a meeting in Lisbellaw Orange hall in May 1920 to form a 'civilian force' to guard the town. That very night the force experienced its first engagement when a raid was made on the house of Clendinning. The militia drove off the raiders. The subsequent attack on the barracks was thought to be a response to the failed attack on Clendinning's house.[59] In their patrols, the group demonstrated the military experience of their members. They allowed for their small size by prioritizing pre-selected defensive positions that allowed them to guard houses and key points in the town such as the railway station, courthouse and police barracks.

The best known of these groups was the 'Fermanagh Vigilance' which was established by Basil Brooke, future prime minister of Northern Ireland, in the summer of 1920. The group quickly became the largest in the county and formed the basis of the revived UVF in Fermanagh as well as heavily influencing the subsequent formation of the USC. The group was also significant for the way in which it effectively launched Brooke's career. Following the armistice, Brooke returned to his family estate in Colebrooke in December 1918. As Brian Barton has emphasized, he was essentially a stranger to the county, having been away for most of the previous twenty-two years. His strongest connection was his involvement with the UVF. In December 1912, while on leave, he had been heavily involved in setting up the first UVF brigade in Fermanagh and he had seriously considered resigning his army commission in March 1914 to 'return to help the loyalists in Ulster'. The outbreak of the First World War rendered this decision moot.[60] Colebrooke, too, was a highly significant centre for the UVF in Fermanagh, holding about one quarter of all arms in the county and being the primary distribution centre for arms following the Larne gun-running. Given Brooke's background and the rising political tensions that coincided with his return, it was unsurprising that he quickly reintegrated himself into the loyalist militia tradition in Fermanagh.

Brooke's distrust of the RIC reflected that of many Fermanagh loyalists. In the 'Battle of Lisbellaw', local unionists had been outraged that the RIC had only arrived the morning after the attack.[61] In addition, the force was seventy to eighty per cent Catholic and, as Michael Farrell has noted, 'to a movement calling for a separate state for Protestants, all Catholics were suspect'.[62] Therefore, in June 1920 Brooke established 'Fermanagh Vigilance', a loyalist militia designed to resist republican raiding in the locality. His wife, Cynthia Brooke, described it as 'an arrangement for the mutual defence against Sinn Féin, two in each townland on sentry duty each night'.[63] The broad duties of the group involved setting up roadblocks at night on key roads, keeping watch over the towns where it had been established, and opposing the IRA militarily should a raid take place. The Cole monument on the Forthill was the sentry point for Enniskillen. In the event, military resistance was never required of the Vigilance before it was subsumed into the USC.[64]

While this force was strongly coded as a continuation of the UVF, Barton notes that it was given the more neutral name 'Fermanagh Vigilance' to encourage Catholic nationalist enlistment, at least in theory. This set it apart from its predecessor, the UVF, and its successor, the USC, both of which to varying degrees discouraged Catholic enlistment.[65] Fermanagh Vigilance represented the first large-scale reorganization of loyalist militias in Ulster, pre-dating the general order to reorganize the UVF of July 1920. The establishment of the Vigilance was a product not only of rising tensions but also of significant demobilization after the war. Returning soldiers had the necessary experience to organize drills and patrols for others.[66] Brooke was keen to portray his new organization as primarily a defensive one; his commitment was to 'maintain order' in the face of an increasing threat of IRA raids.[67] One of his primary motivations for founding Fermanagh Vigilance was a fear that without a structure to control the 'hotheads on the Ulsterman's side', unrestrained violence might erupt.[68] The group provided a Protestant alternative to the IRA's organized violence. Brooke expressed an apprehension that unprotected Protestant families might turn to SF.[69]

The Vigilance were armed with Larne guns that had not been surrendered. Brooke was keen to acquire more arms and estimated that he only had about forty per cent of what he required. Privately, he expressed concern about sending men out to patrol, and thereby attract attention to themselves, if they were insufficiently armed. To this end, he persistently lobbied General Nevil Macready, commander of British forces in Ireland, to provide his group with more arms. Macready was reluctant to support the establishment of another armed group in Fermanagh and initially suggested to Brooke that the company be issued with whistles and armbands. This proposal was greeted by the nascent

Vigilance with laughter and chants of 'Dublin can go to hell, we'll look after ourselves'.[70] Although initially established without official approval, Brooke believed the best way to acquire arms from Macready was if Vigilance was constituted as an official oath-taking organization under the British government. He spent a large portion of July 1920 lobbying Macready and Hamar Greenwood, Irish chief secretary, to this end.

Barton has highlighted that Brooke did not pioneer the new wave of unionist militarism. The threat of a revived UVF had been an ever-present rhetorical tool for Carson since the end of the war. In Fermanagh, the resistance at Lisbellaw in May 1920 also pre-dated the Vigilance. However, Brooke and the Fermanagh Vigilance were significant for a number of reasons. First, they were the most prominent militia before the UVF was reorganized. While the Lisbellaw militia, like other town guards, had existed in secret and only came to prominence after it had successfully ambushed an IRA raiding party, Brooke was keen to publicize the Vigilance to secure high-level political support. In the weeks leading up the re-establishment of the UVF, Fermanagh Vigilance essentially functioned as the face of the new wave of loyalist militias. Second, Fermanagh Vigilance was significantly more ambitious than many of the other Fermanagh defence forces, which were decidedly local in focus. Although Fermanagh Vigilance had started in this similar vein, Brooke quickly expanded its scope and it began to incorporate pre-existing militia. Within a few weeks there were branches at Brookeborough, Lisbellaw, Maguiresbridge and Lisnaskea.[71]

The effects of the 'Battle of Lisbellaw' and the establishment of the Vigilance were immediately apparent. The raids on Belleek and Tempo barracks were significantly complicated by the resistance of local loyalists.[72] Belleek barracks was, however, later burned in response to a warning by local loyalists against attacking the town.[73] William Copeland Trimble recorded that the revolution in Fermanagh might have been much worse were it not for 'the nightly watch in certain districts of volunteers, who ... warded off danger.'[74] Francis Tummon of the Wattlebridge company recalled that 'it was difficult to go off in broad daylight without being identified by some loyalist'.[75] IRA attempts to burn Belcoo and Carngreen were thwarted by the strength of unionist opposition.[76]

The establishment of these groups, and particularly the revival of the UVF, encouraged many loyalist groups to threaten reprisals against local republicans. After the attack on Lisbellaw, it was reported that 'more drastic measures' were being considered in response to the attacks.[77] In September 1920 a 'second in command of a defence body in the county of Fermanagh' warned the *Impartial Reporter* that reprisals were already being planned for outrages that had yet to be committed: 'If they try it again there they will suffer ... If one life be taken we will have two ... and we won't confine ourselves to laymen'.[78] This threat of reprisals was echoed by the CI who warned of 'a very serious encounter ... involving considerable loss of life and very bitter party feeling'.[79] In the aftermath of Lisbellaw, Robert Barton, the SF TD for Wicklow West, was forced to make a hasty retreat from the town after shots were fired at his vehicle.[80] In Ballinamallard in October 1920, over 100 Ulster Volunteers lined the streets during the funeral of Captain Alan Lendrum, a member of the RIC killed in Clare.[81] The Lendrum murder became a major rallying point for the unionist community and prompted strong recruitment to the USC in Fermanagh.[82] The willingness of loyalists to commit serious reprisals can be seen following the raid on Tempo barracks in October 1920. Philip Breen, captain of the Tempo company, did not take part in the raid and, to provide himself with a public alibi, remained at home that evening, occasionally stepping out on the street.[83] Following the shooting of Sergeant Lucas, Breen was shot dead on the street. His killers were never caught but his father maintained: 'it was the civilians who killed him. I am not going to mention names'.[84] The IRA later attempted to kill one of the perpetrators – a postman named Potter who survived the initial attack but died later. Breen's other killer was not identified although an Ulster Volunteer named Beatty was suspected.[85] Following the killings of Breen and Lucas, the CI described sentiment in the county as 'embittered' and noted the proliferation of 'covert threats of reprisal' from both sides.[86]

The revival of the UVF often manifested itself in a willingness to fight off raids such as at Pettigo in September 1920 when the intended victim invited the raiders into his house on the pretence of handing over his rifle before shooting them.[87] In some cases, the response was more directly coded as an anti-IRA reprisal. In November 1920 an IRA convoy driving through Roslea was fired on and forced to retreat in response to an attack on a Monaghan loyalist at the same spot a day earlier.[88] In other instances, the response was a threat issued, both to those directly involved in revolutionary activity and those whose political associations suggested they might be. Dr John Carraher, a Catholic with SF associations on the Enniskillen Board of Guardians, refused to return to the Tempo district following the shooting of Breen. By his own account, in a letter presented to the board on 23 November 1920, after the shooting, he had noticed he was being ignored by his former unionist friends before being held up by a 'drunken policeman' who verbally abused him and threatened him with death if he did not clear out of the district. Carraher had it on good authority that he was wanted 'by the same men that shot Breen'.[89]

The commitment of these loyalist groups and individuals to resisting the IRA should not be underestimated. An unnamed officer issued a warning in the *Reporter* that 'if they interfere ... it will not be an eye for an eye and a tooth for a tooth with us, but two eyes and two teeth.'[90] Local knowledge was used in the same manner as it was by the IRA. The same interview concluded by stating that a list of targets had been created. Atypically, the *Reporter* placed itself against this policy and instead pleaded for preservation of the peace. The 'insurmountable' difficulties faced by the IRA in Fermanagh during this period were summarized by James Smyth: 'It must also be remembered that the majority of those who were opposed to the IRA were fully armed and constantly on the lookout for any movement on the part of the IRA.'[91]

The RIC was active, if ineffective, in responding to these initial outrages. In February 1919 Samuel Hanna had been replaced as CI by Ivon Henry Price, a veteran intelligence officer and unionist hero of the Easter Rising. His personal qualities earned him admirers on both sides of the aisle but he was unable to improve the Fermanagh RIC's flagging fortunes due to his short time in the role. He served creditably and uneventfully for a year before being promoted to assistant inspector general and leaving the county.[92] It is unclear if he would have been able to improve the fortunes of the RIC, but his successor Frederick Tyrell proved unable to do so. The police were hampered by a significant 'lack of men and motors'.[93] This was compounded by a persistent failure to recognize the scale of the threat they faced. As late as January 1920, Price still asserted that SF was 'dying out' in Fermanagh.[94] Following raids by the IRA's Wattlebridge company on a number of bread vans, a large police crackdown was undertaken. Tummon recalled that practically 'every house was raided several times. It became necessary to keep clear at night'.[95] His neighbour, John Tummon (no relation), was arrested by the military and held for three days in a case of mistaken identity. Francis Tummon relocated to a byre in Derryelvin for a number of months. While on the run, he avoided arrest during a Crown forces raid while Mass was celebrated in Connons Catholic church over the county boundary in Monaghan. Each Mass-goer was searched as they left, and a number of arrests were made but none were IRA and only a few supported SF.[96] Cahir Healy recalled an amusing incident in the summer of 1920 where the police attempted to raid a Dáil court in Pettigo nationalist hall but mistakenly targeted the local Orange hall due to a 1916 banner displayed over the door (in this case commemorating the Somme). This allowed members of the court to escape by pretending to be part of a passing funeral procession.[97] Fermanagh's relatively low level of IRA activity was matched by a relatively low level of reprisals by Crown forces (although it should be remembered this was coupled with a much higher occurrence of reprisal and resistance by the loyalist community). In the Dáil's own publicity materials only two attacks against property were recorded between September 1919 and March 1921.[98] The first was when the drilling hall of the Wattlebridge company was burned by the RIC in 1920 in reprisal for an IRA ambush.[99]

The most significant challenge to the IRA came not from the RIC but from the USC. In October 1920, after outbreaks of loyalist violence in Belfast, Lisburn and Banbridge, the British cabinet agreed to James Craig's request to establish a volunteer auxiliary police force in Ulster – the USC – to combat the IRA. The USC was based along the organizational lines of the UVF, which had itself been reorganized across Ulster in July 1920 at the behest of the UUC.[100] There were three classes of 'Specials'. The A Specials were full-time and paid, functioning in a similar role to the RIC, although they could not be deployed outside their home area. The B Specials were part-time and had their own command structure. This was the largest and most flexible group and would come to represent the worst excesses of the USC. The C Specials were reservists and often used for guard duties and other static roles.[101] The A Specials were divided into squads of about fifty men with bases at Enniskillen, Newtownbutler, Florencecourt, Churchhill and Clonelly.[102]

Fermanagh's various unionist militias influenced the creation of the USC. In September 1920 Brooke submitted a detailed proposal for the organization of the putative USC to Sir Ernest Clark, assistant under-secretary for Northern Ireland. The proposal was based on the organization of Fermanagh Vigilance under which a county commander was elected by district commanders, who in turn were elected by townland commanders, each of which led a squad of fourteen men. The proposal also gives an insight into how Fermanagh Vigilance functioned. It leveraged the local knowledge of its townland commanders. Any suspicious local figures were watched and capable men were put in charge of patrols, which took place only close to the homes of members to reduce the burden of active duty. Barton suggests that this proposal had a formative influence on the USC structure. Clark deemed it 'the most valuable information I have received'.[103] In any case the relative autonomy of the unionists militias would become a major point of contention with the USC. Cormac Moore has noted how unusual it was that the body was able to act without any real oversight from central government.[104]

Despite this, Brooke was not the initial choice for the role of county commandant. Instead, Wilfrid Spender, head of the UVF, received a petition from 'leaders of the county' in Fermanagh who requested Viscount Cole, heir to earldom of Enniskillen, to take the role. Both Clark and Spender were surprised by this and expressed regret that Brooke had not been selected. Barton suggests that this may have been due to the deferential nature of Fermanagh unionism and Brooke's extra-legal actions that had made him somewhat unpopular in the mind of 'respectable county opinion'.[105] In any case, Cole was unwilling and Brooke was selected as Fermanagh's first county commandant on 18 November 1920. Alongside him, Fermanagh's main USC officers were Colonel Henry Richardson (the future county commandant), Major Hal Butler of Innisrath and Guy Richardson, the county adjutant.[106] Brooke was regarded as the most active and competent of the county commandants. Craig later lauded him as 'one of the finest leaders in Ulster today'.[107] Prospects for USC recruitment in Fermanagh were not initially regarded as positively as they had been in Tyrone.

However, by mid-1921 Brooke was able to boast that Fermanagh had more of its 'unionist population enrolled ... than any other county'.[108] The new body greatly enhanced unionist power and their control of the prospective Northern Ireland since it was designed to be Protestant and loyalist and to supplant the largely Catholic, 'disloyal' RIC as the primary tool in the fight against republicanism. Indeed, while the initial call referred only to 'law-abiding citizens', McCluskey has underlined that this was an implicit call to loyalists and local leaders, and did not anticipate any nationalist applicants.[109] Additionally, all applicants had to be verified by a local selection committee, which was comprised of JPs who were invited to co-opt other members.[110] The USC was nominally under the dual control of General Tudor in Dublin and Sir Ernest Clark in Belfast, but in practice, the head of the USC, Lieutenant-Colonel Sir Charles George Wickham, had significant independence to run the new force as he saw fit.[111]

Recruitment was strong in Fermanagh from the outset, reflecting the solid tradition of loyalist organization in the county and the active role various militia had taken against the IRA.[112] By the end of November 1920, 28 A Specials, 93 B Specials and 16 C Specials had been enrolled.[113] John Porter-Porter declared that the county's impressive record was 'the sequel to the people of Lisbellaw doing their own police work'.[114] Local leadership played an important part in initial recruitment with county commandant Brooke to the fore. In November he welcomed one of the first groups of Fermanagh recruits in the following terms: 'By answering the call of the Empire you are helping your country and defending yourself.'[115] The popularity of the USC in Fermanagh can be linked to the sense of vulnerability felt by the loyalist community due to their peripheral position on the edge of Protestant Ulster, their sense of isolation and their numerical minority. As the *Fermanagh Times* noted at the first recruitment call, 'the response to this call to duty in Enniskillen and Fermanagh will form a real test of the loyalty of our male population ... talk and sentiment in themselves are not worth a straw if not backed up by action'.[116] Tellingly, Tyrone with its similar population split was the only county that resembled Fermanagh in terms of recruitment.[117]

Discipline was a significant problem for the USC in its early days and especially so in Fermanagh. Even the loyalist *Impartial Reporter* criticized the unprofessionalism of the Enniskillen platoon on its first parade through the town, going in for an ill-disciplined 'Irish whoop'.[118] From the beginning the actions of the USC displayed sectarian intent. Catholic houses inevitably fell more heavily under suspicion than Protestant ones, the inverse of what was seen in the south.[119] John McHugh, a member of the IPP, recalled that he had been 'stripped in broad daylight by Specials who shouted: "You are a Papist and you should be shot"'.[120] IRA men in Fermanagh and Tyrone recorded the growing frequency of raids on their houses and the holding up of any men suspected of an IRA connection whenever they were passed on the road.[121] The *Fermanagh*

Herald disparagingly referred to the organization as 'the dregs of Orange lodges, equipped to overawe Nationalists and Catholics and with a special object and special inclination to invent "crimes" against nationalists and Catholics'.[122] On one day in December 1920 shots were fired at St Michael's church in Enniskillen by a USC platoon while another marched up and down the town shouting 'to hell with the Pope'.[123] Brooke was forced to apologize for the incident.[124] However, for most unionists in the county, these events were resolutely defended as an exaggeration. At a meeting of Enniskillen UDC, James Cooper denounced the chairman, J.P. Gillin, as 'out of order' and 'indulging in a political harangue' when Gillin brought forward a motion criticizing the USC.[125] The *Impartial Reporter*, meanwhile, noted that of the three USC arrested after the incident, two were Catholic.[126] The most serious breach of discipline came when the Newtownbutler platoon of the USC engaged in a firefight with the RIC in Clones. The USC had arrived in the town at 3 a.m. on 23 January 1921 after a patrol. They blockaded Fermanagh Street before going to John O'Reilly's shop and off-license and demanding that he come out. O'Reilly refused, escaped through the back door, and reported the incident to the local RIC. The USC were looting the shop when the RIC arrived and were fired on when they ordered the USC to stop.

James McCullough, a special from Belfast, was killed and another, a Capel Archdale from Enniskillen, was seriously wounded and taken to Monaghan Infirmary. Two other special constables were injured and then arrested. A report subsequently recorded that the USC lorry contained large quantities of ginger wine, which the raiders appear to have mistaken for whiskey.[127] Dale and Hezlett suggest that the RIC fired first but the subsequent reaction from official Unionism makes this unlikely.[128] The platoon, denounced as 'armed burglars', was disbanded, although only those members implicated were banished from the force. The rest of the platoon were simply reassigned elsewhere in Ulster.[129] The USC quickly generated antipathy among nationalists of all colours who feared this development would marginalize them politically while furthering unionist interests. In October the house of E.D. Kerr, a former drill instructor of the Enniskillen Horse, was attacked and stones thrown through his window.[130] In December 1920 the RIC reported two cases of threats being sent by post to members of the USC. That month, Edward Keenan of Lurganboy was taken out of his home by two armed men and forced to swear not to join the USC.[131]

The labour movement saw significant growth in Fermanagh, and especially Enniskillen, after a relatively quiet first half of the decade. While there were no strikes in the county during the First World War, between the end of the conflict and 1921 three significant strikes took place in the building, metal and textiles sectors.[132] As discussed in the previous chapter, the catalyst for this growth was the establishment of an Enniskillen branch of the NAUL in January 1918. By the end of its first year, it boasted 400 members in Fermanagh with branches in

Blacklion, Derrygonnelly, Irvinestown, Lisbellaw and Florencecourt. Jim Quinn has also noted that this upsurge was not specific to the NAUL. He identifies the National Union of Life Assurance Workers and the Vintners' Assistants Association as two others that expanded in 1918 and early 1919.

This increase in labour agitation led to the establishment of the Enniskillen Trades and Labour Council in February 1919 at a meeting in Enniskillen town hall. The Trades Council was affiliated to the Irish Labour Party and Trade Union Congress and boasted 800 members. William Clarke again appears to have been the significant figure in this development. As he was involved in the anti-conscription campaign, he presided over the initial meeting that established the council and became a part-time assistant Irish official delegate of the NAUL. The council had strong representation and support from all the unions in Fermanagh. At its first business meeting in March 1919, in the Enniskillen Irish National Foresters' hall, Clarke was elected chairman.[133] The Trades Council and the NAUL were prominent in the building strike in 1919. Both pushed a number of Enniskillen construction firms to improve wages and conditions for their workers after a boom in the industry. The strike lasted from late March until July and achieved its objectives as new rates were agreed for labourers and tradesmen, and reduced hours and increased overtime were also secured.[134]

Labour in Enniskillen became increasingly confident throughout 1919. In July it was able to break up a council sanitation scheme that was availing of strike-breaking workers. The Trades Council secured representation on the UDC's sanitation and housing committees. In December 1919 they were invited to nominate three members to the council committee to oversee the implementation of the Profiteering Act. Labour's political presence on local bodies was primarily utilized to exert pressure on employers in pay disputes. This extended to the Enniskillen UDC itself, which committed to a 10s. pay increase for its workers as well as a half-day holiday on Saturday. Beyond this, Quinn has identified two key priorities for the labour movement in Enniskillen: the improvement of street lighting and house-building schemes in the town.[135] Consequently, the Trades Council felt confident enough to contest the 1920 municipal elections. Five candidates ran under the Labour banner in the elections. Walter Campling, Frank Carney, Thomas Trotter and William Clarke were officially endorsed by the Trades Council, while Bernard Keenan ran as an independent Labour candidate. The Labour candidates attracted 281 votes, enough to elect Keenan, Carney and Campling.[136]

As commander of the Fermanagh Brigade IRA, Carney's election for Labour placed him in an ambiguous position. He was primarily known for his republicanism and his focus during this period was on the IRA rather than on Labour issues. Indeed, in a debate on replacing him in October 1921 after his internment, Seán Nethercott of SF argued that Carney should be viewed as a republican and that his replacement should be a Sinn Féiner.[137] While Campling disputed that the seat belonged to SF, he agreed that Carney had been a most disappointing Labour councillor and was on the cusp of being asked to withdraw from the council when he resigned. Carney was 'elected under the guise of Labour but did not act and work for Labour'.[138] Labour politics in Enniskillen had more cordial relations with nationalism than unionism and the two often allied on an informal basis. The Nationalist Election Association was happy to support Campling and Carney as they did not threaten nationalist seats, but did not do the same for Trotter, Clarke or Keenan. This coalition was partially due to the conservative alignment of political unionism in the county. While the unionist *Fermanagh Times* expressed sympathy for the general cause of labour, it also wished that its representatives would 'cease to talk what, after all, is twaddle – wishy washy orations about the "plutocratic" merchants of the town walking about the streets with fat cigars in their mouths'.[139] Despite this, Trotter was a loyalist himself and held only an uneasy alliance with the other labour candidates. He would later cross the floor and in 1921 was co-opted as a Labour Unionist candidate to Enniskillen UDC.[140]

There was a strong nationalist strain in Fermanagh Labour irrespective of the hostility of unionism. In March 1920 Carney proposed an anti-partition resolution, which was supported uniformly by the nationalist and labour members of the UDC and opposed by unionists. An outraged James Cooper reminded the labour members that they had been supported by Protestants as well as Catholics as 'non-political representatives'.[141] Fermanagh's narrow political split caused significant problems for labour in the county. While nationalism was willing to support labour as a means to bring members of the unionist working-class into a broad coalition, it was unwilling to tolerate this aim if it risked splitting the vote in an already tight contest. Jim Quinn posits that William Clarke's candidature for Enniskillen Board of Guardians and Fermanagh County Council was harshly targeted by the nationalist press for this reason. The *Fermanagh Herald*, for example, speculated that Clarke was running on a quasi-Orange platform as he seemed to be primarily pitching his speeches to them.[142]

Labour's nationalist leanings (and specifically the NAUL) caused it significant problems with the growing presence of the Ulster Workers' Union (UWU) in the county. Founded by unionist labour activist James Turkington in 1918, the UWU was an attempt to 'establish a sectarian rival to the ITGWU'.[143] A branch was founded on 13 May 1919 at a meeting in Enniskillen Orange hall. In Fermanagh, where the ITGWU was not strongly established, this rivalry was focused instead on the NAUL, although most unions in the county regarded the UWU as sectarian and refused to co-operate with it.[144] For its part, the UWU and Turkington utilized the NAUL's support for the anti-conscription campaign as leverage to convince Protestant and unionist workers to join. They also struck a number of atypical labour positions such as criticizing stoppages on May Day (International Labour Day) as 'Bolshevism' which further underlined their perception by the rest of Fermanagh labour as a yellow union (one dominated by employers).[145] Nonetheless, the NAUL's arguments were sufficiently convincing to turn a sizeable portion of the Protestant working class away from it. In February 1921 construction workers in Enniskillen refused to finish a building project that employed five non-union workers. Four agreed to join the NAUL but a fifth was already a member of the UWU and refused to leave it. Construction ground to a halt for a number of weeks until a compromise was negotiated.

As 1919 progressed, the prospect of a six-county partition settlement grew ever more likely. Such a settlement had been part of the British coalition government's manifesto at the 1918 general election and the success of nationalist candidates in South Fermanagh, Tyrone North West and Tyrone North East in the same election seemed to have done little to change their mind. Despite IPP opposition in the House of Commons and the War of Independence in Ireland, little seemed to change the mind of Lloyd George and his cabinet. By December 1919 it was widely expected that the Government of Ireland bill would be introduced in the new year. It allowed for two separate parliaments for a six-county Northern Ireland and a twenty-six county Southern Ireland.[146] The bill was met with flat opposition from Fermanagh nationalists. A strong showing in the 1920 local elections was seen by some as the best political path to undermine the settlement while outright military victory in the War of Independence was preferred by others. For unionists, however, the passage of the bill, especially after its acceptance by the UUC in March 1920, engendered more complex feelings. Fermanagh delegates to the UUC did not join in the protests of their Tyrone counterparts and no Fermanagh delegates resigned from the UUC in the way Brigadier-General Ricardo of Sion Mills did.[147]

Fermanagh UUC delegates did sign a petition requesting a meeting to reconsider exclusion. This was motivated by the threatened resignation of delegates from Cavan, Monaghan and Donegal. However, while eighty-six delegates from the six counties signed the document, only six were from Fermanagh.[148] These delegates were James Cooper, Cecil Lowry-Corry, C.C. D'Arcy-Irvine, Colonel Robert Doran, Brigadier-General Ricardo and R.W. Strathearn.[149] In a petition on behalf of the three counties from northern allies, no signatories were from Fermanagh. The majority came from Down and Antrim, areas with sufficient Protestant majorities that they did not need to fear continued inclusion of the Catholic-heavy three counties.[150] Nor did any Fermanagh delegates resign in protest at the decision.[151] James Cooper later claimed he signed the petition more out of concern for the Protestants of Pettigo than for three-county loyalists as a whole.[152] Fermanagh unionism was roused to a far greater extent a year later when the county's Unionist Association unanimously passed a resolution opposing any change in the boundaries of a six-county Ulster.[153]

1 William Copeland Trimble (1851–1941), editor of the *Impartial Reporter* and founder of the Enniskillen Horse.

2 Jeremiah Jordan (1831–1911), MP for Fermanagh South, 1895–1910; an early titan of Fermanagh nationalism.

3 Edward Archdale (1853–1943), MP for Fermanagh North, 1898–1903, 1916–22. He later became Northern Ireland's first minister for agriculture.

4 Cahir Healy (1877–1970), NI MP, 1925–65, the most prominent Fermanagh nationalist of the period.

6 Charles Falls (1860–1936), MP for
Fermanagh-Tyrone, 1924–9.

5 Godfrey Fetherstonhaugh
(1858–1928), MP for
Fermanagh North, 1906–16.

7 Orange Order Derrygonnelly Star of Freedom, c.1910.

8 Seán O'Mahony (1872–1934), MP for Fermanagh South, 1918–22; he was the most significant anti-Treaty voice in the county.

9 Enniskillen Town Hall, c.1900. From here in 1918, Edward Archdale delivered a speech whipping the unionist crowd into a frenzy.

UNION
IS
STRENGTH

ULSTER
WOMEN'S
UNIONIST
DEMONSTRATION.

———◆———

ENNISKILLEN,
1st August,
1912.

O God, our help in ages past,
    Our hope for years to come,
Our shelter from the stormy blast,
    And our eternal home.

Beneath the shadow of Thy Throne
    Thy saints have dwelt secure ;
Sufficient is Thine arm alone,
    And our defence is sure.

A thousand ages in Thy sight
    Are like an evening gone ;
Short as the watch that ends the night
    Before the rising sun.

O God, our help in ages past,
    Our hope for years to come,
Be Thou our guard while troubles last,
    And our eternal home.

8620—F.T.

10 Postcard for a demonstration by the Ulster Women's Unionist Council, 1 August 1912.

11 Enniskillen Horse outside the former jail, *c.*1912.

12 6th Battalion, Inniskilling Dragoons, 1914.

13 Women's Branch, Florence Court Star of Victory, *c*.1920.

14 Orange Hall, Enniskillen.

15 3rd Battalion of UVF Enniskillen, 1914.

16 Royal Irish Constabulary officers with man at a checkpoint, *c*.1920. The photo is likely staged, and the man with his hands held high is Mr George Hazlett from Co. Monaghan.

17 Cumann na mBan pin badge.

18 Commemorative Belleek pottery vase with portrait medallions of Michael Collins and Arthur Griffith inlaid. Belleek pottery was one of the most famous of Fermanagh's industries.

19 Arthur Griffith (1871–1922), MP for Fermanagh-Tyrone, 1921–2. Griffith also represented a southern constituency (Cavan East) during the Treaty debates. The same was true for Milroy, Collins, de Valera and McNeill. Consequently, only Seán O'Mahony exclusively represented Fermanagh's interests during the debate and he opposed the Treaty, unlike the majority of the county.

20 Main Street, Roslea, Co. Fermanagh, after the burning of the village on the night of 21 February 1921 by the Black and Tans. The burning of Roslea (itself a reprisal) sparked a vicious series of raids and murders that threatened to escalate into a wider conflict.

21 Frank Carney (1896–1932) and Eoin O'Duffy (1890–1944). Carney was the most significant IRA leader in Fermanagh during the War of Independence. His health never recovered from his active service and subsequent imprisonment.

22 Train derailed on the Great Northern Railway line from Dundalk to Enniskillen, 1922. Attacks on trains were common to enforce the Belfast boycott.

23 Seán and Mollie Nethercott, *c.*1920. Nethercott was a significant figure in Fermanagh republicanism and paid the price for this when he was interned on the *Argenta* from 1922 to 1924.

24 B Specials outside Coulter's grocery shop in Letterbreen, *c.*1920. The USC was central to how the Belfast government established its control over Fermanagh.

25 B Special patrol beside a destroyed Crossley tender, date unknown.

26 The *Lady of the Lake*, *c*.1900. Rechristened HMS *Pandora*, this pleasure barge played a critical role in ferrying the USC across Lough Erne during the occupation of the Pettigo–Belleek triangle by the IRA in 1922.

27 Boundary Commission first sitting, 9 December 1924. For Fermanagh nationalists the Commission would promise much and deliver little.

28 Basil Brooke (1888–1973). Brooke was crucial in the establishment of the UVF in Fermanagh and across Ulster. He was prime minister of Northern Ireland from 1943 to 1963.

This is not to say that the plight of Cavan, Monaghan and Donegal was ignored. It met with significant sympathy in Fermanagh but, as elsewhere, this was coupled with very little resistance. While Trimble and the *Impartial Reporter* were less concerned about those counties left behind, the *Fermanagh Times* had greater misgivings. In April 1920 it reported that 'some of the staunchest unionists in County Fermanagh fully share this opinion [against exclusion] and are altogether in sympathy with the Loyalist population of Cavan, Monaghan and Donegal'.[154] In April 1920 Colonel Robert Doran, head of Brookeborough unionist club, wrote to Richard Dawson Bates that he could not 'go against the three excluded counties in whom without a doubt there are true hearted loyalists.'[155]

A nine-county, Ulster-based settlement was decried as impractical and could lead to future nationalist domination while a four-county, demographics-based settlement would see them stranded in the south. Fermanagh unionism had a complicated relationship with the three 'southern' Ulster counties. Cavan, in particular, was described as being only marginally of Ulster. As Trimble wrote dismissively: 'County Cavan was not in the ancient Ulster, it was in Connaught.'[156] The *Fermanagh Times* began to refer to the nine counties merely as 'geographical Ulster'.[157] The paper also frequently referred to Fermanagh as the 'outpost of Ulster'.[158] James Loughlin has described how Ulster unionism was persistently constrained by the lack of clear geographic boundaries for their supposed Ulster homeland.[159] Trimble, when discussing the electoral map of Fermanagh, claimed that South Fermanagh would have returned a Unionist MP in all previous elections were it not for the western shores of Upper Lough Erne; such an area was unnatural as it 'formerly belonged to the province of Connaught'.[160] For Trimble, the Catholic majority in this area and its supposed non-Ulster status were therefore linked. Following the East Cavan by-election, Fr Michael O'Flanagan of SF referred to his audience as 'hard-headed men of Ulster, you shrewd unemotional, un-Irish people'. The *Reporter* was swift to remind the priest that men of Cavan and Catholics of Cavan, in particular, are 'native and Irish, not of Ulster as the phrase is generally understood'.[161]

For Fermanagh unionists it was far more important that the Government of Ireland bill was passed quickly given their demographic weakness, a point well known to their opponents. In the House of Lords, as the bill was passing, Lord Killanin had formally proposed a four-county Ulster only to be rebuffed.[162] As a result of this insecurity, Fermanagh unionists sought to bring forward a particular version of the history and character of the county that placed themselves immovably at its centre. This was articulated most clearly by William Copeland Trimble in the *Impartial Reporter* in December 1920. In an editorial titled: 'Fermanagh a Protestant County: Notwithstanding the Population'. Trimble's claim was that 'in a matter of this sort heads do not count.' To his mind the bulk of the Catholic population was made up of two overlapping groups: servants and outsiders – people who are 'not of the soil'. He identified key communities as being majority Protestant – 'the landowning, land-occupying, professional, commercial, farming and industrial communities.' These were the dominant groups as voters and ratepayers.[163] References to these ideas were common on the campaign trail and in local government. In a debate at a meeting of Enniskillen guardians on the payment of workhouse officials, a frustrated William Elliott exclaimed 'we are the ratepayers. These are the men who pay the rates. I am a heavy ratepayer and you [Edmund Corrigan, SF] are not'.[164]

What this represented was a non-negotiable Fermanagh identity that was defined in traditional Protestant terms. History and the control of it were crucial to Trimble's perception of the county. Fermanagh, before the planters came, did not exist in Trimble's view. It was just a loose collection of farms that were loyal to The Maguire and subject to constant raids. Only Protestant rule and Protestant law brought peace and allowed the emergence of the county. This was an argument echoed in a letter to the *Fermanagh Times* by a 'Descendant of a Planter' who made the case for a chaotic pre-Protestant Fermanagh even more forcefully: 'The followers of these less or more warlike chiefs lived in wattle and mud huts much like what modern travellers find in Central Africa.'[165] These arguments were used against them too, such as during a county council debate in November when Cahir Healy said of the unionists present that 'there is not a member on the other side of the table that has not been imported.'[166]

In the context of the looming prospect of partition, the local elections of January and June 1920 were extremely significant in Fermanagh and across Ireland for a number of reasons. Nationally, they were the first political bellwether since the establishment of the Dáil and the beginning of the War of Independence. In Fermanagh the IPP hoped that the campaign of violence undertaken by the IRA had turned many moderate voters against SF. The UIL and AOH had also resumed meetings following the end of the First World War and it was hoped that their newly energized base would see them reverse their setbacks from the previous election. In addition, the 1920 election was the first to use the proportional representation system of voting after the passage of the Local Government (Ireland) Act, 1919. On a national level, it was hoped this would undermine support for SF, but it also allowed smaller parties such as Labour to secure local government seats.

These factors were magnified in Fermanagh where the prospect of partition, as in 1918, heightened the electoral stakes. Control of the councils was seen as critical for making the case that the county was inherently nationalist or unionist and, therefore, ought to be included on one side or the other of the upcoming political settlement. It should be noted that between the municipal elections in January and the county and rural elections in June, the Government of Ireland bill passed its second reading in the House of Commons and was accepted by the UUC. The local election was, therefore, fought in the context of nationalists trying to disrupt the political situation and unionists trying to maintain it. Nationally, these elections confirmed the dominance of SF, which won 338 out of 393 local government bodies, while labour candidates also performed well and frequently formed coalitions with SF.

The introduction of proportional representation was another unknown factor that presented complications and opportunities. This was accompanied by a restructuring of the county and district council electoral areas by the LGB, the electoral impact of which was uncertain.[167] The IPP hoped that the new system, which removed fear of the nationalist vote being split between the IPP and SF, would allow them to conduct a full campaign rather than running a single candidate along with SF as they did in 1918. Conversely, unionists feared that the absence of a split nationalist vote removed their greatest prospect of electoral success. They also hoped that the new system would allow them to secure representation in southern areas where they traditionally had been locked out. For SF, the new system would be a test of the party's popularity in Fermanagh and of its ability to break the IPP machine that persisted more strongly in Fermanagh than elsewhere in Ireland. Unionists were the most vocally opposed to the new system. Before the UDC elections in January 1920, the *Impartial Reporter* complained that under the 'usual lines' the unionists would secure a two-thirds majority. It further reported that the whole system of proportional representation 'was said by some people to have been introduced to destroy the unionist control of Ulster'.[168] However, as with the other newspapers in the county, the *Reporter* devoted a great deal of space to explain in detail how to vote properly under the new system to minimize spoiled votes.[169]

While the election (with the exception of the Labour campaign) was mostly fought on the broad socio-political divide in the county, there were some efforts to draw a distinction between the parties. Unionists were keen to portray themselves as the party of sensible local government. The *Reporter* suggested that the Unionist Party should be 'more correctly described as the Ratepayers body hence their policy all through has been *to keep down the rates*.'[170] The *Fermanagh Herald*, meanwhile, trumpeted the success of the previous five years of nationalist control of Enniskillen urban council: 'the rates have been kept at a comparatively low figure, notwithstanding the increased cost of all materials and the increase in wages'.[171]

However, it was the broader symbolic significance of the local elections that held the greatest sway in the election. Whichever side controlled the county, urban and rural councils, it was believed could plausibly claim to speak for the area and, therefore, wield influence during the partition process. This assumption proved false. Despite nationalist success in the local elections, they were unable to translate this into any change in the proposed partition settlement. Notwithstanding their desire to outperform each other, SF and the

IPP were keenly aware of the importance of maintaining nationalist control of the councils and entered into an informal electoral pact. Before the municipal elections, the *Fermanagh Herald* advised its readers to vote not only along 'Nationalist' but also 'Catholic' lines.[172] Both parties also agreed to nominate only a limited number of candidates in each district to maximize transfers between them.[173]

In January 1920 municipal elections were held across Ireland but in Fermanagh the only contest was for Enniskillen UDC with Enniskillen divided into east, south and north wards. Unionists held a strong majority in the south ward while nationalists dominated the north ward. Control of the council usually came down to who won the east ward. The *Reporter* noted that under proportional representation the turnout of the minority in their respective wards would prove crucial.[174] In the same article the *Reporter* excoriated the *Fermanagh Herald* for advocating a 'Catholics only' electoral policy in Enniskillen, while also denouncing the 'silly and dangerous' unionists of the town who had previously not voted exclusively on party lines.[175] While Unionists were ultimately able to secure ten seats to six for the IPP and two for SF, they were still in a minority in the council due to the three Labour and independent labour seats.[176] At the first council meeting, J.P. Gillin was unanimously returned as chairman. For the vice-chairmanship the Unionists nominated George Whalley while the nationalists and labour supported Thomas Gordon. Recognizing that they could not win a numerical contest, the unionist members appealed to the nationalists to return Whalley on the basis that he represented a significant minority on the council. The tone of the meeting was striking. In nominating Whalley, Councillor Samuel Clarke was keen to assert that he had no problem with Gordon and spent much of his speech praising the latter. When the Unionists were defeated on this vote, Gordon himself apologized to the room for the friction caused by this vote and referred to the role dismissively as a 'sinecure'.[177] In general, it was noted that the urban council elections were conducted in surprisingly good humour by both sides.[178]

In June 1920 Fermanagh County Council and rural council elections took place. Much like the UDC elections, neither side significantly over or underperformed. Nationalists successfully parlayed their majority on the voter register into a bare majority on the county council, reflecting the population split. No rural council changed hands either. The nationalist vote was roughly evenly split between SF and the IPP. Fermanagh and Tyrone were the counties where the IPP had the best showing in the elections, taking five of the twenty available county council seats and also securing the chairmanships of the UDC and Lisnaskea RDC. Ten Unionists, six IPP and five SF candidates were elected to the county council. Nationalists also took Belleek and Lisnaskea RDCs while no contest took place in Clones No. 2 Council. Unionists successfully (albeit narrowly) held Enniskillen RDC, where Lord Belmore was extremely influential, and they held Irvinestown RDC by virtue of there being no contest.[179] Enniskillen Board of Guardians also showed a strong nationalist vote, returning two SF candidates, two IPP and three Unionists.[180]

The first meeting of the new county council took place on 17 June 1920 with only Archdale absent due to his parliamentary responsibilities. Joseph Gillin of the IPP and Cahir Healy of SF were co-opted onto the council while the Unionist nomination of James Cooper was defeated.[181] With these co-options and the presence of the chairs of the rural councils, the final distribution of county council seats stood at sixteen nationalist (nine for SF and seven for the IPP) and eleven Unionists.[182] For Unionists, this was a major failure. A 'Unionist Ratepayer' writing to the *Impartial Reporter* after the election bemoaned the 'want of proper organization on the day of the poll' and blasted the unionist organization in the county as 'blundering'. A meeting of subscribing unionists was demanded to review the campaign and reprimand those responsible.[183] Such insecurities were present among nationalists too. The *Fermanagh Herald* regretted the inability of nationalists in Florencecourt to 'express their preferences in a proper manner'. This meant that they had failed to return an extra nationalist to the Enniskillen rural council which would have allowed them to unseat Lord Belmore as chair and hold an even greater majority on the county council.[184]

For the election of the chair, the nationalists unanimously supported the outgoing John McHugh while unionists proposed Archdale. McHugh was elected by sixteen votes to ten. For vice-chair, the IPP proposed Joseph Gillin while SF proposed Cahir Healy. The unionists meanwhile reintroduced Archdale as a candidate and argued that they should secure the vice-chairmanship 'under the principle of Proportional Representation'. After two rounds of voting, Gillin was elected with the support of some of the unionist councillors. This prompted Healy to 'offer sincere condolences to Mr Gillin upon the position he finds himself to-day, elected by Unionists!'[185] Despite their electoral alliance, relations were strained between the two strands of Fermanagh nationalism as was revealed in Gillin's reply to Healy: 'I am in the town where I was born and reared and when I want to look for a character I will go to the people of the town for one and not to you.'[186]

While Unionists held roughly the same proportion of local government seats as before the election, they were concerned that the new political circumstances would lead to the loss of positions on the various committees that undertook much of the actual governance of the county. There was a legitimate reason to be concerned about this. When the Unionists had controlled Fermanagh County Council before 1914, the IPP often complained that they were inadequately represented on important groups such as the county emergency committee or the finance committee, and had been limited to one or two seats. In this regard, the nationalist alliance was surprisingly conciliatory when it offered unionists two of the four seats on the emergency committee. Even this caused some discord, however. Unionist councillors complained that they had not been allowed any choice of nominee as the nationalists had simply proposed Archdale and Belmore, the senior Unionists in the county. After some discussion, McHugh agreed to have Archdale substituted with A. Cathcart. This may have seemed like pointless quibbling over positions but there was the possibility that an emergency committee with Archdale as a member would frequently have a nationalist majority given Archdale's commitments in London as an MP.[187]

McHugh's first speech as chairman of the council left little doubt as to the political aims of the county council. He declared strongly against partition:

> the people of Fermanagh will not have Partition, the County Council will not have it, and I, as your Chairman, say we will not have it. To use a phrase of Sir Edward's own – 'We will not have it'.[188]

McHugh used his position as chairman to campaign against the implementation of partition. In November 1920 he was a signatory to a letter, along with the chairmen of Cavan, Monaghan, Donegal, Armagh, Antrim and Derry County Councils, the mayor of Derry and a member of Belfast Corporation, protesting partition. Partition was, it declared, 'a purely political device designed to weaken the Irish nation and break its unity and is so abhorrent to the views and wishes of the vast majority of the people of every province in Ireland that the British Government dare not take a plebiscite'.[189]

In September 1920, in response to the growing number of SF local bodies that recognized Dáil Éireann, the LGB sent a letter to each county, urban and rural council asking for an assurance that the councils would submit all accounts to the board as usual and only use LGB grants for the intended purpose. The implied threat was the cessation of grants to local government bodies that refused to recognize the authority of the LGB. At this stage, owing to the strength of Unionist and IPP members in the councils, no Fermanagh councils had broken with the LGB. Nationalist and labour members, however, were reluctant to state a position definitively on the matter, preferring to continue to receive money from the LGB and keep open the possibility of splitting with the board later on.[190] When the letter was read at a meeting of Enniskillen UDC, James Cooper attempted to force the issue by proposing a motion that the council would accept the jurisdiction of the LGB and 'otherwise fall in line with their requirements'. It seems this was pre-emptively aimed at scuppering the plans of the nationalist contingent simply to ignore the letter, offering no confirmation or denial of the authority of the LGB. SF and labour members responded to the letter with outrage, declaring it an insult to a council who had not repudiated them. When Gillin, the chairman, suggested as a compromise that the letter simply be marked as read and a decision be taken on another date, Cooper insisted on a vote on his motion. In response, the nationalists proposed an amendment to the motion, overwriting it and changing it to a motion that no action at all be taken. Both this amendment and Gillin's amended motion were passed.[191]

Nationalists made good use of the councils that they dominated in this regard. In March 1920 Enniskillen UDC passed a resolution protesting the latest wave of internments undertaken by the British government. The motion, which referred to many of the internees as 'cultured men and delicate ladies', passed by a single vote in a division that fell along party lines.[192] The previous week the same council passed a motion protesting the imposition of partition. James Cooper had unsuccessfully proposed a wrecking amendment that would instead declare Fermanagh's 'joy' to be part of the Northern Ireland parliament and which ended with 'County Fermanagh is largely populated by Unionists, who pay two-thirds of the rates and taxes, and who abhor to be grouped with the anti-British element'. The amendment failed and the main motion passed again by a single vote.[193] The same motion was passed in Lisnaskea rural council but only after the meeting had similarly descended into petty squabbling.[194] In 1920 the nationalist members of Enniskillen Board of Guardians were able to pass a vote recognizing Dáil Éireann by waiting for the Unionist members to leave following normal business but holding that until the chairman left his chair, the meeting had not finished. They were then able to pass a resolution 'unanimously'.[195] When the stunt was discovered in the minute books, Unionist member F.R. Carson demanded the record be expunged. There followed an extended 'duel' in which Carson refused to sit down to allow the meeting to continue while Corrigan used his gavel to interrupt Carson's attempts to talk. The incident was resolved when Carson put forward a notice of a motion to excise the record from the minutes and resolved to write to various unionist groups to encourage unionist members to attend.[196]

Unionists for their part still doggedly brought forward resolutions they knew would be unpopular with their nationalist colleagues, often framing them as inoffensive or common sense proposals. In July 1919 George Whalley, a unionist, brought forward a proposal that the council should organize celebrations for 'Peace Day', an Empire-wide celebration of the victory in the First World War. He had gotten as far as discussing possible avenues for LGB funding before he was interrupted by nationalists who opposed the idea in principle. Councillor James McGovern asked why should the Irish people celebrate the freedom of small nations in Europe when 'the majority of their people were military ridden'. Whalley then declared there was 'no use' in continuing the discussion before adding he 'thought it would have been received in a different spirit altogether'.[197]

At the 1918 election of chairmen for the boards of guardians, the election for the Enniskillen guardians proved contentious. The discussion began in a conciliatory tone as the Protestant chairman John Crozier announced his intention to step down and nominated a Catholic, Patrick Crumley, the IPP MP,

as his successor. Crumley was seconded by two unionist members in Lord
Belmore and Robert O'Hara. Belmore was effusive, saying they 'could not have
a better man than Mr. Crumley.' The move was opposed by another unionist,
F.R. Carson, who nominated his fellow unionist W.J. Brown. When the voting
began, only O'Hara among the unionists voted for Crumley. Belmore reverted
to party lines. The previously cordial tone swiftly changed. Nationalist member
Meehan shouted across the table to Brown that he was 'well pleased you got a
beating. To grab a seat is a thing our side of the house would not attempt'.[198] As
the main Fermanagh body held by Unionists, Enniskillen RDC became their
only outlet for passing political motions of their own, although they did so with
greater infrequency than nationalists. In May 1920 the council passed a motion
with the support of some IPP members, denouncing the 'outrageous conduct of
some unknown persons in burning unused police barracks and other acts which
serve no good purpose whatsoever'.[199]

Importantly, these acrimonious divisions in local government were the
exception to the rule. In most cases local councillors were able to unite in the
governing of the county. Indeed, the most frequent object of the ire of the local
councils in Fermanagh was not the British government or the IRA but the LGB.
In August 1919, for example, all councillors expressed significant discontent
when they were informed that the employment of two ferrymen for Lough Erne
may be illegal as councils were only legally entitled to fund ferries over rivers
and it was unclear which of these the Erne was.[200] In September 1919 both
nationalists and unionists united in a vote protesting the administration of war
pensions in Fermanagh. These motions were characterized by the symbolic
proposing and seconding of the motion by members of the different
communities.[201] Similarly, the council united in December 1920 to protest
increases in the price of gas.[202]

The issue of patronage and of limiting the boons of local political power to
within one's own community was a recurring source of contention. In November
1921 John McHugh made a speech calling for the introduction of competitive
examinations instead of appointments to all future council jobs. 'His experience
of public Boards was that each party that got into power believed that its friends
should be placed in the positions whether they were fully qualified or not'.[203] In
this he was correct. Livingstone had noted that under Unionist domination,
nationalists only earned £43 15s. of the £2,100 wage budget of the council. In
1916, after two years of control, nationalists earned £1,409. The issue was
particularly prominent on the boards of guardians, which were responsible for
appointing and setting the wages for a number of important positions. Older
office holders were more likely to have been appointed by Unionist-dominated
councils and so the degree to which preference should be given to incumbents
became politicized. In McHugh's speech, Protestant and Catholic were split
cleanly as to whether some preference should be given to pre-existing office

holders.[204] This was a complaint voiced in Cavan and Monaghan but only from the unionist community railing against Catholic domination of local bodies. One such complaint by Colonel Madden suggested: 'Whenever a place is going to which a salary is attached then I say the principle acted upon is that no Unionist need apply.'[205]

The political element of this was often explicit. In July 1921 attempts were made to secure for Thomas Corrigan, the county accountant, the position of county secretary following the death of the previous holder. Corrigan was a noted republican and objections to his suitability were raised by unionist councillors. This appointment was particularly sensitive for unionists as the other candidate, W.H. West, a unionist, had been the assistant secretary for twenty years and it was felt that he was being unjustly overlooked. Corrigan too was a particularly obnoxious candidate to local unionists due to his strong republicanism. The *Impartial Reporter* dismissed Corrigan's record as county accountant, noting that he had barely carried out his duties while drawing a generous salary.[206] In response to a remark made by the chairman of the council that if Corrigan had been a staunch Protestant he would not have had such trouble, it was stated that if Mr West (assistant secretary at the time) had been Catholic, he would not have been passed over.[207]

Unionists were generally able to counter nationalist control of the council through their stronger networks with the British administration. After Corrigan was confirmed in his role, Unionist councillors contacted Sir Henry Robinson, vice-president of the LGB in Dublin Castle, and Corrigan was forced to pass a much more rigorous test than was normally required. After passing this, the LGB claimed his papers had been lost in Dublin which delayed his appointment.[208] Three months later, six nationalist councillors signed a resolution demanding West's resignation and the immediate appointment of Corrigan.[209] Cahir Healy disingenuously claimed they put forward the resolution as a 'business proposition and he hoped that there would be no political heat or recriminations'. He assured West that he had no issues with how he did his business but that he held five public offices and had sufficient responsibilities while Corrigan had been elected and therefore was entitled to the position.[210] Ultimately, Corrigan was appointed on a temporary basis and served until 31 March 1922. Corrigan continued to vex Fermanagh unionists through his political usage of the office. On 22 June 1921, the day that King George V opened the new Northern Ireland parliament, he removed a Union Jack that had been flying above the courthouse. It was later reinstated by the RIC. In response, Corrigan closed the council offices, leaving a public notice complaining of the 'invasion and commandeering, by Crown forces, of the offices of the Fermanagh County Council'.[211]

By New Year's Eve 1920 the future of Fermanagh looked both uncertain and certain. The Government of Ireland bill had settled the UUC and the British government's position regarding partition – it was uncompromisingly along six-county lines. While this was cause for rejoicing among forty-five per cent of Fermanagh's population, it was viewed as a disaster by the nationalist fifty-five per cent. While still in control of the county's important establishments, Fermanagh nationalists watched the approach of 1921 with something akin to dread. The sudden organization of the USC not only constituted a direct threat to nationalists, but it also hinted at something more sinister – that the year to come would see a unionist power-grab both before and after partition.

6 'A unionist coup': Fermanagh and the Treaty in 1921

1921 was a year of two halves in Fermanagh. The period before the truce in July witnessed an ever increasing pattern of reprisal and counter-reprisal as the IRA began to come to terms with its new foe – the USC. This period served to divide further nationalists and unionists as the actions of the IRA and USC profoundly alienated both communities from each other. The most important republican action of this period was not, however, an act of violence but rather the widespread implementation of the Belfast boycott in Fermanagh. The boycott, more than any other factor, drove both communities apart and sparked countless smaller acts of violence and intimidation. The second half of the year was relatively peaceful but no less transformative. Encouraged by the passage of the Government of Ireland Act and in anticipation of the establishment of Northern Ireland, unionists began steadily to assert their control over Fermanagh. Enniskillen UDC was taken in a 'coup' and local government bodies were revised to remove the nationalist majority on the county council. By December 1921, when Fermanagh County Council, in effect, voted itself out of existence by recognizing Dáil Éireann, it was too late to reverse unionist political gains. Accusations of malpractice were common in the Northern Ireland general election of May 1921, which was a qualified victory for unionists. While the Anglo-Irish Treaty in December may have seemed like the final bitter blow for nationalists in a year of disappointments, in actuality Fermanagh nationalism largely supported it. The pro-Treaty stance of official nationalism in the county was surprising given that the Treaty left them on the wrong side of the border and both Derry and Tyrone came out as strongly against the settlement. Fermanagh nationalists were generally tired of the war and reprisals by the USC. Many genuinely believed that the Treaty was as good as could be hoped for and had confidence that most of the county would be returned to Dáil Éireann by the Boundary Commission.

Despite the growing likelihood of a truce, the early months of 1921 saw no significant reduction in the scale of violence in Fermanagh. The most significant outbreak of violence occurred in Roslea.[1] The area around Monaghan had been the most unsettled part of the county for several months. In January 1921 the CI recorded that thirteen outrages had taken place in Fermanagh, primarily along the borders with Cavan and Monaghan.[2] The following month he observed that Fermanagh was peaceful except for that portion bordering the south.[3] The Roslea attack can be seen as part of a cycle of attack, reprisal and counter-reprisal. The affair began when George Lester, a local B Special, was shot in February 1921. A party of B Specials entered Roslea at about 10 p.m. on 21 February and burned a number of nationalist homes. In response, Eoin O'Duffy, commander of the 2nd Northern Division, ordered a series of raids on the houses of B Specials believed to have taken part in the raid. In total, four unionists were killed, three during the IRA's reprisal and one accidentally in the initial burning of Roslea. For both sides it confirmed implicit biases about the looming partition situation: that nationalists in a unionist state were inherently unsafe and at the mercy of a loyalist militia; and that nationalists in a unionist state, emboldened by southern support, were fundamentally disloyal.

The affair also represented the first significant, violent challenge to the newly constituted USC. Fermanagh had continued to lead the rest of the province in USC recruitment in early 1921. By March the force was estimated to be 2,200 strong.[4] By late January most platoons were sufficiently equipped with transport – two cars and four Crossley tenders – to undertake policing operations. The officer in charge was also supplied with his own Ford car.[5] Nevertheless, the force had been on edge following an ambush in Crossmaglen, County Armagh, on 13 January when Special Constable Robert Compston became the first USC member to be killed. A wave of arms raids on and near the Monaghan border near Roslea had further enflamed tensions among the local USC.[6] The unit continued to struggle with discipline in its early days. Even Hezlett acknowledged that 'some of the officers of the A Specials were poor', although he qualified this with the remark that this was because 'less than half were Ulstermen'.[7]

The circumstances of the shooting of George Lester that caused the Roslea outrage are contested. Both the *Northern Standard* and the *Impartial Reporter* alleged that he had received a warning letter from the IRA approximately two weeks before he was shot.[8] The unionist press also emphasized Lester's respectability and popularity among his community.[9] Later accounts from the RIC undermine this by describing Lester as a 'hysterical Orangeman'.[10] Lester also claimed that prior to joining the USC, he refused to sign up to the Belfast boycott and had been targeted ever since.[11] Nationalist accounts make Lester a more active participant in his own shooting but they are not entirely consistent. Patrick McMeel of Carrickroe company in Monaghan and John McKenna of Newbliss suggested that Lester had passed on information about IRA volunteers.[12] The most detailed account and probably the most accurate was that of John T. Connolly, a captain in the Roslea Battalion. He claimed that Lester had threatened a local IRA man who was handing out Belfast boycott notices. Whatever the specifics of the shooting, Lester's attackers were immediately fired on by Lester's brother Thomas and other USC.[13]

Most accounts indicate that the reprisal burning of nationalist homes in Roslea took place on the same day but beyond that, there are significant differences. A USC detachment arrived in the afternoon to make enquiries and warned the people that they (the specials) would not be responsible for what was to happen next. The town was then visited by a group of UVF from Fermanagh and Monaghan who discharged their guns.[14] This was followed by the arrival of USC in lorries who proceeded to shoot at houses and start fires.[15] The *Impartial Reporter* carried a report about the shooting of Samuel Finegan, a member of the UVF from Smithborough. The circumstances of his death were unclear. Initial reports suggested that he had attempted to smash the door of the Catholic parish priest with his rifle when it discharged.[16] James Mulligan, a member of the Monaghan IRA, later claimed that Finegan was shot by B Specials who were pursuing four IRA men and were startled when he emerged suddenly from an alleyway.[17]

A total of ten properties were burned and many others were damaged. The losses incurred were substantial. For example, Philip Trainor suffered £1,000 of damage to his grocery shop and Matthew Finnegan's recently opened drapery suffered £4,000 in damage. Other victims included James McMahon, James Flynn, Dan McEntee, Patrick Tully, Anne Carron, J. McElvaney and Hugh McCaffrey.[18] That only nationalist houses were burned suggests local involvement and the speed with which the houses were burned, almost simultaneously, hints at a level of preselection.[19] It was later asserted that some of those targeted were members of SF or the IRA, but this was not borne out in compensation applications.[20] The *Northern Standard* noted that the burnings did not lead to any nationalist fatalities. The terrified inhabitants had fled en masse and sought refuge in Clones.[21] From the field in which he was working, Connolly recalled seeing families move all their furniture and belongings onto the road before an exodus.[22] The *Irish Independent* reported that some sought the safety of the surrounding hills and could see their homes go up in flames.[23]

The burnings were broadly condemned. It was characterized later by the Fermanagh unionist judge James Johnston as a 'savage and inhuman reprisal'.[24] Fermanagh officialdom disassociated itself from the attack, claiming it had been committed by unknown out of county forces while the police had only arrived afterwards to restore order.[25] Whereas the *Standard* expressed horror at what had happened, the *Reporter* was not only unrepentant but also painted the reprisal in quasi-official terms when it declared: 'The Sinn Féiners must understand that reprisal in Fermanagh will be prompt and vigorous for any of their actions.'[26] The *Fermanagh Times* focused primarily on the assault on Lester as the crime most worthy of comment.[27]

That the IRA would respond to such a provocation was not immediately obvious. A few weeks elapsed before Eoin O'Duffy, who had been organizing in Tyrone at the time, called a meeting of the officers of the Clones Battalion in Derryheanlish on the Monaghan border to decide on a response. The initial discussion was mindful of bringing further trouble on the nationalists of Roslea. O'Duffy specifically asked Connolly about whether they would stand beside the IRA if a reprisal was conducted. Connolly answered in the affirmative, although in his BMH statement he attributed this to his own youth and desire for revenge on those responsible.[28] The strongest initial opposition to an IRA reprisal came from Frank Aiken who feared it would spark counter-reprisals. However, he was won over by O'Duffy's argument that a sufficiently strong action would deter local unionists from responding in kind. Aiken's response was curt: 'Well, burn them and their houses.'[29]

Each house was preselected and assigned to a different raiding party of up to ten men. The raids themselves were to take place roughly simultaneously.[30] There were to be sixteen in total, two for every Catholic house burned and a clear statement of intent from O'Duffy. McKenna was clear that at least some of the victims were chosen because of their association with earlier burnings.[31] McLean of Smithborough, the late Finegan's employer, was selected precisely for that reason. The only four people otherwise specifically chosen were the four USC sergeants known to reside in the area.[32] 'Orangemen', 'loyalist' and 'special' were all muddled together in the various accounts of the reprisals and the direct thread of culpability between perpetrator and victim was not always apparent. Some houses targeted, like those of the Magwoods or Thomas Lester, had previously opposed IRA arms raids. Most attacks focused on Roslea itself but, as Tim Wilson has noted, they spread to Smithborough and Scotshouse in County Monaghan as well.[33] Philip Marron noted that the three areas had a large unionist population and that 'all young unionists were armed and trained in the use of arms'.[34]

The Roslea company's sole role in the raid was to scout the houses in case any USC patrols were about. Some local unionist families were vulnerable because of their association with nationalists. As McKenna noted, the IRA's guides were poorer mountain men who were frequently employed by unionist farmers.[35] The IRA was supported by members of the Monaghan brigade of Cumann na mBan who had been responsible for smuggling arms and ammunition into the area before the attack.[36] Two houses escaped being burned: that of Rowland Beatty, which stood in an open field and was thus more difficult to approach undetected, and the McClean household in Smithboro, which had seen off previous IRA raids and was likened to a fortress.[37]

The raiders met variable resistance. McKenna recalled the raid on the 'Larmour' household (this seems to have been an error in memory and he meant the Leary household). His recollections indicate the degree to which the IRA portrayed these reprisals as a form of sectarian justice in which they were the defenders of the nationalist community. 'Larmour's' response, if true, also provides us with an insight from the other side as to why Roslea was burned after the shooting of Lester:

> I again knocked and shouted, 'are you there Larmour?' and he shouted, 'who is there?', I said the IRA friends of the Catholics you turned out in Roslea and we are about to burn your house so come out at once. I heard the door being unlocked [and] my men moved up beside me, two men and

a woman came out. I asked Mr Larmour where his second son was, and he responded, 'out on duty', 'on armed patrol?' I asked, he replied 'yes' I said 'if you had kept your sons at home from the sack of Roslea we would not be here tonight' he replied heatedly 'you though you could have it all your own way when you shot Lester'.[38]

McKenna told his men to shoot the elderly man if he spoke again and only gave the family time to take out essentials. This raid included an unusual interaction with one of the younger sons of the family, who asked and received McKenna's permission to remove a treasured mirror that had been presented by the Orange lodge. In return for some information on the size of the local USC patrol, McKenna agreed to a request to burn only the house and not stables or carts required for rebuilding. McKenna was shocked: 'I told him we were not that bad.'[39]

At the unsuccessful McClean raid, Marron noted four brothers of the family had been in the British army between 1914 and 1918.[40] As a result, they were both trained enough and numerous enough to defend their home, as they had done in the past. Marron's plan to take the house involved stealthily breaking and entering instead of an open assault on the isolated property. For some unknown reason, Marron chose not to follow his own plan. He knocked on the door to demand that the family open up before releasing the horses in the stable. Awoken, the McClean brothers fired on the raiders. After half an hour of continuous fire, Marron resolved to burn the hay loft in the hope that the flames would spread. The operation descended into farce when the IRA forgot to open the windows and 'the fire got suffocated for the want of air and smothered itself'.[41] The IRA departed when Marron's men heard gunshots from surrounding unionist households to raise the alarm.

Over the course of the night, three men were shot and killed. William Gordon, a 34-year-old married man from Rathkeevan, was shot through the window of his parent's home.[42] He was an active unionist and had served as the master of the local Orange and Black lodge.[43] An attempt had been made to burn down his home two weeks previously.[44] Gordon's pregnant wife gave birth five days later.[45] Samuel Nixon was a 35-year-old farmer from Tattymore and a member of the local lodge. He had received a threatening letter from the IRA at the same time as George Lester, also warning him against any further dealings with the police.[46] Nixon was wounded in the first volley of shots fired at his house. He and his wife lay on the floor until the raiders threatened to burn the property if they did not come out. The couple were disarmed when they emerged. Nixon was shot without warning by a raider who ran towards him from the back of the house which was left untouched.[47] For Harry Macklin, an IRA member, Gordon and Nixon 'were a pair of bad boys and richly deserved what they got'.[48] The third fatality was James Douglas of Aghafin who lived with his mother and was drawn out by a threat to attack the house. He was shot and left for dead but was removed to Clones hospital after the raiders had left.[49] In other cases, the threat to clear out was either not offered or did not work. The house of Edward Nelson of Mullaglass was set alight while he was inside and he only escaped with his sons by jumping from an upper window.[50] William Andrews, also of Mullaglass, met with a lucky escape. He had been disarmed following a threat to harm his parents if he did not surrender. Andrews was then tied up and blindfolded and told he was going to be shot. However, the raiders were drawn away by commotion elsewhere and he escaped.[51] Thomas Lester and his sister were similarly threatened with execution. In the immediate aftermath of the attack, both the RIC and USC poured into the locality. The IRA went to ground. Connolly recalled: 'We could take no chances of either being seen by B-men or being captured by Crown forces.'[52] Nationalists in the area were fearful of reprisals and requested protection from O'Duffy should that arise.[53] With characteristic understatement, Dublin Castle recorded that 'a general attack was made by Sinn Féiners on loyalists in Roslea district. Some arms were taken from loyalists'.[54]

The *Anglo-Celt* and *Fermanagh Times* provided the first list of victims: Samuel Nixon, William Gordon, James Douglas, Edward Nelson, Mrs Magwood, Thomas Lester, William Andrews, John Johnston, William Leary.[55] Both Leary and Douglas were located just over the border in Kilcorrin and Aghafin respectively while Nixon and Gordon were killed in townlands on the border itself. Gordon and Nixon were both buried on 29 March 1921 in Clough parish in Monaghan. Their coffins were covered by a Union Jack and accorded 'semi-military honours'.[56] Gordon's grandson stated in an interview in 2015 that his grandfather was carried over the border 'by Protestant and Catholic neighbours alike'.[57] Heightened tension in the district played itself out in various ways. In mid-April the Roslea AOH hall was raided by uniformed men said to be USC and the AOH had their drums and other items seized.[58] A Specials playing football on the streets of the town would strike nationalists walking by with the ball or deliberately aim to smash the windows of nationalist houses.[59] In March DI McMonagle was shot at by the IRA four miles north of Roslea and CI Tyrell was warned that McMonagle would be 'shot with a bullet' if he were not removed.[60] Thomas Lester was fired on as he left his house a few weeks after the attack but was unharmed.[61] Despite nationalist fears of an escalation, the Roslea burnings proved the high-water mark of violence. The most significant military consequence of the IRA operation was the capture of local commander Matt Fitzpatrick after he was injured during the attack on the Magwood household. Two IRA men were pursued by a USC party after the raid and Frank Connolly was shot dead.[62]

Local leaders of both faiths organized a peace conference in Clones chaired by Canon Ruddell, rector of the town. It was agreed to appoint a committee to heal the rifts between Catholics and Protestants in Roslea. Members included both Thomas Toal and M.E. Knight, the local leaders of Monaghan nationalism and unionism, and Reverends Morris and Martin of Clough and Smithboro, both prominent unionists.[63] Roslea became an important symbol for the Fermanagh unionist community as a cautionary tale of the dangers posed by unchecked nationalist aggression. Commemorations of the Gordon and Nixon murders were common with the two painted as martyrs – a process seen in the semi-military funeral procession accorded both men. The biannual meeting of the Monaghan Black Chapter in June 1921 passed a vote of sympathy with Gordon's family.[64] Nixon's death, due to its dramatic nature, became particularly prominent – his defencelessness and the closeness of his family were central themes. As the *Impartial Reporter* put it: 'Of mercy there was none. A gallant man, after surrendering, was treacherously riddled with bullets in the presence of his wife and little ones.'[65]

The propaganda importance of Roslea to unionists should not be understated. William Copeland Trimble started a relief fund for unionist families affected by the raids (especially for the period before compensation was awarded). The fund was also for the commissioning of a memorial. No consideration was given to nationalists who had lost their homes or to unionists in Monaghan.[66] An early and popular method of raising money for the fund was to organize collections in Protestant churches of all denominations on politically important days such as the opening of the Northern Ireland parliament.[67] On 5 May 1921 it was decided to amalgamate the fund with the County USC benevolent fund and to expand its scope to all special constables and their families injured through enemy engagement in Fermanagh.[68] While the fund represented a genuine charitable impulse (at least towards loyalist families), it was important for another reason. No other organization so promoted or exaggerated the cause and suffering of Roslea loyalists (and by extension any loyalists who suffered at the hands of the IRA):

> Picture women and children hoarded together for a night's rest behind barricades; there is through the night the dread of the bullet; the accommodation is the most primitive as several families under one roof cannot have the same comfort as in their own homes. The district is experiencing a state of war.[69]

Despite the tendency to prioritize such outbursts of violence, it should be remembered that for many in Fermanagh, even those within the IRA, their experience of the War of Independence was not defined by explicit violence but rather by social pressure and implied threat. For many, the primary experience of the War of Independence was enforcing the Belfast boycott or having the measure imposed on them.[70] The boycott was a response to sectarian violence in Ulster, in general, and to the expulsion of Catholics from their workplaces in

Belfast over summer 1920 in particular.[71] A boycott was first suggested in August 1920 when Seán MacEntee, TD for Monaghan South, read a petition calling for the boycotting of goods from Belfast and the withdrawal of money from Belfast-based banks. Following the continuation of anti-Catholic riots in the city, the boycott was instituted in September.[72] This was in spite of the warnings of Monaghan's other TD, Ernest Blythe, that such a tactic would forever alienate neighbouring unionists.

Fermanagh's experience of boycotting was inherently different from the rest of the country. First, the county's geographical and cultural proximity to Belfast meant that there were more and deeper connections between the two that made conforming to the Belfast boycott a far greater economic and cultural burden. Second, the greater proportion of Protestants (and consequently loyalists) meant that the communities being targeted were larger and more coherent than was the case in Munster counties for example. Additionally, the larger Protestant community in the county heavily undercut the efficacy of the boycott as a parallel market emerged. Gemma Clark has emphasized that while isolated loyalists were most vulnerable to boycotting, larger, more cohesive communities could still come under threat when the boycotters were sufficiently organized.[73] The boycott in Fermanagh served to heighten and make explicit the differences between the county's two political communities. Dooley, looking at Monaghan, identified similar factors when he noted 'given both Monaghan's border location and its long tradition of sectarianism, it was inevitable that the boycott would have significant consequences'.[74]

Livingstone characterized the attempts to enforce the Belfast boycott in Fermanagh as sporadic and slow to start, much like earlier attempts to establish the Dáil courts. By the end of September 1920, the unionist *Derry Sentinel* declared that 'no attempt has been made throughout Fermanagh to enforce a boycott of Belfast'.[75] An initial meeting on extending the boycott to Enniskillen on 17 September 1920 met with an ambivalent reaction.[76] In November 1920 Fermanagh County Council received a letter from the Irish County Councils General Council asking its members to accept a recent resolution against religious tests in employment and to discontinue business with 'the city in which such an illegal test is now attempting to be enforced'. While Cahir Healy vocally supported the motion, Lord Belmore declared that it would be 'impossible for any Protestant or unionist member' to do so. IPP discomfort with the boycott was revealed when John McHugh, the chairman, moved that the first part of the resolution regarding religious tests be adopted and the second part ignored.[77] Like the Dáil courts, efforts to implement a boycott were more effective in the south and east of the county along the Monaghan border, where Eoin O'Duffy was particularly strict about enforcing it. Monaghan was one of the only Ulster counties able to implement the boycott effectively.[78] In August 1920 O'Duffy wrote to all traders who did business with Belfast to stop.[79] Monaghan saw a much stricter boycott than Fermanagh. Many of the boycotting operations around Newtownbutler and over the county boundary in Clones were directed more at disrupting trade in Monaghan that went through Fermanagh than trade in Fermanagh itself. South-eastern Fermanagh was also a major throughfare between Belfast and Clones, and between Clones and Enniskillen and saw significant traffic.

Due to its position along the border, the Wattlebridge company of the Monaghan Brigade, led by Matt Fitzpatrick, was the most active. The company was involved in holding up a goods train and arresting its guard, named Wallace from Clones, due to his repeated defiance of IRA orders to quit serving on trains with prohibited goods.[80] In late 1921 Fitzpatrick was notified that a van from a Belfast bakery called Inglis would not be permitted to pass through after a set date. Nevertheless, deliveries continued. Francis Tummon recounted how 'These Belfast firms had got so well rooted through their efficiency and service that most shopkeepers at any rate regarded them as indispensable.'[81] Consequently, the company decided to ambush the van as it passed near Wattlebridge national school. The ambush demonstrated the problems experienced by the IRA in Fermanagh during the War of Independence. The initial ambush went well. The driver was held up. But before the company could set the van on fire, a USC Crossley tender from Newtownbutler was observed. A firefight broke out and Fitzpatrick was almost captured after he took refuge with another Volunteer in the house of Pat Smith a couple of miles away. The RIC arrived at Smith's house a few of hours later, surprising the Volunteers and a shootout took place that ended in the wounding of Constable Farrelly and the retreat of the RIC.[82]

While the initial efforts at boycotting were relatively sporadic and relied on the initiative of local republican leaders, greater momentum and centralization came in the early months of 1921 with a renewed push from Dublin by Joseph MacDonagh in the Department of Labour.[83] However, in Fermanagh even this was slow to take hold. Only in August 1921 was the Enniskillen committee of the Belfast boycott established.[84] It was not until September that the CI conceded the boycott was 'being felt in the towns to a small degree'.[85] That month, James Cooper MP raised the issue of 'a criminal conspiracy' underway in Enniskillen to impose the boycott.[86] Although efforts were made to institute a widespread boycott like that in Monaghan, the size of the unionist population in Fermanagh rendered this impossible.[87] Apart from the border near Clones, Enniskillen was the primary focus of the boycott. In August 1921 the Enniskillen boycott committee published a 'whitelist' of traders who abided by the boycott. This list initially contained only six names but it had increased to fifteen by September.[88] These activities occurred in mid and late 1921 during a lull in violence that followed the truce in July. Initial attempts to impose a boycott directly were foiled by the police raiding the SF headquarters in the town and in the swift response of the USC. A more subtle approach to boycotting was then adopted in which it was publicly announced that certain houses were being 'watched'.[89] In Irvinestown, Catholic traders were asked to sign a commitment to not engage with Protestant custom while in Kinawley it was reported that even the local Orange lodge master was abiding by the boycott.[90]

The boycott was broadly ineffective. Donal Hall noted in Louth that it was a failure both in regard to hurting Belfast merchants and those willing to trade with them.[91] It drove a deeper wedge between the nationalist and unionist communities in Fermanagh due to its disproportionate targeting of unionist traders and what Brian Hughes has described as 'the difficulty with which politics was disentangled from economics'.[92] Unionist businesses suffered heavily in the boycott, as they did in Monaghan and Tyrone, and this 'embittered' feeling significantly between the two communities.[93] The *Impartial Reporter* denounced the boycott as 'a religious boycott to capture business from the Protestant business houses'.[94] Despite denials from the boycott committee, numerous unionists, including James Cooper, claimed that the sectarian aspect of the boycott was evident as only nationalists received demands to abide by the whitelist.[95] The *Reporter* also noted that many Protestant businesses had been placed on the blacklist despite undertaking no trade with Belfast, while others that had been whitelisted were openly trading with the city.[96] By October 1921 the *Reporter* was openly speculating about the scale and power of a unionist response to the boycotting committee:

> What if Protestants were to retaliate? What if they closed down the Nursing Society tomorrow? … What if Protestant employers were to reduce their staffs and see that the first to go were Roman Catholics? What if the Protestant landlords were to put their Roman Catholic tenants out of their house?[97]

Mouthpieces of unionism like the *Reporter* and the *Fermanagh Times* attempted to discount how widespread or endemic such boycotting was, preferring instead to portray it as a pernicious invasion from the lawless south. The Enniskillen boycott was understood more easily by unionists if it was blamed on servant boys from Leitrim as it was by an anonymous writer 'Fermanagh Radical' in a letter on 15 November 1921.[98] That month, 'South Tyrone Radical' made the same claim but also suggested that servants were betraying their employers to the IRA by providing information to raiding parties. Their recommendation was to fire all foreign labourers and let them return over the border 'and serve Roman Catholic masters, where their pay will be lighter and their diet too'.[99]

In April 1921 the Government of Ireland Act came into force and formally established Northern Ireland as a separate entity, which was viewed with suspicion by nationalists. Cahir Healy dismissively referred to the new Belfast

government as a 'parliament of Planters'.[100] Unionist control of national
government initiated a new phase in the struggle between nationalist and
unionist for control of local government. Unionists were increasingly able to
convert power in Belfast into power in Fermanagh.

Throughout 1921 the number of USC in Fermanagh continued to grow in
an attempt to control IRA outrages. Initially, this was counterproductive as the
USC provided a new, easily identifiable target for the IRA. Its reputation as a
sectarian force made the USC an attractive target for militant republicans. In the
first half of 1921, the IRA frequently raided the houses of B Specials in an
unsuccessful effort to deter potential recruits. On 29 May a USC patrol was
ambushed at Mullaghfad and Special Constables Robert Coalter and John Hall
were killed.[101] The attack took place at Hall's home. He had allegedly crawled to
his Catholic neighbour for help but they refused to open the door and Hall was
later found dead outside.[102] Basil Brooke, who had himself nearly been part of
the Mullaghfad patrol, both warned and threatened Craig that should such
outrages continue, 'nothing can stop reprisals on a large scale'.[103] In this case,
three men were arrested shortly afterward, which allayed some of Brooke's fears
of reprisals. In April 1921 Craig himself had visited Fermanagh in a significant
test of the security capabilities of the county. The visit passed off without issue,
largely due to Brooke's policy of surrounding Craig with 'lorries armed to the
teeth'.[104]

The security efforts of the USC were characterized by a greater willingness
to enact harsh punishments and to engage in sectarian-coded reprisals for IRA
activity. On 21 February 1921 the Catholic Temperance Hall in Teemone was
burned down in reprisal for a raid on the house of Revd F.W. Grant of Aghintra
the day before. The reprisal was much more extreme than the outrage it
punished. Grant had not been injured and only some food and a bicycle were
taken. The house of Edward Fitzpatrick of Clonaroo was also burned in
February, having been deemed a 'harbour of armed rebels'.[105] The USC was
reported to have prepared lists of all SF leaders in Fermanagh. On 18 March
Patrick Doonan of Carlare reported shots fired into his house by the
B Specials but the RIC insisted the IRA were responsible.[106] Later in March,
Knocknarooney SF hall was burned in reprisal for the burning of the vans of
William Little for breaking the Belfast boycott.[107] The reprisals reached their
peak in June 1921, following the Mullaghfad ambush. Five Mullaghfad
nationalists – John Monaghan, Hugh Lowry, Henry Lowry, Thomas Coulter and
Annie Connolly – alleged that their homes and out offices had been burned by
'five or six policemen wearing coats and carrying rifles'.[108] Hugh Lowry began
to suffer a co-ordinated campaign of intimidation. On 6 June he discovered that
fifty hens, nine ducks and six chickens had been stolen from him. The heads of
the ducks had been left nearby. In response, the IRA burned the hayshed of
George Godler, a local B Special.[109]

In April 1921, in anticipation of partition, the local government areas within Fermanagh were reformed. The parts of the county under Ballyshannon and Clones guardians were transferred to Irvinestown and Lisnaskea guardians respectively. Enniskillen guardians was put under unionist control when its Cavan members were transferred to Manorhamilton. Joseph Geddis was put forward as a candidate and was defined in traditional unionist terms as 'a large ratepayer'. Lord Belmore expressed regret at losing the services of Corrigan as chairman but attributed it to 'the fortune of war'. He hoped that in the future one of the Catholics may be put in as one of the lower chairmen but 'the Unionists had not had a chair for 21 years, and it was time now that they got one'.[110]

More significantly, Belleek and Clones No. 2 RDCs were dissolved and their areas were transferred to Irvinestown and Lisnaskea. This was controversial for a number of reasons. First, it deprived nationalists of two seats on the county council and reduced their majority. This proved a significant obstacle to nationalist business in the council. Second, Belleek was transferred to Irvinestown rather than Enniskillen rural. This was seen as suspicious as Enniskillen was nearer and much more convenient to access for the Belleek councillors. It also meant that the unionists kept their majority on Enniskillen RDC, which would otherwise have been threatened.[111] Livingstone reports that this was done at the specific request of Lord Belmore.[112]

Unionists were able to take control of the tightly contested Enniskillen UDC in October 1921. After the arrest of Frank Carney, O/C of the Fermanagh Brigade, one seat on the council fell vacant. While the council was now divided evenly between the nationalist–labour alliance and unionists, with ten seats apiece, nationalists controlled the chair and should have been able to use the tie-breaking vote to co-opt one of their own. However, the failure of Thomas Gordon to appear gave the unionists a majority that they used to co-opt Thomas Quinn and gain a majority. They used their new majority to declare Gordon's seat vacant as he had recently obtained a post as a technical instructor for shoemaking in Enniskillen and holding a paid municipal position while also being a councillor was not permitted. Nationalists left the chamber in protest. As they now held the majority, the unionists declared the chair vacated and elected George Whaley to hold it for the remainder of the meeting. Thomas Trotter, a Unionist member, was co-opted to fill Gordon's seat.[113] Trotter had run unsuccessfully as a Labour candidate in 1920. Although he still professed to be a 'labour man', he consistently voted against Bernard Keenan and Thomas Campling in the council. Enniskillen UDC now had a majority of three unionists and with future boundary changes, they would hold this council for decades.[114] For nationalists, this violation of precedent was nothing less than a coup. The *Fermanagh Herald* declared it 'an act that any men versed in the ordinary code of political and public honour would be ashamed to commit'.[115] Nationalists, it noted, had not previously co-opted members of their own party when similar vacancies had arisen, nor had they removed any previous unionist office holders from their posts when they could have.

Unionists immediately used their control of the UDC to reduce its expenditure. A common unionist criticism of nationalist local government at all levels was how it mismanaged funds and caused rates to skyrocket. When the IPP gained control of Fermanagh County Council in 1914, the rate had been 11s. on the pound. Seven years later it was 15s. In unionist eyes, as the biggest contributors, they should have the right to set the rates and within a few months of unionist control the rate was again 11s. Nationalists and labour protested the spending cuts. On Enniskillen UDC, a week after seizing control, James Cooper proposed the cancellation of an application for a £66,000 loan to build houses in Enniskillen. While Cooper acknowledged the need for housing, with many of the homes being little more than 'hovels', he claimed that this scheme would bankrupt the town – a claim disputed by the borough surveyor. A large deputation of labourers under William Clarke marched to the courthouse to protest the cancellation. A nationalist deputation proposed a compromise whereby the scale of the scheme would be reduced but this was rejected by unionists and the project was abandoned. While this was done in the name of fiscal prudence, the *Fermanagh Herald* noted bitterly that it was not a coincidence that such a project would have disproportionately benefitted Catholics.[116] When Cooper was accused of bigotry by J.P. Gillin, the *Reporter* and Cooper retorted that Gillin was guilty of bigotry of his own: 'If the present Chairman refuses in future to set houses belonging to the Council to Roman Catholics ... he will only be following the precedent set by his predecessor'.[117]

In May elections were held to select the MPs for the new parliament in Belfast. Both the IPP and SF committed to contesting the election. Despite initial hints from de Valera that he might be willing to engage with some form of northern devolution as part of an independent Ireland, in the end he and Michael Collins agreed on a policy of abstention. SF MPs would take their seats in Dáil Éireann instead of in Belfast City Hall, thereby undermining the legitimacy of the latter. This decision, along with SF's confirmation that only republicans could sit in Dáil Éireann, forced the IPP, now under Devlin's leadership, to adopt a policy of complete abstentionism.[118] De Valera hoped that such a policy would allow new class divisions to form in the all-Unionist parliament, which could be exploited later.[119] De Valera and Devlin had also agreed once again to co-ordinate nationalist candidates to maximize the number of candidates returned. They encouraged their supporters to transfer between nationalist candidates. This was especially important as the Government of Ireland Act had joined Fermanagh and Tyrone in a single eight-seat constituency. There was some uncertainty over how this, combined with proportional representation, would affect the election. Unionists had lost William Coote's South Tyrone – their strongest constituency in either Tyrone or Fermanagh – but they were in a better position to leverage clusters of unionists such as in Florencecourt which had previously been unable to effect the choice of MP in South Fermanagh. Nationalists, however, hoped that their absolute majority in both counties could now be utilized more effectively.

To meet these concerns, unionists deliberately put forward just four candidates: the two sitting MPs, Edward Archdale and William Coote, as well as two prominent county councillors, James Cooper for Fermanagh and William Thomas Miller for Tyrone. These candidates had clearly defined campaign areas which, it was believed, would provide each of them with sufficient votes to get elected and thereby nullify the nationalist majority in the county into a simple 50:50 split of seats. On the nationalist side, the IPP's weakness was reflected in its difficulties mustering a quorum at the UIL convention before the election: 400 attendees had been expected but only forty 'mostly old men' turned up.[120] The party put forward their only sitting MP from either county, Thomas Harbison of Tyrone North East as well as George Irvine's erstwhile opponent from 1918 – J.P. Gillin. SF nominated five candidates – sitting MPs Arthur Griffith and Seán O'Mahony as well as Kevin O'Shiel, Seán Milroy and Seán MacEntee. Seven nationalist candidates competed for the same vote. While this was an electoral misstep in the constituency, it fell in line with the SF policy in the election of trying to achieve a significant victory by exploiting unionist misgivings about partition. De Valera himself expected that nationalists would win at least a third of the fifty-two available seats on the assumption of major success in nationalist areas of strength like Fermanagh and Tyrone.[121]

Prior to the election, the *Impartial Reporter* urged its readers to vote, reminding them that their future domination of Ulster was the potential prize for a strong election: 'no remedial legislation can be attempted unless there be a substantial majority and once having gained that, it will be for all time'.[122] By contrast, nationalists were more pessimistic. J.P. Gillin's speeches denounced partition as 'national suicide' but offered no path out of the current situation beyond pledging to 'work unceasingly for Irish Unity'.[123] O'Shiel held the first large-scale election meeting in Enniskillen and the speeches focused primarily on the economic disadvantages of partition.[124] It is striking, however, that such an important election at a time when political violence was rampant across the country saw little if any disorder of its own. Indeed, the nationalist campaign was derided by unionist opponents for its low energy and lack of enthusiasm.[125]

The results clearly favoured the Unionists and their cautious strategy. While Arthur Griffith was elected on the first count with 21,677 votes, so too were Archdale and Coote with 10,336 and 9,672 votes respectively. By the third count, all four Unionist candidates had been elected and only Seán Milroy had also been returned for SF. The final two seats eventually went to Harbison and O'Mahony with J.P. Gillin losing out on the tenth count. O'Shiel had polled moderately well but Seán MacEntee, future tánaiste under Seán Lemass, was left somewhat humiliated after only polling 179 first preference votes. Both sides were keen to portray the election as a victory. Despite proportionally losing seats compared to the 1918 election, nationalists in Fermanagh emphasized that 57 per cent of the votes cast had been against partition. The optimism engendered by this can be seen in their celebrations after the results were announced when they marched in procession through Enniskillen and held a mass meeting.[126] The *Fermanagh Herald* characterized the result as the best that the nationalists could possibly have achieved in the face of unionist 'jerrymandering' through the creation of the new constituency. The newspaper noted that the anti-partitionists had a majority of 7,899 in Fermanagh.[127] O'Shiel echoed this in a letter to the *Herald* in which he described the constituency as '1,200,000 acres specially carved out to give the Separatists four seats and to prevent the real loyalists from securing five'.[128]

O'Shiel noted several other ways that the election had been set against nationalist candidates. First, the constituency centre had been located in Omagh, which was easily accessible from unionist strongholds in north Fermanagh and south Tyrone but which isolated nationalist campaign directors from key areas of support in south Fermanagh. Second, polling stations had been placed in great abundance in 'Partitionist areas', whereas many nationalists had to walk several miles to vote. The nearest polling station for the strongly nationalist Devenish West, for example, was in Belleek, despite the area being on the outskirts of Enniskillen. The county council had passed a motion of protest against the LGB on the same issue.[129] O'Shiel complained about the same issue in 1918 but was ignored. He also alleged that nationalists had been hindered in acquiring motor vehicles to convey voters to the polls by the newly introduced motor permit system which had been introduced to reduce the IRA's ability to travel in motor vehicles. All drivers were required to obtain a permit from the relevant military authority. O'Shiel maintained that this system favoured unionists who were able to acquire at least sixty vehicles on the day of the election whereas nationalists secured just four.[130]

Despite this, it is difficult to view the results as anything but a failure for Fermanagh and Tyrone nationalism. The relative expectations of both sides can be seen in a false rumour run in the national papers in the week before the election which claimed that a deal had been brokered between all sides in the constituency under which Unionists would return three MPs, Sinn Féin two and the IPP three.[131] The *Belfast Newsletter* meanwhile trumpeted the unionist result in the county as a 'triumph' and a 'huge blow to Sinn Féin'.[132] Following the election of James Cooper, the loyalists of Enniskillen lit a large tar barrel on the prominent Windmill Hill. Bonfires greeted the victory in Mullaghy, Fivemiletown and Garvary. In Ballinamallard, Florencecourt and Maguiresbridge Union Jacks were draped across the town and large drum and fife processions took place.[133]

There was further good news for Fermanagh unionism when Archdale was appointed the first minister of agriculture and commerce for Northern Ireland. John Porter-Porter and Basil Brooke were also nominated to the all–Unionist senate by the new House of Commons. Viscount Cole had declined Craig's invitation on learning of the responsibilities involved.[134] Brooke nearly resigned too after he was informed that he could not simultaneously be the county commandant of the USC in Fermanagh – a salaried position – and a senator. The issue was eventually resolved when Brooke agreed to continue in his USC role in an honorary, unpaid capacity. Unmistakably, the election left Fermanagh under the control of a parliament completely dominated by unionists. The election had been a disappointment for nationalists. Unionists took forty of the fifty-two seats with twelve shared between SF and the IPP.

In June 1921, prompted by King George V's plea for peace as he opened the new northern parliament in Belfast City Hall, talks reopened between the British government and the Dáil. These culminated in a ceasefire which came into operation on 11 July, bringing an immediate end to violence in the county. Under the terms of the truce, British troops were confined primarily to their barracks and could not interfere with either civilians or known members of the IRA. In return, the IRA agreed to cease its own military operations. The USC was stood down but continued to operate unofficially under the umbrella of the UVF.[135] The truce was generally upheld in Fermanagh despite some occasional lapses in discipline. For instance, in November 1921 a number of men from 'the foothills of Leitrim' attacked Kesh RIC barracks when most of the force were attending a boxing match. The raiders stole a number of rifles and made off in the direction of Donegal.[136] The CI also noted throughout August and September that various activities were continuing uninterrupted in the county such as boycotting, the running of Dáil courts and drilling.[137] Many unionists reacted angrily to the idea that the USC were being 'disbanded' to appease SF. John Porter-Porter told an Orange rally in Fermanagh in July that he hoped 'the "B" men will hold on to their guns. Hold on to them as long as you can for we all look to you'.[138] No attempt was made to seize the USC arms. Indeed, by November 1921 it had become apparent that in the absence of the USC and in the context of a growing threat of southern invasion, the UVF was once again in operation.[139]

The start of negotiations between the British government and the Dáil was a source of great optimism among the nationalist community in Fermanagh who believed that these negotiations would, at the very least, see the inclusion of Fermanagh and Tyrone under Dáil Éireann. Northerners were consulted as part of the Treaty negotiations but, according to McCluskey, these consultations 'lacked coherence'.[140] The Fermanagh man most involved was Cahir Healy who advised the northern working group of the Dáil on the impact of partition on local government and education.[141] In August 1921 Fermanagh nationalists sent a cross-party delegation consisting of John McHugh, Cahir Healy and Fr

Lorcán Ó Ciaráin to meet de Valera in Dublin. They were joined by Seán O'Mahony who introduced them to a meeting of the cabinet. The purpose of the delegation was to deliver a joint statement on behalf of all Fermanagh nationalists in favour of including the county in a southern state. The statement itself focused on two key points. First, that Fermanagh was dominated politically by nationalists who held the county council with a two-member majority, three of the five rural councils (with Enniskillen RDC held by a single unionist vote) and the urban council. This was evidence that 'Fermanagh is strongly opposed to inclusion in the area of the Belfast Parliament'. Secondly, nationalists in the county feared how they would fare in a northern state and cited the 'recent treatment meted out to them since the idea of partition became real'. They also noted the removal of Clones No. 2 and Belleek rural councils as proof of an ongoing unionist gerrymander.[142]

Despite nationalist optimism, throughout the second half of 1921 the new Belfast parliament was able steadily to increase its authority in Fermanagh and other nationalist areas. Craig judiciously built up the USC as a means to enforce Unionist political power. USC platoons began to have notable victories in Fermanagh. In April a number of IRA members in Roslea were arrested and fifteen guns were seized. Some IRA men were also chased to an island on Lough Erne and arrested in an amphibious operation.[143] As the initial restructuring of the rural councils would suggest, it was also a priority that local government be brought under control. At the same time, de Valera was keen for the local councils to end their equivocation and come under the authority of Dáil Éireann so as to strengthen the negotiating position of the Dáil in respect of partition. Consequently, in November 1921 Fermanagh County Council, along with Tyrone, voted to recognize Dáil Éireann and not the Belfast parliament.[144] The Northern government had already considered disbanding the 'recalcitrant' councils of Fermanagh and Tyrone and now had the perfect opportunity.[145] On 21 December 1921, as control of local government was formally placed under the Belfast parliament, Fermanagh County Council again asserted that it did 'not recognize the Partition Parliament in Belfast' and ordered the secretary of the council to cease communications with Belfast. Less than five minutes after the close of the meeting, the RIC raided the council offices and told officials to 'have a few days holiday'. Unlike the situation in Tyrone, where the council was allowed to continue once it had repudiated recognition of Dáil Éireann, in Fermanagh the council was dissolved entirely and its functions given to a commissioner from Belfast, Robert McNeill.[146] Lisnaskea District Council, the only remaining nationalist controlled council, was similarly dissolved. Cormac Moore has noted how these actions turned a relative humiliation in the 1920 local elections for unionists into a victory and enabled them to bring the most recalcitrant nationalist councils to heel.[147]

Nationalist troubles deepened on 6 December 1921 when the Irish delegation signed a treaty with the British government confirming that Fermanagh was to be part of Northern Ireland. This result did not come completely out of the blue. Eoin MacNeill had encountered a number of rumours regarding the conduct of the delegation and Collins, in particular, when he had toured Fermanagh in late November.[148] McCluskey has emphasized that these rumours, though unfounded, reflected a very real fear in the area that the delegates had been outmanoeuvred by the British.[149] Confirmation of these fears was a major blow to Fermanagh nationalists. Despite this disappointment, many Fermanagh nationalists were willing to support the Treaty at least provisionally. Livingstone estimated that ninety per cent of the county's nationalists supported the settlement. The same figure was given by the Enniskillen correspondent of the pro-Treaty *Freeman's Journal*.[150] While it is an exaggeration, it does speak to the cross-party support for the Treaty in the county. Cahir Healy viewed the settlement as the best deal that could have been achieved in the circumstances. In this he was supported by one of the most prominent IPP members in the county, John McHugh, the former county council chairman.[151] Most dissenting voices such as that of Thomas Irvine of Lack or John McElgunn, chair of Lisnaskea guardians, did not advocate outright rejection of the Treaty but prioritized other issues over ratification. For Irvine this was a demand for greater clarity as to the status of Fermanagh under the Treaty and for McElgunn it was a call for a resolution that prioritized unity over either ratification or rejection.[152]

For most nationalists their acceptance of the Treaty hinged on Article 12, which provided for a future commission to be established to redraw the boundary between the two states.[153] This, it was hoped, would recognize demographic realities and place nearly all of Fermanagh south of the border. That view was echoed by an anonymous Fermanagh Sinn Féiner quoted in the *Freeman's Journal*: 'it may not be an ideal settlement but what hope is there of obtaining better terms if the Treaty is rejected. Personally, I can see no way out of the morass that rejection would create'.[154] Arthur Griffith, as both one of the plenipotentiaries and an MP for Fermanagh–Tyrone, utilized his contacts to help win over key figures in the county. In December 1921 he met Fr Eugene Coyle, parish priest of Garrison and later a prominent pro-Treaty figure, in the Gresham Hotel in Dublin to answer personally his concerns about where the Treaty had left northern nationalists.[155]

On 7 December a delegation of northern nationalists met Eoin MacNeill in Dublin's Mansion House to discuss the settlement. While others, such as the mayor of Derry, denounced the Treaty, Healy supported it on the principle that the future Boundary Commission would inevitably save Fermanagh and Tyrone and, in doing so, render the northern state unviable.[156] A special meeting of the county SF executive was held on 30 December 1921 to discuss the Treaty. A motion calling on the TDs for Fermanagh–Tyrone to support the agreement was proposed by Healy and seconded by Fr Patrick Cullinan of Belcoo. An opposing motion was proposed by Fr Terence Caulfield of Ederney and seconded by Patrick O'Hart. The motion in favour was carried by a strong majority of thirty-four to eight.

The *Herald* estimated that nationalists were 'overwhelmingly' in favour of the Treaty and noted sourly that many unionists were 'jubilant' at the prospect of the Treaty being rejected.[157] The paper also expressed concern that the will of Fermanagh and Tyrone nationalists might be underrepresented on this issue in the Dáil. Two of their MPs, Arthur Griffith and Seán Milroy, were also TDs for Cavan and thus could only cast one vote. This would be cast for Cavan as votes were cast alphabetically by constituency name. That would leave the pro-Treaty voice in the county 'totally disenfranchised' as, of their other two representatives, Thomas Harbison belonged to the IPP and thus could not sit in Dáil Éireann, and O'Mahony had already made it known that he opposed the Treaty.[158]

O'Mahony's opposition was the subject of significant local controversy. He received numerous petitions from SF clubs in Fermanagh and Tyrone recording their own vote in favour of the Treaty and urging him to change his vote as their representative.[159] The resolutions passed at a local level reflected a reluctant acceptance of the Treaty among Fermanagh nationalists as the best available option. For instance, the Rossinure More club unanimously passed a motion describing the Treaty as providing the 'essentials of freedom' and warned that its rejection was the goal of the 'Orange and ascendancy party' since this would destroy national unity and leave them 'masters of Ulster'.[160] Magheraveely SF club passed a similar motion by ten votes to three (although the club secretary Patrick Harte was keen to assure O'Mahony that 'I was one of the three').[161] Comparable resolutions were sent to O'Mahony by the Derrygonnelly, Derrylin, Brookeborough and Ederney SF clubs.

During the Treaty debates, O'Mahony acknowledged the strong pressure on him from Fermanagh to ratify the Treaty but claimed the petitions he had received were 'only individual opinions' and that no mandate from a local SF club or even the county executive was stronger than 'our Republican mandate, our national mandate'.[162] Despite his assertion that he had 'yet to be convinced – resolutions, letters and telegrams like those I have already received will not convince me – that the people have turned down the Republic that seven short months ago they elected me to maintain and uphold', O'Mahony received no letters of support from Fermanagh. The most positive communiqués explicitly rejected either side of the vote. The Shaun McDermott SF club in Arney refused to pass a motion either for or against the Treaty and stated that it would abide by whatever decision the Dáil made. In his letter to O'Mahony on the result of this vote, club secretary Peter Cassidy was very careful to emphasize that the club's refusal to ratify the Treaty was not an implicit vote against it: 'we were as much opposed to one as to the other'.[163]

It is perhaps surprising that Fermanagh should have supported a settlement that confirmed, at least temporarily, their separation from the rest of Ireland. This is particularly unusual when the county is compared to Tyrone which, despite similar social and political circumstances, saw widespread anti-Treaty sentiment, including a revolt among many rank-and-file republicans against the county's moderate pro–Treaty leadership.[164] There were a number of reasons for this attitude. First and most important was the Boundary Commission. Fermanagh's position directly on the border as well as the relatively even distribution of its nationalist population meant that a reasonably conservative commission would surely return most of the county to Dáil Éireann. Second, the nationalists in the county were keenly aware of the threat the USC now posed should violence flare up again. The Fermanagh IRA had not been able to operate effectively given unionist opposition even before the USC had been established. It seemed much less likely now that they would be able to oppose the Northern state militarily in a way that did not bring significant hardship upon the civilian population of Fermanagh. Third, several of the most influential republican figures in the county such as Cahir Healy and Lorcán Ó Ciaráin were strongly pro-Treaty and carried many of the SF clubs with them. The abiding strength of the IPP in the county (which retained a majority of nationalist seats on Fermanagh County Council) also lent itself to support for ratification. John McHugh and J.P. Gillin both supported the Treaty and publicly endorsed it.

Many influential voices who were ambivalent or opposed to the Treaty were outside of the county. Frank Carney, who refused to take either side in the Civil War and was later a Fianna Fáil TD, was in Ballykinlar internment camp in early December 1921, and on his release was assigned to Beggar's Bush as chief supplies officer for the National army.[165] George Irvine, who vocally opposed the Treaty and later joined the anti-Treaty IRA, had been based in Dublin since the early 1900s.[166] In contrast, the two most prominent IRA divisions in the county were Dan Hogan's 5th Northern Division and Seán Mac Eoin's 1st Midlands (which contained the Fermanagh Brigade), both of whom were strongly pro-Treaty. Local prominent IRA captains like Matt Fitzpatrick, while not vocal in their support of the settlement, entered into active service with pro-Treaty forces. James Smyth recalled that while some in the IRA may have been 'inclined towards the extreme wing', these differences were largely smoothed over by the Collins–De Valera pact of May 1922.[167] Finally, Phoenix suggests that the strong unionist opposition to the Treaty may have convinced many local nationalists of its merits.[168]

It is often forgotten that SF MPs elected in the 1921 Northern Ireland elections were entitled to sit in the Dáil and were present for the Treaty debates. Of these, only O'Mahony exclusively represented a northern constituency since Griffith, Milroy, Collins, de Valera and MacNeill all represented southern constituencies as well. However, even O'Mahony's speech opposing the Treaty made little mention of partition and was instead focused on the 'inviolability of the republican oath'.[169] This was in common with the majority of the debate in which, as McCluskey notes, 'partition barely registered ... primarily because few recognized the ambiguities contained in Article 12'.[170] When the Dáil voted on 7 January 1922, the Treaty narrowly passed with sixty-four in favour, fifty-seven against and three abstentions. For Fermanagh–Tyrone, Griffith and Milroy had voted in favour while O'Mahony abstained.

The news was greeted by nationalists in Enniskillen not with pleasure but with some measure of satisfaction. The previous year had been transformative for Fermanagh as republican violence had rapidly flared up and then died out, the Northern state had begun to assert itself inexorably, and nationalists faced greater challenges than ever from the USC, the loss of local power and growing internal division over the Treaty. For both communities, the coming few years would prove critically important as they aimed to either capitalize on or depower the looming Boundary Commission.

7 'Ulster is awake': the establishment of the northern state, 1922–3

The signing of the Anglo-Irish Treaty ushered in a new stage in the Irish Revolution in Fermanagh. While the Civil War largely passed the county by, the new Irish border became a significant source of violence throughout 1922. In response to the threat of the USC, most of the Fermanagh IRA either lay low or decamped across the border. Throughout early 1922 the IRA launched frequent raids across the border, most famously kidnapping a number of prominent unionists in March. In June 1922 the Donegal IRA occupied parts of Fermanagh around Pettigo and Belleek for a number of days before being driven off by the British army.[1] For unionists this constituted an invasion and a major breach of their territorial integrity. For local unionists in Pettigo and Belleek, the border represented a source of danger. It was a new frontier beyond which lay a wild and dangerous land. Security was, therefore, a dominant concern for unionists. The USC was deployed to control access to Fermanagh, trenching roads and destroying bridges – in effect creating a border where before there had been none. As part of a wider crackdown on republicans, a large number of prominent nationalists in Fermanagh were arrested. This further limited the capacity of Fermanagh nationalism to respond to emerging challenges. Nationalists in Fermanagh hoped that the Boundary Commission would deliver them from unionist control.

After the passage of the Treaty, Collins turned his attention to the northern border and the nationalists beyond. On 21 January 1922 he and Craig agreed a wide-ranging deal to resolve ongoing issues between north and south. The Collins–Craig pact agreed to end the Belfast boycott in exchange for a commitment from Craig to allow expelled Catholic shipworkers in Belfast to retun to their jobs. More importantly for Fermanagh, it also enabled Dublin and Belfast to bypass the Treaty and the Boundary Commission by bilaterally agreeing a new shape for the border. Among Fermanagh nationalists this led to fears that the Boundary Commission was being abandoned. There was also discontent over Collins's volte-face recognition of Craig's government after Fermanagh County Council had already suffered the consequences of the Dáil's previous non-recognition policy only a month before. The pact itself survived for just over a week until another meeting of Collins and Craig in Dublin on 2 February. It then emerged that Lloyd George, characteristically, had promised entirely different degrees of boundary changes to both men.[2]

The pact had also been undermined by the almost immediate outbreak of violence in Northern Ireland, something that Fermanagh had not been immune to. While the USC had enabled the unionist establishment to gain firm control over Fermanagh and nullify the security threat of the Fermanagh IRA, the border itself became a significant source of instability in the county. These events occurred just as the first generation of USC was put on active service. In February 1922 the distribution of arms to the entire force was completed. Each B Special was given a rifle and bayonet and one hundred rounds of ammunition.[3] It was also at this point that the B Specials received their distinctive dark green uniform. This escalation of violence was precipitated by the arrest of a number of prominent republicans while returning from playing a Gaelic football match in Derry in January 1922. The match itself had been their cover for a reconnaissance mission for a planned attack on Derry jail.[4] These men were all based in Monaghan and included Dan Hogan, O/C 5th Northern Division.[5] In retaliation, the IRA began to raid over the border into Fermanagh and Tyrone. While these raiders were predominantly from the south, they were aided by local scouts. In early February 1922 an ambulance requested by the CI in Enniskillen passed through Monaghan and was held up by the IRA. While the ambulance was released, the five specials onboard (four patients and one guide) were detained.[6] On 8 February 1922 the IRA attacked the home of James Cooper in Enniskillen but were driven off.[7] This was repeated at the home of George Elliott, Cooper's neighbour and a unionist member of Enniskillen UDC. At Glengreen the Allingham family also held off the IRA but Samuel Laird, a workman and a local B Special, was killed.[8]

The mixed success of these raids demonstrated growing unionist control of the county due to the USC. Cooper was able to defend himself with the assistance of local B Specials.[9] The IRA did, however, have some success. Ivan Carson, a prominent unionist and high sheriff of Fermanagh, was kidnapped, taken to Ballyconnell, and released on 21 February.[10] Cahir Healy was anonymously informed that he was personally responsible for the return of Carson.[11] The house of Richard Ward of Kinturk was attacked by the IRA and a Crossley tender of USC was ambushed near Wattlebridge.[12] Robert Worrell, head of the B Special company at Tully, was also captured but escaped when the IRA's car struck a trench in the road.[13] In total, some forty unionists were kidnapped and taken south as collateral to secure the release of the IRA men arrested in Derry.[14] These men were not randomly chosen Protestants but were prominent unionists and USC. In certain instances, the IRA focused on familiar targets. For example, in Roslea John Connolly was instructed to kidnap Thomas Lester.[15] That those kidnapped were primarily USC was contested by both the *Reporter* and the *Standard*.[16]

Four special constables were also taken from Roslea.[17] The number would have been greater had Thomas Lester been located but he had left town. Instead, Connolly opted to seize a policeman and on eventually finding one was obliged to buy the man a whiskey in Scotstown to calm his nerves.[18] For Robert Lynch this example captures the 'opportunistic' nature of many of these raids.[19] To the *Reporter*, the kidnappings represented the natural spread of violence from the wild south across the weakly secured border. It called for curfews, increased road patrols, and the seizing of 'lay and clerical Sinn Féin leaders as hostages'.[20] The newspaper warned starkly:

> The marauders brought from the now provisional Irish Free State and their masters will find that Ulstermen will not tolerate such lawlessness as we have suffered from; and if by dint of an unexpected raid some of our people are seized or murdered that REPRISALS WILL BE MADE.[21]

The paper also made the exaggerated claim that over 100 unionists had been kidnapped.[22] There were also rumours that the IRA planned to kidnap Basil Brooke's 22-month-old son Julian.[23] One *Fermanagh Times* editorial stated: 'Ulstermen are coming rapidly to the conclusion that their only hope of self-protection or security is to band themselves together and rely upon their own strength.'[24] In a speech delivered at Aughnacloy Methodist church, William Coote MP, whose son had been kidnapped, warned it was 'very difficult to restrain their people from seizing the persons of active Sinn Féiners within their border and holding them hostage'.[25] Following the kidnappings, Brooke returned to Fermanagh from a holiday in London and resigned from the Northern Ireland Senate to focus on directing the loyalist response through the USC.[26] He was met on his arrival in Fermanagh by a deputation of USC who threatened 'bloody murder' if the kidnapped men were not quickly released. Brooke advised caution because a reprisal could result in the killing of the kidnapped men and restrained the USC in the county.[27] On their release, the kidnapped men revealed that they had been treated courteously but that crowds in southern towns had come out to taunt them.[28] This idea of rabid southerners jeering proud Ulstermen had great currency in the pages of the *Reporter*. It contrasted sharply with the positive account of the release of the constables seized with the ambulance in Clones who were cheered and given food for the journey as they left Carrickmacross.[29]

On 7–8 February 1922 the Fermanagh A and B Specials were mobilized to seal the border and guard all crossings. In essence, a state of war existed with an extremely limited no man's land across the border. In this environment of heightened tension on 11 February, word was received that a party of nineteen USC travelling by train from Newtownards to Enniskillen had stopped in Clones. While the Specials themselves were not acting provocatively on their arrival, they were in uniform and six were armed. Unlike earlier forays by the USC into Monaghan, this seems to have been an innocent journey, one that ignored the border out of habit, but in the context of increased frontierization it was inherently provocative.[30]

On learning about the USC, Matt Fitzpatrick rushed to the station and entered the train. He walked down the carriages until he came to the main company of USC whereupon he shouted something to the effect of hands up. In what became known as the Clones affray, shots were exchanged during which Fitzpatrick was fatally wounded in the head and four special constables were killed: Sergeant William Dougherty and Constables Robert McMahon, James (John?) Lewis and Joseph Abraham.[31] All but two of the others were wounded. The IRA removed everyone from the train and separated USC from civilians. The train was eventually allowed to continue on its journey. Its arrival in Lisbellaw, bullet holed and bloodstained, sparked outrage.[32] That night a drunken shouting match took place between Sinn Féiners and USC on the Clones road which the *Impartial Reporter* tried to reconstruct as a clever diversionary tactic through which their comrades were able to sneak into a field behind the town and rescue two constables who had lain there since Friday (there appears to be no other record of such an incident).[33]

The unionist press was split in its response to the events. The *Northern Standard*, which was based in Monaghan, asserted that there were 'many conflicting accounts' of the event and depicted the affray as the most serious political incident amid a series of graver moral ones.[34] The *Reporter* did not have to be so measured, describing it as a 'massacre' and 'treachery'.[35] While the paper did not explicitly claim that the attack was an unprovoked ambush, they defended the Specials' right not to surrender, stating that 'we would have been ashamed of them had they done anything else'.[36] Unusually, the *Fermanagh Times* was the more extreme of the two newspapers, describing the incident as 'planned and carried into execution by a horde of uncivilised savages'.[37] The aftermath of the Clones affray was similar to Roslea in that it polarized nationalists and unionists by providing both communities with an incompatible set of narratives and martyrs.

The most serious reprisal occurred on 22 March 1922. Two special constables from near Trillick in Tyrone – Samuel Laird and George Chittick – were killed during the IRA raids in February. The USC then killed three nationalists in Trillick – William Cassidy, Edward McLaughlin and Francis Kelly. The latter was reportedly shot at close-range as a part of his skull had been blown away.[38] Cassidy's murder shocked his local community in Drumharvey near Irvinestown because of his popularity and because he was only twenty-four. While the attack was condemned, the *Impartial Reporter* betrayed some of its own vengeful attitude when it ran a headline: 'an eye for an eye'.[39] At Cassidy's inquest, the coroner ruled as *ultra vires* a claim by R. Herbert, solicitor for the next of kin, that he had been given information that identified the killers. Cassidy does not appear to have been active in the IRA and his family had traditionally been loyal, with his father serving as a recruiting officer during the war. His father had no illusions about what had motivated the attack: 'I did good military service but the reward for my loyalty is that when I come back home my son is murdered. When I was recruiting in 1915 the people who are interfering with me now would not come near me.'[40]

Across Fermanagh, several reprisals took place in 'revenge' for Clones. On 11 February 1922 a number of nationalists in the Ballinamallard district were reported to have been variously held up, threatened and attacked. John Keown of Drumavaughan was shot in the leg, while others were warned that their houses would be burned. In Tullyrain, eight men playing cards were dragged outside and marched with their hands up into Ballinamallard town. One of them, Dominick Murphy, was blindfolded and forced onto his knees and asked if he was 'ready to die'. He was then let go and told to 'run' while the group was warned that if they were caught on the road in the coming week they would be shot.[41] Similar actions were repeated elsewhere in the county. For example, on 15 March James McHugh was stopped by A Specials near Derrylin and allegedly ordered to curse the pope and say 'God Bless the Specials'. After he refused to curse the pontiff, three shots were fired over his head and he was let go.[42] In the House of Commons, cases were reported of nationalists being forced to spit on pictures of republican figures such as Terence MacSwiney or kiss the Union Jack. In another incident, Alfonsus Gallagher was reportedly stripped of his clothes by a USC patrol when returning home from Pettigo.[43]

The best known post-Clones reprisal occurred in the loyalist stronghold of Lisbellaw. Two nationalist houses were attacked by a large mob immediately after the arrival of the train that had been attacked in Clones. The main target was the house of Bernard Hughes, a tailor, and his brother John. The brothers resisted the initial attack during which their windows were smashed. They later told the county court that the mob comprised about 290. Although probably exaggerated, the number involved was substantial. As the Hughes brothers attempted to flee to their father's house beside the police barracks, they were seen and set upon by 'a gang of young rowdies' who left them semi-conscious. Their mother subsequently testified that they were covered in blood and barely recognizable to her.[44] The Hughes family were one of just four nationalist households in Lisbellaw and an easy target. After the attack and despite their serious injuries, they were too scared to seek a doctor. Bernard Hughes later made an unsuccessful application to the Irish Grants Committee when he was no longer living in Lisbellaw and estimated his loss to be £130.[45]

It was in this context that Collins and Craig met again in London in March 1922. The meeting focused on the role of the USC. Collins, increasingly positioning the south as the protector of northern nationalists, unrealistically demanded that Catholics be included in the USC and that patrols in mixed areas should be comprised of equal numbers of Catholics and Protestants. Much of what was agreed was on mediating community relations and moderating the excesses of the USC. Arms searches could only be performed by mixed patrols and the weapons of the USC were to be put 'in charge of a military, or other competent officer' when not being used.[46] Other proposals included the gradual release of prisoners for offences committed before 31 March 1922 and the establishment of 'conciliation committees' with alternating nationalist and unionist chairmen. In return, Collins ordered the IRA to refrain from operations in Northern Ireland, although, as Hopkinson has observed, IRA GHQ probably had no real intention of any large-scale operations along the border.[47]

Many unionists in Fermanagh regarded the Collins–Craig negotiations and subsequent agreement with distrust. James Cooper claimed that his constituents were 'very suspicious of the tone of these terms'.[48] The most controversial aspect was clause III, which allowed for Catholic recruitment into the USC. This criticism was particularly fierce in Fermanagh and Tyrone. William Coote argued that it would destroy the USC, while Cooper suggested that the Fermanagh specials would refuse to work with Catholic recruits.[49] The clause was only insipidly defended by Craig and his cabinet who were both worried about the strength of opposition to the clause and to the deal in general. The proposals contained in the agreement failed nearly as quickly as those contained in the earlier pact. When it became apparent that no serious effort was being made to implement the proposals on the USC or on prisoner release, the northern IRA began to increase activity again.[50]

Outside of its political consequences, the Clones affray and the subsequent reprisals draw attention to a different form of violence that became increasingly prevalent in Fermanagh in early 1922 – mob violence. This tended to be even less specific in its targets than the raids described above. In Pettigo on 27 January 1922, six months before the conflict between the IRA and USC, five nationalists were attacked by a gang of unionists who had apparently been drinking. Attempts to intervene by other nationalists were prevented.[51] Mob violence had more far-reaching consequences. The attack on the Hughes family of Lisbellaw led to the abandonment of attempts to build a Catholic workhouse in the town.[52] These acts were not spontaneous grassroots actions removed from the official government or the USC or other loyalist groups. In the case of the Hughes family, the inability or unwillingness of the police to stop or punish those who attacked the brothers was an important element in the attack. Equally, in Pettigo the *Herald* reported policemen arriving but refusing to intervene.[53]

While the post-Clones reprisals were the most significant examples, throughout 1922 and 1923 there was a marked increase in organized and targeted violence against nationalists. This was distinct from the organized resistance to the IRA. Writing in May 1922, an *Irish Independent* correspondent reported that 'so aggressive have all sections of the Special Constabulary become no Catholic will now venture out at night'.[54] The reporting of these events in the press was inherently politicized. Southern newspapers such as the *Freeman's Journal* and the local nationalist *Fermanagh Herald* recorded far more incidents than the *Impartial Reporter* or even the *Northern Standard* (which felt much less affinity to the B Specials and was far less predisposed to defend them). For example, reports would appear in the *Freeman's Journal* about drunken USC searching Catholics in Fermanagh and in following editions the *Reporter* would disavow that any such events happened, labelling it 'anti-Protestant propaganda'.[55] The *Reporter* was not, however, an unthinking defender of loyalism. In response to a letter ordering J. Goodwin, a prominent Catholic from Dernavore, to clear off over the border, Trimble personally commented: 'we would like to see the writer of that letter driven across the border out of the Ulster he disgraces by his acts'.[56]

The type of acts reported in Fermanagh are variable but broadly match what occurred in the south. Raids, firing on passing traffic, and threats were common. Kate McGovern reported that her hotel had been raided by masked men looking to turn a guest, IRA liaison officer Brennan, out of the town. The attack was marked for its loudness and the unnecessary rudeness of the raiders who eventually left after realizing that Brennan was not there.[57] Fr O'Daly, parish priest of Roslea, stated that he had been fired on without warning while cycling through the district of Magherarney.[58] Although such attacks were not overtly sectarian, they had a sectarian element to them – this was demonstrated when those interrogated by USC patrols were asked their religion.[59] In July 1923 sacred vessels in Derrygonnelly church were destroyed by two special constables. Both claimed to have been under the influence of drink, which was a common factor in many such cases and raises questions about a systemic lack of discipline and the role this played in their reputation.[60]

Threats were often not delivered personally but sent in anonymous letters. In February 1922 the *Fermanagh Herald* reported that four nationalist families in Ballinamallard received threatening letters. Typically, these letters were signed 'Ulster Defence Association' or the 'Protestant Defence Association' and gave threatened households so many days to clear out.[61] Unusually, in Florencecourt in early 1923 an ex-special named James Black was brought to trial for sending a threatening letter to Frank McGarvey, a local farmer.[62] Some letters to nationalists included a certain dramatic flair. James Magee of Killymitten was warned that if he disregarded 'this notice you will get Waterloo'.[63] A letter to Patrick Gilroy of Aghavea in May 1923 advised him to 'prepare his coffin'.[64] James Hackett of Whitehill meanwhile received a letter that was signed simply 'Death' in 'large capital letters'.[65] Frank McGarvey had both of those features combined in his letter, which featured a drawing of a coffin and a bullet with the postscript 'every time this speaks you know what it means, Death'.[66] Magee's letters and those of James Green, also of Ballinamallard, were framed in very traditional Ulster iconography, to a far greater degree than we see with southern threats and nationalist iconography. Green's read: 'remember the Boyne and Croppies lie down under, for if they rise up they will be shot like a dog', while Magee was warned: 'We don't forget Wexford's Bridge and Scullabogue's barn'. The letters to Green and Magee were also signed: 'The Men of Ulster. For King and Country' and 'Descendant of William the Third since the Boyne Battle', respectively.[67]

The border featured prominently in threatening letters and victims were warned to leave Northern Ireland. In the Ballinamallard cases, Hackett was told to go to 'h*** across the border', while Magee and Green were told to 'clear out of Ulster'.[68] On 8 November 1923 the assistant manager of the creamery in Pettigo and a Catholic was approached by armed men and advised to leave the country. He fled to Ballyshannon.[69] In February 1923 Patrick Drugan, a shopkeeper in Macken, claimed that he had been targeted by unionists after he had complied with the Belfast boycott, which had culminated in the burning of his shop in November 1922. He reported that multiple customers had received 'threatening letters' and as a result had ceased dealing with him. The extent of these threats is difficult to determine but Drugan claimed that many of his 'best customers were told they would be shot'.[70]

In the Ballinamallard cases all the men involved were referred to by various rebel pejoratives: 'Fenians', 'blackguards', 'bloodthirsty gang' and disloyalty is cited as the reason for their expulsion.[71] Fr Coyle, parish priest of Garrison, claimed to have received a threatening letter due to his position as local curate.[72] Local concerns such as land disputes were less common than in Cavan or Monaghan. Patrick Gilroy was threatened when a Protestant milesman had been fired from his work gang.[73] James Green was informed that 'It's over with you now earning from Protestants'.[74] Edward Fitzpatrick of Clinaroo was warned off seeking compensation in the courts for a previous attack by USC.[75] In no cases were the threats followed by any degree of land occupation or boycotting of auctions. William O'Brien, the parish priest of Drumskinney, alleged a USC patrol had interrupted an Irish class he had been teaching at the local school and dismantled the classroom while searching for unspecified contraband.[76]

Following Clones, violence along the border increased significantly. In particular, as tensions grew between pro- and anti-Treaty factions in the south, leaders of both groups began to consider an attack on Northern Ireland as part of an effort to unite the IRA. Were such a campaign to be undertaken, Fermanagh would have been on the frontline. On 29 March Belcoo barracks was seized and 22 rifles, 21 revolvers and 5,000 rounds of ammunition were removed. Sixteen policemen were also taken prisoner, including eight specials. As with the raid on Tempo barracks in 1920, it was suspected that the raiders had been helped by one of the guards.[77] On 11 April a USC patrol was attacked in Newtownbutler and one of the special constables wounded.[78] That there was an awareness of this vulnerability can be seen in the growth of tensions in Belcoo after the barracks raid. Belcoo was right on the border and after the barracks raid, the IRA and USC patrolled within feet of one another. Brooke and the local USC commander were worried about the potential for violence and agreed on 11 April 1922 to move both their patrols at least 400 yards from the border.[79]

Most seriously, in April 1922 a patrol of seven A Specials was ambushed near Garrison. One was killed and two wounded. This attack was part of a wider campaign by the anti-Treaty 1st Northern Division based in Donegal.[80] Later unionist histories recorded that the ambush party numbered close to seventy men and had opened fire immediately with a machine-gun.[81] Brooke, normally keen to maintain order, enflamed tensions by declaring that the dead constable, James Plumb from Albertbridge Road in Belfast, had been 'mutilated beyond all recognition'.[82] The *Impartial Reporter* described how 'the head had been battered in with the butts of rifles ... while the skull has been beaten into one continuous fracture.'[83] The mutilation claim was disputed by Fr Connolly, parish priest of Garrison, who had retrieved the body along with the town's Protestant rector. Connolly reported only a 'cut on his face, that might be caused by a fall'.[84] However, these accounts of mutilation were widely reported on both in Fermanagh and nationally.[85] This account has also been accepted by Tim Wilson who has noted that while cases like Plumb were exceptional, they were not unheard of. A few months earlier, across the border in Cavan John Finlay, the 78-year-old former Church of Ireland dean of Leighlin, would also be battered to death by raiders. Significantly, as Wilson observes, such reports were believed by most nationalists who expressed similar revulsion at the brutality.[86]

Livingstone claims the attack was perpetrated by a company of anti-Treaty IRA located just over the border in Kiltyclogher. This unit had been active in the area since early 1922, raiding into Fermanagh and firing over the border. When investigating the ambush, the CI was himself ambushed by a force of about twenty which appeared from over the border about 300 yards distant. The men fired on Inspector Tyrell and his escort but were unable to capture or kill them.[87]

In April 1922 the USC in the county was mobilized in response to a perceived massing of the IRA on the border.[88] All enlisted members were ordered to report to their local barracks. While this appeared to be in direct response to the Clones affray, it had actually been planned by the Northern government for some time as a key component of securing control over the increasingly volatile frontier. It was thought that the local knowledge and strength of the USC was sufficient to control Fermanagh itself. The general scheme involved using local squads of Specials to control the border in their locality, reinforced by patrols from further afield where necessary. In February 1923 the Fermanagh's border defence scheme was tested in a county-wide exercise. At 7 p.m. the order to mobilize was issued from Enniskillen without any warning. USC near the border were expected to take up positions and close all roads with the Free State within fifteen minutes. The A platoons, reinforced by the reserve B Specials, took up positions further inland and liaised with the border scouts by bicycle. The exercise was regarded as a significant success and was continued in subsequent years.[89] By March 1923 there were 3,200 B Specials in Fermanagh.[90]

In summer 1922 actions shifted from raiding to cross-border sniping. While this was more heavily focused along the Tyrone border, near Clogher, it was sufficiently intense along the Clones border for the A Specials from Newtownbutler to commandeer Loughkillygreen Orange hall so as to have a base of operations nearer to the Monaghan border.[91] Areas fortified by either the USC or the IRA such as Castlesaunderson and Belcoo became flashpoints.[92] Bertie Kerr recalled that such firing forced his family to live away from their home on the Leitrim border for nearly two months.[93] Cross-border shootings tended to be indiscriminate with regard to religion or political orientation. Which side of the border the victim was on was often the only factor used in the decision to shoot.[94] In some cases, the cars fired on by the USC were even found to have contained loyalists.[95] Ironically, by doing this the IRA was inadvertently aiding the consolidation of the border. In March 1922 John Davidson, for example, was denied passage into Monaghan before being told explicitly to 'return over the border'.[96] In the same month three northern businessmen in Clones named Knaggs, Conn and Barrett were judged to be of suspicious character and were ordered 'to get out of the Free State'.[97] Northerners in the Free State often had their cars stolen. Unionist reporting of the fighting portrayed the border as a frontier of a wild and violent land from which they were constantly threatened.[98]

In April 1922 the most significant disruption to the territorial integrity of Northern Ireland occurred in what has since been called the Pettigo–Belleek affair. Fundamentally, this was an invasion of Fermanagh by the IRA. For unionists, it reinforced the view that Fermanagh was the new borderland and the frontline in a nationalist–unionist, north–south conflict. It also served as a symbolic first test of the integrity of the new unionist state. The area being contested in this incident was a roughly triangular patch of land (sometimes called a salient) that ran about twelve miles along the Fermanagh–Donegal border from Pettigo in the north to Belleek in the south and to Lough Erne in the east. This land was largely wooded and boggy with limited communication links with the rest of Fermanagh. Indeed, even before the occupation of the village by the IRA unionist authorities had struggled to exert control over the region.[99]

The impracticality of a border drawn along arbitrary and out-dated county lines served as a catalyst for this violence. The two towns in question, Pettigo and Belleek, were both pierced by the new border and divided awkwardly between the two new jurisdictions. While Pettigo had a unionist majority, it lay predominantly on the Donegal side of the border; this included the RIC barracks, the train station and most of the shops. Belleek, meanwhile, was largely nationalist but most of its infrastructure and population lay in Fermanagh. Crucially, however, on the Free State side of Belleek was an old military fort that occupied a strategic position over the town.

On 10 April 1922 Belleek and its surrounding area came under the control of the IRA through no action of its own when the RIC withdrew from the town. Much like Drummully in Monaghan, Belleek was left stranded by partition without a route to elsewhere in the county that did not first pass over the border. This meant that republican forces controlled access in and out of the town and did so with the compliance of the local nationalist population. Consequently, the area was seen as ungovernable by the local RIC inspector who departed with twenty men, having first asked the IRA for permission to pass through its territory.[100] Control of the Belleek–Pettigo area was crucial should a conflict between north and south erupt in 1922. The National army placed official garrisons in both villages and pro- and anti-Treaty forces cooperated in their operations along the border. Control of the fort also allowed the IRA to stage raids into Fermanagh and provided a safe haven for IRA men on the run. After the collapse of the 2nd Northern Division in May, large numbers of Tyrone IRA men ended up in the district and were put on patrolling duties.[101]

The response to this development came not through the military or the police but through the USC. Barton suggests the initial catalyst was the assassination of Unionist MP William Twaddell on 22 May 1922.[102] A week later a force of USC assembled and crossed into the triangle on a pleasure barge *The Lady of the Lake*. The men occupied Magherameena Castle in Pettigo which was the home of the local priest – Lorcán Ó Ciaráin, a prominent Sinn Féiner who was unpopular with Pettigo unionists. Ó Ciaráin was ordered to clear out.[103] This act, influenced by local vendettas, religious prejudices and strategic considerations, demonstrated the ambiguous layers of identity that informed so much military logic in this period. The initial invasion was beaten back by an IRA counter-invasion from Donegal and the force was effectively besieged in Magherameena Castle. A relief force of A Specials sent from Garrison was fired on as it approached the castle, and one driver, Albert Rickerby, was killed.[104] Three IRA men were also killed. The USC retreated to Buck Island in the middle of Lough Erne. An attempt by another USC party to rescue them was also defeated.

These incidents prompted an escalation on both sides. Brooke declared a general USC mobilization in Fermanagh, calling the entire body of B Specials into active service.[105] The IRA and Cumann na mBan flooded into the Pettigo–Belleek triangle, taking possession of both towns and effectively establishing a frontline on the River Erne.[106] The USC successfully evacuated the Magherameena garrison after *The Lady of the Lake* was pressed into service and renamed HMS *Pandora*. The boat's owner, Mrs Laverton, saved the expedition from disaster when she noticed the level of water in the lake subtly decreasing. The IRA had opened the sluice gates of Lough Erne in an attempt to strand the boat. Under Mrs Laverton's direction, the USC retreated to Rough Island and took up positions there.[107]

While this had the appearance of a border skirmish that had simply escalated, abetted by the unique geography of the triangle, it was a significant event. A sizeable portion of Fermanagh now lay in southern hands. Northern Ireland had, in effect, been invaded, just as many unionists had always feared. Naturally, the event caused major alarm in both London and Dublin where the Provisional government was keen to assure the British government that this was not an officially sanctioned attack. Winston Churchill ordered the triangle to be retaken which was done with considerable caution by General Macready who instructed his troops to avoid entering the Free State itself unless they had no other option. The operation was carried out by General Cameron and consisted of a dual assault along the northern and southern banks of the Erne. The British force included the 1st Battalions of the Lincolnshire Regiment and the Manchester Regiment with a number of howitzers.[108] They encountered no serious resistance. An isolated paramilitary force in such a situation could not hope to hold out for very long, nor did the IRA have any realistic long-term goals. The IRA fled Pettigo after a day of combat on 5 June 1922.

Belleek held out slightly longer, but it was inevitable that the town would fall. The IRA withdrew from the fort on 6 June. It also abandoned Cliff lodge, a fortification even further into Donegal. On 8 June, after shelling the area, the British forces arrived at a largely empty Belleek and took the fort.[109] The IRA suffered a number of casualties, three men were killed during the British shelling and fifteen others were taken prisoner.[110] The British, by contrast, had only one soldier wounded. Special Constable Thomas Dobson was killed by a sniper firing across the border.[111] The IRA prisoners were later exchanged for a number of USC prisoners.

Controversially, the British army hoisted a Union Jack atop the castle. Even in a time when the border was barely formed, such a provocative action was a deliberate and obvious violation of the Treaty. It was the last time a military fortification was taken by British troops in independent Ireland. It was justified by the British as being a strategic necessity, although the symbolic act of raising the flag somewhat undermined a purely utilitarian argument. This also heightened the alarm that Lloyd George had felt at the belligerence of Churchill's response when he proposed an expeditionary force that would hold Belleek indefinitely. Lloyd George advised Churchill 'if they wanted to carry domestic and imperial opinion, they were better off fighting with the Free State over the oath of allegiance or the constitution'. The case of Ulster 'was not a good one'.[112] Churchill threated to resign if the prime minister interfered but ultimately backed down.[113] It is important to emphasize how close the Belleek–Pettigo affair came to igniting a much larger conflict.[114]

Peace returned to the area, aided by the IRA becoming distracted by the Civil War. By late 1922 troops were withdrawn from Pettigo as Gardaí arrived to police the town and in January 1923 official control was returned. Belleek fort remained in British hands until 1925.[115] Aware of the fears of the loyalist population following the previous occupation, Captain Joyce, head of the local National army garrison, made particular efforts to liaise with the local Church of Ireland rector, E.W. McKegney.[116] For unionists in Pettigo the recapture was cause for celebration. They had been virtual prisoners during the entire engagement and were vocal in their desire for the British forces to retain the town. Indeed, following recapture, they published a letter in the *Fermanagh Times* appealing for inclusion in Northern Ireland. They listed some of the indignities suffered, including being made to remove the motto 'Fear God, Honour the King' from a gable and having their houses searched for pictures of the king or British soldiers. They indicated as their dread 'that any future time the protection of the military might be withdrawn and that we would again be at the mercy of [the IRA]'.[117]

The IRA asserted that they had implemented a normal and impartial policy in the village, although there was perhaps something of an implicit admission that unionists were targeted when Captain Joyce acknowledged in December 1922 that he could not guarantee that the unionist population of the town would avoid unfair arrest and advised them not to engage in political activity.[118] Some of their number, the able bodied men, had been prevented from fleeing the town and forced 'to dig trenches and suffer every insult'.[119] Most unionist refugees fled to Enniskillen where they were taken in by locals and had charity provided by the Freemasons.[120] The *Reporter* stated that divine service had continued in the Church of Ireland all throughout the occupation, a remark intended to convey the resilience of Pettigo Protestants rather than nationalist or Free State tolerance.[121]

Nationalists meanwhile both in Belleek and Pettigo found themselves in the opposite position.[122] They were only allowed to leave their homes if they could obtain a permit from the local British commander.[123] Following the occupation, a local woman, Jane Gallagher, sued for compensation for the religious artefacts in her house that were allegedly burned by British forces.[124] A report on 2 November 1922 to Richard Mulcahy noted that conditions for nationalists in Pettigo had become very bad and they were subject to 'all kinds of terrorism'.[125] Later reports of the incident found little tension between the unionist and nationalist inhabitants who both regarded the issue as an outside blunder.[126] The Anglican rector McKegney expressed resentment over insinuations of 'Northern bigotry' made by a Free State delegation to the area in December 1922 and stated that relations between the two communities were excellent.[127] However, the *Fermanagh Times* did note that the town's loyalists had established a new post office over the bridge in the Northern Ireland territory which was patronized almost entirely by them while nationalists paid two pence more at a post office a hundred yards away.[128]

Tales of the unfair treatment meted out to unionists trapped in Pettigo became commonplace in the unionist press.[129] The *Impartial Reporter* described an 'exodus' of unionists from the town. It carried stories of unionists being arrested and held without charge before being released.[130] The *Fermanagh Times* reported how they had been 'reduced to a condition of worse than slavery for one of Ulster stock'.[131] The narrative put forward was not that unionists in Pettigo were forced out of their homes but rather made the decision to leave because of the dangers in staying due to the invaders' disregard for human life.[132] This was portrayed as an inherent feature of nationalist rule. The *Reporter* sarcastically referred to the unionist community as having gotten its first 'sample of Free State "government"'.[133]

In broader rhetorical terms little attempt was made to distinguish between being forced out and leaving voluntarily as all were classed as 'refugees'. According to one estimate, 100 Pettigo unionists left the town following the start of military engagements. The *Reporter* carried accounts of those who departed such as Albert Anderson who fled with his 80-year-old mother by boat to Boa Island.[134] The narrative again centred on a few key symbolic points. Prominent among these was the Specials, who served as a wider metaphor for unionist defence. Not only was their conduct during the affair praised but stories were also reported of young men enlisting because of the episode.[135] The idea that the USC would be targeted directly as they were such a threat to the IRA was also promoted and this added to their prestige.[136]

The reaction to Pettigo–Belleek was different to Roslea. While Roslea's response mirrored the reactions to social violence in the rest of Ireland, the aftermath of Pettigo–Belleek was informed by the fact of a border and the putative concept of national territory. The *Reporter*, taking the initial occupation of the salient and the Clones affair in one editorial, declared the incident a moment for Ulster to arise and assert that 'Ulster is awake. We shall not have any truck with traitors nor truce with outrage-mongers. If those men from the South come up North to stir up strife on the border, let them come out and meet the British soldiers in the open.'[137] Ulster 'territory has been violated.'[138] The *Fermanagh Times* similarly characterized the initial occupation as 'Free State rule in Fermanagh'.[139]

More importantly, Pettigo represented the high-water mark of an external threat to Northern Ireland. Following the victory at Pettigo, Brooke was confident that the major danger to the county from a southern invasion had dissipated. By mid-1922 there were 3,500 A and B Specials in the county and plans had been drawn up to create a neutral zone occupied by British troops in the south of the county to avoid any tension between the IRA and the USC.[140] From mid-1922, instability in Fermanagh began to decline. The only IRA attacks on government forces after September 1922 took place in March 1923 as a reprisal for a raid in Monaghan by Fermanagh B Specials.[141] By October the maximum number of USC on daily patrols had fallen to thirty from 360 in June.[142] In August 1923 the USC recommended restoring a number of bridges that could be safely operated. In April a policy to reduce the force was introduced but few withdrew in Fermanagh. Many unionists still feared an attack from the south and were unwilling to do away with the USC.[143]

The USC formed the centrepiece of the Northern Ireland government's strategy to control both Fermanagh and reinforce its border. On 9 June the RIC was disbanded in Northern Ireland and replaced with a force that unionists hoped would be more reliable – the Royal Ulster Constabulary (RUC). Sir Charles George Wickham, head of the USC, was appointed inspector-general of the new force. Only 1,100 of the old RIC were accepted into the RUC and only 400 of them were Catholics. The new RUC was initially 21 per cent Catholic, although this number would subsequetly fall steadily.[144] It was hoped that this new force would free up the USC to focus more on reinforcing the border and ensuring security in the province. Craig's desire to avoid a full military confrontation with the south also led him to use the USC as Northern Ireland's key instrument for defending its border. That responsibility was beyond what Brooke had initially envisaged for the USC and was a major source of concern to him.

This increase in the scope of the responsibilities of the USC can be seen in the growing ambition of the Northern Ireland government for contingency plans in case of a southern invasion. On 7 April 1922 General Arthur Solly-Flood took up his position as a military adviser to the Northern government to supervise its paramilitary preparations. Solly-Flood threw himself into his role, even petitioning the RAF to provide him with planes and bombs. Of greatest significance for Fermanagh, however, was his proposal to deal with serious trouble along the border. He maintained that a significant portion of Cavan and Monaghan should be seized, including Cootehill, Ballybay, Castleblaney and Monaghan town. At the same time, a strip of land should be annexed to the west linking Fermanagh to the ocean. This new border, Solly-Flood argued, would be more defensible. However, it would also have positioned Fermanagh as the beachhead for a southern invasion and, in the case of the western sea connection, would have invited significant conflict along its western border.[145] Ultimately, the Belfast cabinet accepted the bulk of Solly-Flood's proposals but delayed making any decision on a southern occupation.

Fermanagh USC had one of the most onerous tasks of any contingent in the province – the defence of eighty-three miles of the new border. Consequently, nearly all companies were deployed on active border duty for most of 1922 and 1923. Only three companies were kept in reserve and none was assigned to protect RUC barracks.[146] The key work of the USC in early 1922 involved reinforcing the border. Roads were trenched and bridges were blown up.

Destroyed roads were often smaller routes into the county with the intent of funnelling traffic through more easily monitored main roadways.[147] By early March 1922 all but seven roads leading across the border had been trenched.[148] General blockades on the border were also instituted by local specials and enforced with violence where necessary. For northern nationalists these moves had a more sinister purpose. As the *Northern Standard* described it, 'the boundary was boldly defined … Fermanagh is now isolated from the Free State'.[149]

Fermanagh was disproportionately represented in lists of USC fatalities. Between 1920 and 1923, sixteen special constables based in the county died: five in Clones, three in Roslea, two in Pettigo–Belleek, two in ambushes at Mullaghfad and Garrison, and four in accidents.[150] This represented roughly a third of the forty-nine USC fatalities during the revolutionary period.[151] The four accidental deaths also demonstrated some of the amateurism present in the newly-established force. Special Constable Murray was killed at Kinawley in June 1922 by the accidental discharge of a rifle. William Leggett was killed when the Crossley tender he was in overturned due to a burst tire. Special Constables McEnnis and Graham were accidentally shot by other members of the USC.[152] Brooke later recalled an early arms inspection at Moan's Cross where one man presented his double-barrelled shotgun to Brooke loaded and with both hammers up. When it was pointed out to him that this was probably unwise, the man replied: 'I suppose I better put her away, she's a bit aisy on the let-off'.[153]

Unionist papers were also keen in this period to distinguish the new Northern Ireland from the Free State. The violence of the Civil War in the south was used to emphasize their sense of separation from there (and thus strengthen their case for inclusion in Northern Ireland). The *Impartial Reporter* expressed fears that Fermanagh would be converted into a 'King's County or Clare or Monaghan or Cork'.[154] Donegal was experiencing a 'reign of terror', in Cavan there was a 'War on Protestants' while the Monaghan Twelfths were cancelled because of a 'vendetta against Protestants'.[155] The *Fermanagh Times* constantly expressed fears that the southern border of the county, particularly south of Lough Erne, was being 'surrendered' and the whole area 'subject to Free State rule'.[156] There was sympathy for the individual Protestant victims of revolutionary violence although this sympathy was put to a political use as evidence of the inherent sectarianism of the south and therefore as an argument to exclude Fermanagh from the Free State. Cases like that of Johnston Hewitt of Cloverhill, Cavan, were promoted under headlines like 'chasing the Protestants out of Cavan'.[157] As in Cavan and Monaghan, it was held as true that Protestants were being specifically targeted in the south. The paper also published a poem by an undetermined author in March 1922 that captured this sense of paranoia:

And motor cars are dashing
Each packed with men at post haste speed
To the border racing madly
For time means gain and the pace is hot
With the roads cut up so badly

And terror filled each village
For treach'rous foes at dead of night
With fire and sword were trying
To kill all those of English blood
Who in their bed were lying.[158]

Politically, after the major successes of 1921, unionists further consolidated their power in Fermanagh. Nationalist members of local bodies were constantly replaced. On Enniskillen UDC, unionists continued their policy of ignoring precedent and filling vacated seats with their own. In June 1922 James Kelly and Frank Carney were barred from the Fermanagh joint technical instruction committee for not attending meetings (it appears that Carney had been living in Dublin for some time). The UDC replaced both nationalists with unionists at a special meeting attended by only two nationalists.[159] In September 1922 Walter Campling was forced to resign from Enniskillen UDC due to non-attendance. Injured in the First World War, his health had never been good and increasingly affected his ability to work. He later established the Enniskillen branch of the British Legion and died in 1931 at the age of thirty-four.[160] In line with the new policy of maximizing unionist representation, a unionist, David Reilly, was co-opted to replace him instead of a labour member. The decision allegedly only took two minutes and a number of nationalist councillors, entering the chambers a few minutes late, expressed surprise that the voting had already concluded.[161] Even a full complement of nationalists and labour could not have defeated the unionist majority. This left Bernard Keenan as the sole labour councillor for the remainder of the council's term and the unionist majority now stood at five. Campling was also replaced on the Fermanagh technical committee; the *Fermanagh Herald* sarcastically lauded this '"tolerant" policy'.[162]

The nationalists on the council were unable to stage much of a protest, but in January 1922 they formed a united front and attempted to enter Enniskillen's courthouse to hold a meeting. On being stopped by the duty RIC sergeant and told to see Robert McNeill, John McHugh declared the council 'did not recognize McNeill here at all or any other representative of the Northern Parliament'. In this he was supported by Cahir Healy who declared McNeill had 'no right whatever to exclude us, except the right of the rifle and bayonet'.[163] In 1923 John McHugh declared that 'during these two years there has been a determination, by brutality and other means, to stifle our opinions'.[164]

In late December 1921 McNeill travelled to Enniskillen to interview a number of county council officials before returning to Belfast. Archdeacon John Tierney, a prominent nationalist, was turned away when he attempted to enter Enniskillen courthouse for a meeting of the education committee. He had been asked whether he recognized the 'Northern Parliament' and, on answering in the negative, was told that until he did so he was to be refused admittance.[165] In general, the new commissioner appears to have tried to keep the nationalists onside and maintain as much of the old local government structure as he could. In January 1922 he sent apologies to J.P. Gillin after learning that the Fermanagh insurance committee had been refused entry to the courthouse due to a ban on most of them engaging in public business. He assured Gillin that he had been unaware of this and had made arrangements for entry in future.[166] Most of the staff retained their jobs, although Thomas Corrigan was dismissed as county secretary and replaced by his unionist rival for the position, W.H. West. Corrigan was, however, retained as county accountant.[167]

Nationalists still opposed unionism where they could, even to the extent of pulling the same tricks that they had in the period of unionist domination before 1914. In January 1922 nationalists on the Enniskillen guardians put forward a motion that the minutes of the board be sent to Dáil Éireann and not Belfast. The chairman, Joseph Geddis, refused to accept the motion and cancelled the meeting amid uproar. After the unionists left, the nationalists who remained declared that the chair had not correctly ended the meeting and therefore business could still be done. They put Mr Corrigan in the chair and passed their resolution. This move was inspired by similar manoeuvring at the Enniskillen UDC where the unionist councillors had installed their own chair following an adjournment.[168]

On discovering this, unionist opposition focused on a blanket refusal to even hear the minutes as following an adjournment, there should be none. Thomas Elliott took the position that the Enniskillen UDC had been incorrect to act as they did but as the guardians were an unrelated body, this should not matter. The meeting was noted later for its bitter tone, with Corrigan in particular shouting over Geddis whenever he attempted to assert order. This culminated in Corrigan and Geddis bellowing directly into each other's faces across Geddis's desk. The meeting descended into further squabbling before it was agreed to sign the minutes relating to everything that happened before the adjournment and deal with the rest at a later date.[169] Lisnaskea guardians made the same decision with far less opposition from the unionist contingent and was then dissolved.[170]

The guardians, which had been spared dissolution, now became a major political battleground. Motions of condemnation, consolation and support became equally contentious. To SF dissent, Enniskillen guardians attempted to pass a motion of sympathy with the widow of Henry Wilson following his assassination.[171] Similar dissent came a year later in the same council when a motion was proposed to welcome the duke of Abercorn to the town.[172] These resolutions were often a means to provide the members of the bodies with a speaking platform. A resolution to welcome the new governor of Northern Ireland at a meeting of Enniskillen guardians in February 1923 became an opportunity for W.J. Brown, a unionist member, to denounce 'Romanism' in all its forms.[173]

The reverses suffered by Fermanagh labour were not limited to its declining representation on local bodies. As Jim Quinn has noted, by 1921 the post-war economic boom was well on its way to collapse in Ireland. Unemployment had grown to 78,000 in Northern Ireland by October 1921. In common with all unions, this had a deleterious effect on membership of the NAUL which had fallen to 53,000 in 1923, a drop of 63 per cent.[174] In Fermanagh there was a concerted effort by employers to reverse many of the improvements in conditions. In November 1921 six construction firms in Enniskillen locked out their workers after they had refused to accept a wage reduction and an increase in working hours. The dispute lasted until March 1922 and saw a co-ordinated campaign by unionist councillors, media and the Ulster Workers' Trade Union to defame the dispute as being a political one, orchestrated by the NAUL at the behest of its SF masters.

This was perhaps inevitable, given that labour had been so closely identified with nationalist interests in the county and consistently opposed unionist councillors on Enniskillen UDC. Frank Carney was a good example, serving as O/C Fermanagh Brigade IRA while also sitting as a labour councillor on Enniskillen UDC. The conflation of labour and nationalist interests had long been a feature of unionist propaganda. The *Impartial Reporter* and *Fermanagh Times* had consistently linked Irish republicanism with 'bolshevism' while indicating that the majority of large businessmen in the county (the 'ratepayers' in the words of the *Reporter*) were unionist. Unionist labour leader James Turkington declared that in his view the 'present dispute [was] not legitimate, strike [being] only a form of boycott.'[175] At a separate meeting in Belfast, Turkington denounced the Fermanagh NAUL as a fundamentally nationalist organization because it had voted against conscription.[176]

These accusations were pervasive enough that on 20 January 1922 a public meeting was called to 'give the truth of the matter'. Councillor Keenan held the chair while William Clarke and Sam Bradley of the NAUL spoke.[177] A representative of the National Federation of Building Trade Operatives was also present. All three men emphasized that the dispute was not a strike but a lockout, the employers had chosen to start it and the union was simply defending its own. It appears many in the union regretted their strong association with nationalism. At a Belfast meeting in February 1922, NAUL member Sam Bradley expressed strong regret and embarrassment at the union's anti-conscription stance.[178] The Enniskillen mass meeting had a second purpose – to bolster the flagging spirits of the workers themselves. Bernard Keenan declared to the assembled workers:

'we are not bursted, we are not down and out. We will fight for another twelve months if need be.'[179] It would appear that the lengthy smear campaign was affecting the willingness of many union members to persist with the dispute. Certainly, the employers had found it easier to employ scabs during this lockout than they had in the disputes of 1919 and 1920. These scabs were also reported to have been forcibly enlisted in the Ulster Workers' Trade Union to undermine the power of the NAUL in the town.[180] In January two of the workers were convicted of following a scab worker home after work, although this conviction was overturned on appeal.[181]

Ultimately, by mid-February 1922 four of the six firms in question had agreed to negotiate with the union. However, such victories were harder to come by for labour activists in Fermanagh, especially after unionist control of Enniskillen UDC was entrenched. In February UDC workers had their wages reduced by over two shillings with a similar reduction threatened for May. In June the ministry of commerce had to overrule Enniskillen guardians' attempt to cut outdoor relief by a quarter. In January 1922 local tailors had their wages reduced by ten shillings a week by the drapers. Despite initial rumblings of industrial action in all of these cases, nothing came of it.[182] Beyond their loss of two urban councillors, the most significant development for labour in Fermanagh in this period came in March 1923 when many members of the NAUL announced that they had joined the newly founded Transport and General Workers' Union (TGWU). William Clarke once again assumed a local leadership role, being appointed as the union's district organizer. Clarke said the NAUL had done good work in the county but was now being led astray by some of its officials.[183] Quinn suggests this probably referred to the issues faced by the NAUL with declining membership as well as the strong-handed tactics of union officials in pushing through an amalgamation of branches in the county.[184]

It was the TGWU (through Clarke) that dealt with the most significant labour dispute of 1923 – a strike by the cleaning workers of Enniskillen UDC. The council had proposed a pay cut of over 5s. a week for the staff. In March the TGWU voted to reject this and go on strike. Under Cooper, the council pursued a severe policy, refusing even to meet with Clarke or any other TGWU members. This was occasionally embarrassing for the council, such as during the visit of Lord Derby to the town in April 1923. Cooper and his associates were forced to organize a group of shopkeepers, 'prominent citizens' and B Specials to clean the streets. However, if this seemed to Clarke to show desperation or weakness on the council side, it came to nothing. At negotiations in Belfast, an agreement was struck to halve the wage reductions as long as Clarke himself agreed to take no part in any future disputes with the council. Quinn has rightly shown that this represented an attempt by Cooper and Enniskillen unionism to silence Clarke 'and with him, they hoped, Labour locally'.[185] Ultimately, the deal fell through after the local TGWU branch insisted on a clause that mandated all council workers should be members of that union.

As the dispute continued, it became apparent that the union was at a major disadvantage against an intransigent unionist establishment that had the full backing of the government. Unlike the other firms in town, the council's primary revenue stream came from the LGB and not from customers. Thus, it was much harder for the strikers to cause major damage to the financial position of the council. Additionally, as had been seen in 1922, it was much easier for the council to find scab labourers in times of lower employment, particularly given the persistent efforts to divide nationalist and unionist labourers. Indiscipline on the part of the strikers in dealing with the scabs also hurt the union, such as when one of the strikers, Alexander Whittaker, was fined ten shillings for abusing a scab. By November it was clear the strike could not be sustained for much longer. The union agreed to seek the reinstatement of the workers but could only secure casual contracts for the former employees as the council was more than happy to keep the scab labourers.[186]

This defeat set the tone for the difficulties faced by Fermanagh labour in the years ahead. The divisive issue of partition, combined with unionist domination of local and national government, made achieving significant victories for the working man difficult. Despite this, the TGWU did achieve some minor victories. They forced the hated UDC to compensate workers on the Ballydoolagh water scheme. They also compelled Enniskillen guardians to give a significant wage increase to the district's ambulance driver.[187] But overall, labour was in major decline and seemed a long way from the high-water mark of 1920.

In September 1922 proportional representation was established for local elections and the constituencies were redrawn to guarantee unionist majorities. The expected returns of the new system can be seen in the table below:

Council	Religion	Population	Members	Effects
Enniskillen Rural	Catholic	9,817	9	Catholic population majority of **720**
	Protestant	9,097	17	Protestant seat majority of 8 seats
Enniskillen Urban	Catholic	2,688	7	Catholic population majority of **529**
	Protestant	2,159	14	Protestant seat majority of 7 seats
Irvinestown Rural	Catholic	8,077	8	Catholic population majority of **1,315**
	Protestant	6,762	11	Protestant seat majority of 3 seats
Lisnaskea Rural	Catholic	9,078	13	Catholic population majority of **4,916**
	Protestant	4,162	18	Protestant seat majority of 5 seats

This majority had only been achieved after numerous nationalist candidates in Florencecourt were struck off when too many of them had been nominated.[188] For unionists this could be explained away as a response to the electoral malpractices of nationalists or as an attempt to preserve the 'natural' order in Fermanagh. In a speech in the House of Commons in February 1922, Captain Charles Craig, MP for Antrim South, claimed that there were many districts with a Catholic majority only because the Protestant population had been disproportionately killed in the war and that therefore any change in electoral representation made due to their absence would be grossly unfair.[189]

The government also began to move against its most dangerous enemies. On 22 May 1922, following the assassination of Unionist MP William Twaddell in Belfast, roughly 500 suspected republicans were arrested across Northern Ireland. In Fermanagh, over fifty individuals were arrested, including Thomas Corrigan, Seán Nethercott of Enniskillen UDC, and Cahir Healy, who later suggested that he had been arrested to undermine the ability of Fermanagh nationalists to assemble their case for the Boundary Commission:

> All my life I have been a man of peace. It is not, therefore, because they feared that I would disturb the peace of Northern Ireland that they dragged me away from my wife and family, but for political reasons. I have been engaged in preparing the case for the inclusion of these areas (Fermanagh and Tyrone) in the Free State. To get me out of the way, local politicians urged my arrest ... to paralyse public opinion along the border.[190]

This assertion is convincing and has been supported by the research of Brian Barton and Éamon Phoenix.[191] The previous month Healy had been appointed by Collins to the 'North-Eastern Advisory Committee', which was to define the new state's northern policy after the breakdown of the Collins–Craig pact. Healy was also viewed by local unionists as the main SF organizer and intellectual force in Fermanagh and the man who would be the most responsible for presenting their case to the Boundary Commission.[192] Craig had received demands from border unionist that he be 'removed from circulation'.[193] Internment also provided the Northern Ireland government with the means to remove other problematic republican figures from the county under the guise of normal governance. Corrigan, for example, was not fired as county accountant for his membership of SF. Rather, when the county council resumed sitting in 1924, he was ordered to resume his role within fourteen days but could not comply as he was interned. He was then dismissed for non-attendance.[194]

Healy and the others were interned on board the *Argenta*, an American cargo vessel moored in Belfast Bay (and later Larne Bay) that had been converted into a prison. The arrests in general were widely protested. Healy, in particular, became the focus of a national campaign. This was further enhanced in November 1922 when he was elected MP for Fermanagh–Tyrone. The Belfast government initially refused to release him, claiming he had been a 'cunning and clever organizer' in the IRA. Despite significant pressure from the Free State, Healy was imprisoned and sidelined from Fermanagh politics until February 1924.

With local councils and the Belfast parliament no longer suitable homes for them, nationalists relied on the two British general elections of November 1922 and December 1923 to demonstrate their actual dominance in Fermanagh. In this they were successful with the elections returning the same results each time. Cahir Healy was returned as a cross-party, anti-partitionist nationalist candidate along with Thomas Harbison. In both elections using first past the post, Healy and Harbison received a majority of over 6,000 votes. The return of a Sinn Féiner and an 'old Redmondite' on the same ticket was significant as it represented the shifting of nationalism in Fermanagh into a more 'northern' perspective as the distinction between IPP and SF was less important in a northern state that both refused to recognize. The goal of both parties now was to defend the rights of nationalists in Northern Ireland and to see a favourable redrawing of the border under the Boundary Commission.[195] This was a realignment that had been going on for some time. On the county council, the IPP and SF had consistently voted as a bloc throughout 1921 to the extent that Lord Belmore suggested that for most political votes they save time and write in the minutes that the vote went along party lines.[196]

After their election in 1923, Bishop McKenna of Clogher sent the men a congratulatory telegram, expressing the hope that 'the injustice of constraining Fermanagh and Tyrone to remain subject to Belfast must now end'.[197] In a letter from the *Argenta* to his election agent George Murnaghan, Healy declared the results a 'splendid victory, greater than even our most optimistic friends imagined to be possible'. As with all previous elections since 1918, it was naively hoped that the result would serve as final proof of the nationality of the county. 'The Tyrone–Fermanagh Election of 1922', enthused Healy, 'may well prove to be the turning point in Irish affairs'.[198] The result was a major disappointment to unionists who had hoped to replicate their 1921 success. The North Eastern Boundary Bureau noted how unionists deployed every available vehicle to maximize turnout.[199]

The election was accompanied by numerous reports of electoral violence, especially of unionists on nationalists. This may have been a consequence of such reports appearing more prominently in southern papers which were keen to undermine the legitimacy of Northern Ireland. But it was also due to the fact that unionists now found themselves with a near monopoly on force in the county. As before, the elections were the biggest propaganda tool available to nationalists ahead of the Boundary Commission and therefore the biggest threat to Fermanagh's place in the Union. The Free State government had been receiving reports about the northern elections, alleging that B Specials, particularly in areas like Tullyhogue and Lisbellaw, were actively raiding houses in an attempt to intimidate the nationalist population from voting.[200]

In Lisbellaw, in 1922 and 1923 nationalist personation agents were attacked by angry crowds following polling. The first of these incidents involved the agents locking themselves in the polling room until police arrived to disperse the crowd. A car was also sent from Enniskillen to rescue them but was turned away from the village by armed men. On the same night an agent cycling home from Ballinamallard was attacked by a crowd of people who cut the tyres of his bike. In Florencecourt, Francis Maguire, JP, was set upon by a large crowd of youths. In Legnahorna, another agent, Michael Carson, was also attacked.[201] That these attacks should happen in areas that were strongly unionist – Lisbellaw, Florencecourt and Ballinamallard – was significant. The *Fermanagh Herald* later referred to those districts as 'storm centres'.[202] Fears had been raised with the North Eastern Boundary Bureau by nationalists in the Marlbank area that they would be prevented from voting in the 1923 election.[203] These areas were identified and given a stronger police presence in 1923 to prevent such attacks. In Ballinamallard and Florencecourt this worked, and agents were greeted with 'groans' but not open hostility. In Lisbellaw, after the close of polls and when the agents and police left the building, they were met by a large crowd (nationalist estimates say between 300 and 400 people) who attacked them. Agents were again forced into the polling station. The *Herald* reported sectarian chants such as 'if they come out we shall make the Papist blood flow'.[204]

As unionist control over Northern Ireland tightened throughout 1922 and 1923, the Boundary Commission grew in importance in the minds of Fermanagh nationalists. The main body of SF in Fermanagh reiterated its support for the Treaty in April 1922 when a meeting was called in Enniskillen to raise funds for pro-Treaty candidates in the Free State election of June 1922 and to 'express our approval of the Treaty and pledge our support to Messrs. Griffith and Collins'. They did so while also reiterating 'our strong objections to the present operations of the Belfast parliament under which life and property are insecure'.[205] The support for Collins was noteworthy given the short-lived threat of the Collins–Craig pact to do away with the Boundary Commission entirely. When the Civil War broke out in June 1922, most Fermanagh nationalists supported the pro-Treaty side. Later, Cahir Healy recorded his frustration with de Valera and the anti-Treaty side for creating a significant delay in the implementation of the Boundary Commission, the sole hope of Fermanagh nationalists: 'for the first year after the Treaty the revolt in the Free State prevented any attempt to carry out Clause Twelve'.[206] The *Fermanagh Herald* was similarly opposed to the anti-Treaty IRA, declaring in 1924 'the position in which the Nationalists of the Border areas find themselves would never have arisen were it not for the ill-considered action of those who opposed the Treaty'.[207]

In November 1923 a large meeting of nationalists was held in Enniskillen and presided over by John McHugh, the former IPP chairman of the county council. The meeting had a number of purposes, reflecting the panoply of issues facing the community. It first passed a protest against the continued internment of Cahir Healy and other Fermanagh men before appointing a committee to decide whether candidates should be run in any upcoming British elections.[208] The speakers at the meeting also expressed a profound sense of isolation from both Belfast and Dublin. The decision of the Free State government to enter into a conference with Craig was roundly criticized as it was feared that it would only lead to the Boundary Commission being shelved. Archdeacon Tierney of Enniskillen noted that with the current 'jerrymandering' of rural districts in the county, nationalists would be in the minority on all local bodies despite being in the majority in every rural district. With such structural inequalities arrayed against them, any negotiations with Belfast would serve to abandon them: they 'should look with distrust on anything in the shape of a conference. They should not allow a red herring to be drawn across the path'.[209]

The goal of Fermanagh nationalism after the establishment of Northern Ireland focused almost exclusively on the future commission. Loyalty to the Free State was entirely dependent on its ability to deliver this commission. As Fr Eugene Coyle of Garrison stated at a meeting in Enniskillen in early November 1923, 'they supported the Treaty because it contained Clause 12, and if it were not put into operation the Treaty was broken'. Importantly, however, Coyle declared his faith in the capacity of the Free State to deliver a fair Boundary Commission and exhorted his audience to 'instead of being downhearted, be of good cheer!'[210] This optimism reflected the feedback that the community was receiving from Dublin. Kevin O'Shiel, now head of the North Eastern Boundary Bureau, told a friend that the Free State was confident of getting South Down, South Armagh and South Fermanagh, and that Derry City might be possible too, albeit contingent upon giving some of Monaghan in return.[211]

Barton has described the Boundary Commission as inducing 'something approaching panic amongst [border] Protestants'.[212] In response, Craig began a major tour of the county to allay unionist fears. In late 1923 he travelled the entirety of Fermanagh, speaking in Roslea, Garrison, Belleek, Lisnaskea, Enniskillen, Irvinestown and Brookeborough, where he assured his audience:

> [In 1914] Carson and myself refused to budge one inch on the subject of Fermanagh and Tyrone. We are now in 1923, all square on the six counties, and as far as it is concerned, not one loyalist within the boundary of the six counties will be transferred into the Free State with my will, unless the loyalists themselves so desire it.[213]

The new British government under the strongly pro-unionist Andrew Bonar-Law was keen to demonstrate its own support for border loyalists. The visit of the earl of Derby, secretary of state for war, in February 1923 provided an opportunity for the USC to demonstrate its strength and dominance of the county. Enniskillen itself was festooned with Union Jacks and bunting and over 2,000 members of the USC gathered at St Angelo on the outskirts of the town. The constabulary and Brooke, in particular, were praised for having kept 'law and order and it is up to you to see that this part of the country feel they can leave their life and property secure in your hands.'[214]

By mid-1923 Fermanagh unionists had, in effect, won. They had taken control of local government, broken the back of labour in the county, and interned most key nationalist leaders. Most importantly, they had strengthened their monopoly on violence through the USC and implemented a border where before there had been none. They had also seen off the single greatest territorial threat to the county at Pettigo-Belleek and had outlived the man they saw as their greatest enemy – Michael Collins. The IRA, ever lethargic in the county, had been well and truly cowed and the nationalist non-recognition strategy had led to the establishment of, functionally, a one-party state. It is striking just how smooth Fermanagh's transition from tightly contested political battleground to secure border county was. No county was more likely to fall out of the six-county partition settlement than Fermanagh and yet, due to significant support from Belfast and London, there never seemed any realistic possibility of that happening. For the disheartened nationalists, 1922–3 had been a series of hammer blows one after the other. As time went on, it became harder for them to see any salvation from either within or from the south. As Adrian Grant has noted in respect of Derry, for most nationalists the Boundary Commission was their sole, 'forlorn hope'.[215]

8 Fermanagh in 1923 and beyond

The conditions in Fermanagh were a laboratory for a revolution that could not have happened anywhere else. It was rare to have two large, confident communities that were evenly balanced enough to frustrate each other frequently. It was even rarer to combine that with a precarious position right on the border of a partition settlement and a great distance from the unionist and nationalist heartlands. In Fermanagh both communities could organize militarily and still feel under threat from the other. Both felt entitled to sole mastery of the county's political fate and were enraged when they failed to achieve it. This was also a history of uncertainties. More than any other county in the period, the ultimate fate of Fermanagh was unclear and this ambiguity continued until the disappointment of the Boundary Commission in 1925. This uncertainty influenced the shape of the entire Fermanagh revolution. Neither side was confident about which side of the border their county would end up on. As a result, both felt they had very real power in influencing its final destination. For both, the revolutionary period was characterized by two deep but incompatible convictions in their visions for what Fermanagh was and should be. The Fermanagh story does not fit into the patterns typical of the rest of Ireland. Arguably, Fermanagh's revolutionary experience did not end until the Boundary Commission in 1925. Many of its key players in the revolution such as Cahir Healy and Basil Brooke were only at the start of much longer careers, which went beyond the revolution but were forever shaped by it. While most of this book is the story of two communities in close parallel, by the end it describes two radically diverging paths – unionists in the ascendancy and nationalists at the start of a long struggle that continued for decades. This chapter provides a postscript. It brings the history of the revolution in Fermanagh to a close with the Boundary Commission before looking back at the two communities and the different uncertainties that led them to that end.

The Boundary Commission began life as a sleight of hand. Bedevilled by the intransigence of both sides during the Treaty negotiations over the issue of Fermanagh and Tyrone, Lloyd George reverted to his tried and tested policy of proposing an ambiguous settlement and selling it as two different things to both parties. In this case, his great innovation was the idea of determining the shape of the border at a granular DED level 'in accordance with the wishes of the inhabitants, so far as may be compatible with economic and geographic conditions'.[1] This was problematic but acceptable to Collins and Griffith on the assumption that the nationalist majorities in Fermanagh, Tyrone and parts of Derry and Armagh would see large swathes of territory transferred. In actuality, clause 12 of the Treaty, which mentioned the Boundary Commission, had a significant wrecking effect on any chances for Fermanagh or Tyrone to be included in the new Free State. First, as Kieran Rankin has observed, it implicitly established a British government favourable to unionists as the arbiter in matters between north and south.[2] Second and more significantly, it delayed the issue and gave unionists in the six counties enough time to establish control over all of their territory. As time passed, the existing border became more fixed, something seemingly recognized by the Free State when it established customs posts along it in April 1923.[3] Cormac Moore suggests that this move was inadvertently 'key to translating partition into a reality'.[4] Paul Murray has also noted that the unionist power grab in Northern Ireland was facilitated by many border nationalists' view of their position in the state as 'transient'. This informed their policy of non-recognition and contributed to their fatal lack of political representation within the Northern state.[5]

Despite continual delays on the part of the Northern Ireland government to name a representative to the Boundary Commission, by 1924 it had been established and was made up of Richard Feetham, a British-born judge in South Africa, Eoin MacNeill, representing the Free State, and J.R. Fisher, nominated by the British government on behalf of Northern Ireland. Both nationalists and unionists in Fermanagh expended significant energy in preparing for their submissions to the commission. Once again, nationalists were stymied by their previous refusal to engage with the new Northern state. The reconstituted, unionist-controlled Fermanagh County Council became the organizational basis for the unionist case. The county council's submission was one of the largest brought before the commission. It combined the testimony of individual Fermanagh witnesses (generally local notables representing their district) with that of southern loyalists who alleged persecution in the Free State. James Cooper undertook his own private census claiming to have identified some 2,047 individuals who had fled the Free State into Fermanagh between 1920 and the end of 1924.[6] The submission made extensive use of the current unionist control of local bodies, portraying the county as one in flux between two communities rather than one with a nationalist majority. The earl of Belmore's testimony conflated electoral success in the county with control over its identity: 'the County Councils have been very equally divided. Sometimes one side has the majority and sometimes, the other. Fermanagh is sometimes one side and sometimes the other'.[7] Traditional unionist tropes were repeated such as the preponderance of unionists among the ratepayers, the supposedly migratory nature of the Catholic population and the intangible 'Ulsterism' of Fermanagh as articulated by William Cassidy of Tievegarrow: 'all our traditions and history are bound up with Northern Ireland'.[8] However, Éamon Phoenix has emphasized that their most persuasive argument was to focus on the wording of clause 12 of the Treaty and argue that any change in Fermanagh's current status 'would not be an economic proposition'.[9]

On the nationalist side, Cahir Healy worked closely with the North Eastern Boundary Bureau (NEBB) established by Kevin O'Shiel. The NEBB had twin purposes. It was responsible for organizing and putting forward local cases for inclusion in the Free State, and it was responsible for putting out propaganda to encourage a large swing in territory. Through his work, Healy grew increasingly trepidatious about what the commission, with a British appointed 'neutral' third member, would decide. If there was no agreement on the terms of reference going in, then Fermanagh would be, in his words, 'diddled'.[10] For Healy, this agreement would have to insist on local plebiscites (as originally envisaged by Collins and Griffith) as the basis for deciding territory transfers. However, this was dismissed out of hand by Feetham. Nationalist submissions for Fermanagh focused entirely on demographic arguments. They cited the census, conflating religious and political identify, to demonstrate the Catholic majority in most DEDs. The NEBB also undertook informal censuses of its own around border regions to make the same point. When the commission sat in Enniskillen from 22 April to 6 May 1925, Healy put forward their case himself and made much the same points. While his delivery was seen as effective, moving even, the mood among the nationalist delegates was grim. Many observers, including Archdeacon John Tierney, felt that Feetham's questions suggested he was in place to merely rubberstamp the current border.[11]

This pessimism would prove well founded. In November 1925 the British *Morning Star* newspaper leaked the commission's suggestions. They were mostly minor border adjustments rather than the wholesale changes hoped for by nationalists and, worse in the eyes of many, even suggested minor territorial concessions to Northern Ireland. For Fermanagh, a sizeable section of south-west Fermanagh was to be transferred to the Free State (including Belcoo, Belleek and Garrison). The border around Clones was to be extended northwards, incorporating Roslea into the Free State. The border north of Swanlinbar was also to be extended north as far as Derrylin. In return, Pettigo and some sections of its Donegal hinterland were to be given to Northern Ireland.[12] While nationalists had hoped for enough territorial concessions to render Northern Ireland unviable as a state, in the end there were not even enough to render Fermanagh unviable as a county. The proposed adjustments never came to pass as Eoin MacNeill resigned following outrage from nationalists and the commission collapsed. On 3 December the Free State government under W.T. Cosgrave signed the Tripartite Agreement with Great Britain and Northern Ireland, whereby the Free State agreed to the boundary set by the Treaty in 1921 in return for certain financial concessions.[13]

For most Fermanagh nationalists it was not the expected antipathy of the unionists that infuriated them but the weak and ambivalent support of southern nationalists. After the death of Collins, the Free State government had adopted a more conciliatory approach to Northern Ireland as Cosgrave and Blythe felt that to undermine the Northern government was to undermine the Treaty and thereby the Free State. This change of stance indicated an increasingly partitionist mindset on the part of the pro-Treaty side. The policy was deeply unpopular in Fermanagh as it was believed that it removed much of the political pressure on both Westminster and Belfast to give any concessions on the border. Nor were the anti-Treaty republicans more popular. The Civil War was already disliked by Fermanagh nationalists such as Cahir Healy because it was seen as delaying the establishment of the Boundary Commission and entrenching partition. However, in 1924 de Valera chose to run abstentionist candidates in the 1924 Westminster elections in Northern Ireland. This enraged Healy who saw the retention of the Fermanagh and Tyrone seats as crucial to having any chance of a good settlement under the commission. Indeed, Healy was so committed to this principle that in March 1924 he took his seat in Westminster at the expense of many of his personal friendships. With de Valera's abstentionist policy there was no chance that the Fermanagh and Tyrone seats could be retained, and in response Healy and Harbison withdrew from the contest and advised their supporters to stay at home.[14] In this context, the Tripartite Pact was merely the most grievous wound in a series of betrayals. Fermanagh nationalists had, in Healy's words, 'been sold into political servitude for all time'.[15]

Even before the commission's decision, Fermanagh nationalists had been making moves to engage more fully in northern politics. In March 1925 Healy and Devlin had met to discuss cooperation in the April Northern Ireland election. Healy stood as one of Devlin's Nationalists and was elected along with Harbison, Alexander Donnelly and John McHugh. Seán O'Mahony stood for re-election but antipathy towards his anti-Treaty positions ran deep and he received less than two per cent of first preferences. While his campaign may have been damaged by the refusal of many republicans to engage with the elections, the total nationalist vote in the county was 42,265 in 1925 compared with 45,826 in 1921 – a decline of only eight per cent. Thomas Larkin, his SF colleague, received over double O'Mahony's votes. The new MPs were a reflection of the new alliance that would attempt to defend Fermanagh nationalists in the coming years. John McHugh and Thomas Harbison were the old IPP elite which had never been fully subsumed by SF as they had in the rest of the island; Healy was a former member of SF. However, beyond the political past, this was an alliance of two geographies. Devlinites were centred in Belfast and east Ulster and had had no real expectation of deliverance by the Boundary Commission (unless the commission succeeded in making the new state so small it simply died on its own).[16] Healy's supporters meanwhile were the border nationalists who had believed they would only be subject to unionist domination for a short period of time and were now settling in for a longer haul.[17] Healy worked tirelessly to bridge the gap between these disparate groups which were united only by their unhappy circumstances. His new policy was motivated by his belief that nationalists had to 'do something for themselves'.[18] Healy would continue to work with Devlin for the next decade, hoping that eventually the unionist monolith would splinter into factionalism and allow nationalists some meaningful chance of change. In 1927 he abandoned his previous abstentionism and took a seat in the Northern Irish parliament. Unfortunately, Healy's hopes would never come to pass and in 1929 the Northern Ireland government abolished proportional representation. In 1932 Devlin and Healy once again led their followers out of parliament.

Labour in Fermanagh had been dealt a heavy blow by the events of 1921–3. However, it persisted albeit in a form better adapted to the new political realities. For a number of years following partition, the labour movement in the county fell out of prominence – battered by the twin tempests of unionist political dominance and economic depression. Labour candidates did not contest seats for Enniskillen UDC again until January 1926 when they had six candidates returned in Enniskillen North Ward. J.P. Gillin, the former IPP chair of the council, was also returned, having reinvented himself as a 'business candidate'. Quinn has noted that after partition, labour in Fermanagh made particular efforts to run candidates distributed relatively evenly across both political communities. The labour councillors tried to avoid the national question entirely and instead focus their energies on key areas such as the poor quality of housing in Enniskillen. However, even here they found themselves in opposition to the unionists on the council. In 1925, for example, the UDC built sixteen houses, all of which were let to Protestants. In the coming years, they would highlight the failure of the UDC to build houses for common workingmen while having no problem building houses for the 'well to do and moneyed classes'.[19] In 1924 the Enniskillen Workers' Council affiliated itself with the new Northern Ireland Labour Party. Labour continued to campaign on key issues such as the provision of public services and housing, and frequently contested elections to boards of guardians. However, like nationalists, they found themselves persistently stymied by the vicelike grip unionism held over a gerrymandered Fermanagh.[20]

For unionism and its leaders, the period after partition was one of consistent reward. Edward Archdale, who was already sixty-five when he faced Kevin O'Shiel in Fermanagh North in 1918, served as an MP in Belfast until his retirement in 1937, nineteen years later. He was Northern Ireland's first minister for agriculture and was created a baronet in 1929.[21] His brother, John Porter-Porter, was elected to the first Northern Irish Senate where he also served until 1937.[22] James Cooper was an MP in the Northern parliament until his retirement in 1929. However, most prominent of all was Basil Brooke whose time as head of the Fermanagh UVF earned him a great deal of popularity in his home county and across the six counties in general. In 1929 he was elected to the Northern Irish parliament for the new constituency of Lisnaskea. In 1933 he succeeded Archdale as minister for agriculture and in 1941 he became minister for commerce. Finally, in 1943 he succeeded John Andrews as prime minister. For Fermanagh unionism, once so close to being abandoned in a partition settlement, this was a major moment that placed one of their own at the heart of power and a sign of their true place within Protestant Ulster. However, if Brooke represented this for Fermanagh unionists, then for nationalists he embodied a much darker side of their unionist neighbours. At an Orange rally in Newtownbutler in 1933, Brooke infamously warned: 'Many in this audience employ Catholics, but I have not one about my place. Catholics are out to destroy Ulster ... If we in Ulster allow Roman Catholics to work on our farms we are traitors to Ulster.'[23] Such sectarianism had its birth in the very heart of Fermanagh. There was also in Fermanagh unionism a concerted attempt to characterize Fermanagh as a fundamentally Protestant county with its Catholic population merely an aberration. This may have had its roots in the sense of precarity that defined Fermanagh unionism and their determination to remain within a six-county settlement.

The key themes that have emerged over the course of this volume were fundamentally changed by the two factors that made Fermanagh's revolution so unique: its relatively even population split and its position on the border of what would become Northern Ireland. Nationalism in the county was defined by the need to maintain unity in the face of a unionist minority that would take advantage of any internecine strife. As a result, many of the internal splits typical elsewhere in Ireland were muted in Fermanagh. None of the fundamental divisions in Irish nationalism – IPP vs SF, propertied vs unpropertied, pro- vs anti-Treaty – defined Fermanagh. The IPP was dramatically diminished by the rising tide of republicanism post-1916 but it was never totally submerged. Constitutional nationalism maintained a presence on local councils throughout the period, even after the loss of its parliamentary seat. It remained the voice for propertied nationalists. For all its new-found dominance, SF was careful to compromise with such a large constituency. This was demonstrated in the 1918 North Fermanagh election and in the 1922 general election. The IPP for its part generally voted with the broad nationalist-labour alliance in opposition to the conservative ideology of the unionists. This included those like J.P. Gillin who were, by instinct, conservative themselves. The strong central control and discipline of both parties, necessary in the face of such a formidable enemy as Fermanagh unionism, enabled either the suppression or influencing of dissenting voices and allowed both strands of Fermanagh nationalism to remain remarkably consistent throughout this entire period. Indeed, one of the most defining characteristics of the IPP in Fermanagh was its endless confidence that its resurgence was imminent.

Of all these muted divisions, by far the most surprising was Fermanagh's strong pro-Treaty consensus, which stands in marked contrast to Tyrone.[24] Again this is readily explicable when looked at in the context of wanting to maintain essential nationalist unity. Even those SF clubs that wrote to Seán O'Mahony in support of his anti-Treaty stance refused to pass such resolutions themselves and instead committed themselves to following the lead of the Dáil.[25] In most cases, nationalists in the county fell into old habits and followed the lead of prominent local figures. Whereas before Jeremiah Jordan's influence had swayed where Fermanagh nationalism went, now it was Cahir Healy and Lorcán Ó Ciaráin. Indirectly, the persistence of the IPP also allowed its leaders to lend their support to the Treaty. Nor can the influence on the Fermanagh IRA of men like Eoin O'Duffy and Dan Hogan be discounted. In truth, it would have been unrealistic for anti-Treaty elements in the Fermanagh IRA to commit themselves militarily. The IRA in the county had been weak even before the Treaty and the new challenge of the USC would have made a sustained campaign impractical. It seemed by far the more sensible course to believe in Cahir Healy and trust that the Boundary Commission would return Fermanagh to her rightful position in the Free State.

The issue of the weakness of the Fermanagh IRA bears consideration. The easy answer is that the Fermanagh IRA never surmounted the challenge posed by UVF opposition which is why its most successful companies were located near the border. However, counties with similar unionist populations such as Tyrone and Derry sustained far more active IRA campaigns through the War of Independence.[26] It is also tempting to suggest this was the result of a lack of exceptional local leaders. The county produced at least two highly regarded commanders in Frank Carney and Matt Fitzpatrick, although Carney was limited by imprisonment and ill-heath and Fitzpatrick's responsibilities often took him over the border to Clones. In truth, it appears that even without these factors there was a long-term weakness in Fermanagh militant republicanism. The strong central control of Jeremiah Jordan and the IPP had blunted any older traditions of nationalist organizing in the county. The Volunteer split had seen Fermanagh side overwhelmingly with Redmond with the Irish Volunteers reduced to a mere rump.[27] Long before the UVF had reorganized, the Fermanagh IRA had been slow to assert itself, trailing a good four or five months behind the rest of the country when we look at Townshend's model for the expected development of revolutionary violence in the county.[28] Tellingly, the two most significant military operations in the period (Roslea and Pettigo–Belleek) took place right on the border and were undertaken on the initiative of commanders and units from Monaghan and Donegal respectively.

On the unionist side, their experience of militarization and mobilization differed greatly from their nationalist counterparts. Where the IRA struggled to dominate the county, the UVF showed a level of energy and initiative that set it apart from the rest of Ulster. Both before and after the war, the UVF in Fermanagh was at the forefront of defining what the organization would be. In the early days of the Ulster crisis, units like the Enniskillen Horse were among the first to demonstrate the propagandistic value of an active unionist militia, something Alvin Jackson has emphasized.[29] Conversely, in the War of Independence Fermanagh Vigilance and other groups were important in showing that unionists could and would organize even in strongly nationalist areas and that such militias could successfully defeat the IRA. The border experience was fundamental to the foundation of the Fermanagh militias and the UVF. It was motivated by their sense of precarity and peril. In their minds they were surrounded by disloyal nationalists in their own county and on the frontier with a wild and dangerous south. It thus made sense for them to arm themselves in defence against whatever threats may come. This also contributed to the essentially reactive nature of the force. Unlike the IRA or later the USC, which undertook campaigns with clear strategic goals in mind, the UVF in Fermanagh was geared primarily around disrupting the functioning of the IRA. One might reasonably expect that having two hostile armed forces would guarantee an escalating bloody conflict, as occurred in Northern Ireland decades later. In general, however, the presence of the two militias seems to have acted as a deterrent to one another for fear of sparking a series of reprisals. Indeed, in those cases where violence did flare up, it tended to trigger a pattern of escalating action and counteraction as seen in Roslea where an attack on George Lester escalated to a cross-county attack on unionist houses. However, it also meant that as unionists gradually secured a monopoly on violence after the Treaty, there already existed the organizational apparatus to attack and intimidate nationalists.

The case of Fermanagh underlines an often-forgotten aspect of the fight over partition – local government and political representation. Both sides recognized very early on the importance of maximizing not only the number of seats won in Westminster but also those on the county council and district councils which were an effective shorthand for conveying the nationalism or unionism of the county. The extent to which control of the various councils actually influenced policy is debatable. From as early as 1916, Carson and the UUC seemed to have settled on six-county partition as the ideal settlement, representing the largest area they could reasonably control while maintaining a majority.[30] Once it realized the UUC could not be coerced into reducing their demands, the British government also adopted this position. However, at the time both sides fully believed in the crucial importance of each campaign – hence Archdale's vitriol after winning North Fermanagh in 1918 and Cahir Healy's elation after his and Harbison's sweep of Fermanagh–Tyrone in 1922. The election of John McHugh as chair of Fermanagh County Council in 1914 had sparked a riot in Enniskillen and an identity crisis in Fermanagh unionism.[31] However, despite nationalist dominance of local bodies from 1914 onwards, abstentionism proved to be a significant blunder that undermined much of their previous influence. By not participating in the Northern Irish parliament and Fermanagh County Council, SF and IPP MPs, in effect, voted themselves out of existence in November 1921. Through these actions local nationalist politics handed the initiative to unionists to reshape Fermanagh as they saw fit. It is easy to feel sympathy for Fermanagh nationalists as these were not policies of their own design but rather were consistent with general SF strategy. However, they suffered gravely for it.[32] The single most influential use of local politics made by either side in the entire period was how effectively the new Fermanagh County Council organized and assembled their case for the Boundary Commission – one so voluminous that it gave Feetham all the reason he needed to decide against major territorial changes.

For unionists this final settlement was nothing less than vindication. They had struggled politically and ideologically for years against the perception of Fermanagh as a Catholic county. While many of their arguments today can seem somewhat ridiculous or even desperate (such as Trimble's article 'Fermanagh a Protestant county: notwithstanding the population'), at the time they reflected a sincerely held belief. For them, unionists and unionism were more deeply tied to the land and to the identity of the county than Catholics could ever be. They had founded it. They were more invested in its material wellbeing and paid more towards its upkeep. They owned most of it. Yet in spite of this, they struggled to assert themselves politically for most of this period. Fermanagh unionists were often peripheral figures in the UUC with the exception of Archdale. Yet after the Treaty, they were able to seize control of the organs of power in the county remarkably quickly. Some of this was due to good fortune, such as with the dissolution of the county council. However, in most cases it came down to two key factors. First, Fermanagh unionists had backing and support from both London and Belfast to a degree that Fermanagh nationalists could only dream about from Dublin. Challenges such as at Pettigo-Belleek were responded to quickly and with force. The Leech Commission, once established, also redrew the electoral map of the county to entrench unionist dominance. However, just as importantly, the key act of power consolidation undertaken post-partition was the establishment of the USC. This force undertook the crucial task of converting Fermanagh into a border county by drawing on Fermanagh unionism's strengths. These lay not in politics but in mobilization and organization. As McCluskey has observed, the USC's use of intimidation and reprisal in Tyrone were fundamental in securing the county for unionism and this was exactly the case in Fermanagh also.[33]

The years 1912–23 had created a new Fermanagh but it was not necessarily a better Fermanagh. Where once there had been two communities in constant struggle, now one was pre-eminent. Where once there had been ambiguities, now there was certainty. Fermanagh's place in Northern Ireland seemed incontestable. After the Boundary Commission, Fermanagh nationalists no longer held any hope of 'rescue' and lowered their ambitions to reverse the unionist gerrymander and reclaim their influence in public life. Until that happened, in the words of Fr Eugene Coyle of Devenish, they were 'living in pre-emancipation days'.[34] Rather than grievances over the fact of partition itself, it was the inability of nationalists to engage politically with the new Northern state that sowed the seeds of the conflicts to come as the twentieth century progressed.

Notes

CHAPTER ONE *'Outpost of Ulster': Fermanagh in 1912*

1   Jonathan Bell, 'Changing farming methods in County Fermanagh' in Eileen M. Murphy & William J. Roulston (eds), *Fermanagh history and society: interdisciplinary essays on the history of an Irish county* (Dublin, 2004), pp 501–3.

2   'Table 1: The number of inhabitants in each county and province in 1841, 1851, 1861, 1871, 1881, 1891, 1901 and 1911', *Census of Ireland, 1911, Preliminary report with abstract of the enumerators' summaries, &c.* [Cd.5691], p. 1.

3   'Table 48: Showing the administrative counties arranged in order of per-centage of increase or decrease of population between 1901 and 1911', *Census of Ireland, 1911, General report, with tables and appendix, BPP 1912–13 CXVIII* [Cd. 6663], p. 65.

4   'Table 29: Religious professions and sexes of the inhabitants, in each county and county borough', *Census of Ireland, 1911, Area, houses, and population: also the ages, civil or conjugal condition, occupations, birthplaces, religions, and education of the people. Province of Ulster* [Cd. 6051], p. 37.

5   *Belfast and Province of Ulster Directory* (Belfast, 1911), pp 1581–2, 1788–9.

6   Ibid., pp 1464–7.

7   Ibid.

8   George Chambers, 'The rise and fall of an indigenous industry: milk processing in County Fermanagh from the seventeenth century until the present day' in Murphy & Roulston (eds), *Fermanagh*, p. 529.

9   *Belfast and Ulster Directory*, pp 1705–9, 1795–7, 1748–9.

10 S. Maxwell Hajducki, *A railway atlas of Ireland* (Newton Abbott, 1974).

11 *Belfast and Ulster directory*, pp 1581–2.

12 Ibid.

13 'Table 37: Showing, for 1911, as compared with 1901, the number and ages of persons who spoke Irish only, and Irish and English in each county district', Census of Ireland, 1911, Area, houses, and population: also the ages, civil or conjugal condition, occupations, birthplaces, religions, and education of the people. Province of Ulster [Cd. 6051], p. 111.

14 *Fermanagh Times* (hereafter *FT*), 26 Aug. 1920.

15 The earldom of Enniskillen was created on 18 August 1789 while the earldom of Erne was created the next day. The earldom of Belmore was a later creation of 1797.

16 For the first earl this was the Irish House of Commons and he ascended to the Irish House of Lords through the title of Baron Mountflorence as the earldom did yet exist.

17 Patrick Maume, 'Crichton (Creighton), John 4th baron of Erne (Ireland) and 1st Baron Fermanagh', *Dictionary of Irish biography* (hereafter *DIB*).

18 Patrick M. Geoghegan, 'Corry, Somerset Lowry 2nd Earl Belmore', *DIB*; C.J. Woods, 'Cole, Sir (Galbraith) Lowry', *DIB*.

19 C.J. Woods, 'Archdale, Mervyn Edward (1812–95)', *DIB*; Peter Gibbon, *The origins of Ulster Unionism: the formation of popular Protestant politics and ideology in nineteenth-century Ireland* (Manchester, 1975), p. 112.

20 Gerry McElroy, 'Archdale, Sir Edward Mervyn (1853–1943)', *DIB*.

21 B.E. Barton, 'The origins and development of Unionism in Fermanagh, 1885–1914' in Murphy & Roulston (eds), *Fermanagh*, pp 309–10.

22 Alvin Jackson, *The Ulster Party: Irish Unionists in the House of Commons, 1884–1911* (Oxford, 1989), p. 205.

23 Fergal McCluskey, *Tyrone: the Irish Revolution, 1912–23* (Dublin, 2014), pp 9–11.
24 Patrick Maume, 'Jordan, Jeremiah', *DIB*.
25 Kevin O'Shiel (BMH WS 1770, p. 139).
26 *Irish Times* (hereafter *IT*), 1 Dec. 1920.
27 *Fermanagh Herald* (hereafter *FH*), 3 May 1919.
28 Jim Quinn, *Labouring beside Lough Erne: a study of the Fermanagh Labour movement, 1826–1932* (Enniskillen, 2019), pp 5–9.
29 Adrian Grant, *Derry: the Irish Revolution, 1912–23* (Dublin, 2018), p. 20.

CHAPTER TWO *'Both sides may be said to be watching each other': the home rule crisis, 1912–14*

1   *IT*, 25 Jan. 1910.
2   Membership list of the executive council of the Fermanagh branch of the Irish Unionist Alliance, June 1905 (Public Records Office of Northern Ireland (hereafter PRONI)/D989/A/9/33).
3   Ibid.
4   *IT*, 20 Apr. 1911.
5   Ibid.
6   Ibid., 27 July 1911.
7   Brian Walker, *Parliamentary election results in Ireland, 1801–1922* (Dublin, 1978), p. 349.
8   *IT*, 4 Nov. 1910.
9   *Nenagh Guardian*, 6 Jan. 1914.
10 *IT*, 14 Aug. 1910.
11 Ibid., 15 Jan. 1910.
12 Terence Dooley, *Monaghan: the Irish Revolution, 1912–23* (Dublin, 2017), pp 20–1.
13 Pauric Travers, *Donegal: the Irish Revolution, 1912–23* (Dublin, 2022), pp 12, 20–1.
14 David Fitzpatrick, *Descendancy: Irish Protestant histories since 1795* (Cambridge, 2014), p. 243.
15 Barton, 'Unionism in Fermanagh', p. 324; Breandán Mac Giolla Choille, *Intelligence notes, 1913–1916* (Dublin, 1966), pp 19–20.
16 CI Fermanagh, Feb. 1912 (TNA, CO 904/86).
17 Ibid., July 1912 (TNA, CO 904/87).
18 Ibid., Oct. 1912 (TNA, CO 904/88).
19 Ibid.
20 *IT*, 18 Oct. 1911.
21 Ibid.
22 *IT*, 18 Oct. 1911.
23 Ibid.
24 Ibid.
25 CI Fermanagh, Jan. 1912 (TNA, CO 904/86).
26 Ibid., Jan. 1913 (TNA, CO 904/89).
27 Ibid., June 1912 (TNA, CO 904/87).
28 Richard McMinn, Éamon Phoenix and Joanne Beggs, 'Jeremiah Jordan MP (1830–1911): Protestant home ruler or "Protestant renegade"?', *Irish Historical Studies*, 36:143 (May 2009), 363–4.
29 Ibid., 364.
30 Malachy McRoe, '"Honest Pat" – Patrick Crumley DL, MP', *Clogher Record*, 20:3 (2011), 541–2.
31 *IT*, 1 Dec. 1910.
32 *Hansard (Commons)*, 13 Feb. 1911, vol. 21, col. 688.
33 Francis O'Duffy (BMH WS 654, p. 12).

34 Éamon Phoenix, 'Cahir Healy and nationalist politics in Co. Fermanagh, 1885–1970' in Murphy & Roulston (eds), *Fermanagh*, p. 359.

35 Ibid., pp 359–60.

36 Michael Laffan, *The resurrection of Ireland: the Sinn Féin party, 1916–1923* (Cambridge, 1999), p. 63.

37 Phoenix, 'Cahir Healy', p. 360.

38 CI Fermanagh, May 1912 (TNA, CO 904/87).

39 Grant, *Derry*, p. 38.

40 *IT*, 28 Sept. 1912.

41 Ibid.

42 Ibid.

43 CI Fermanagh, Sept. 1912 (TNA, CO 904/88).

44 Ibid.; *IT*, 30 Sept. 1912.

45 Fitzpatrick, *Descendancy*, p. 243.

46 Diane Urquhart (ed.), *The minutes of the Ulster Women's Unionist Council and executive committee, 1911–40* (Dublin, 2001), pp 223–4.

47 *IT*, 20 Apr. 1911.

48 Travers, *Donegal*, pp 20–1.

49 Grant, *Derry*, pp 30–1.

50 Eligible population is calculated as non-Catholic above the age of 16 in the 1911 census. North Fermanagh numbers may be slightly inflated as some North Fermanagh records were grouped together with either mid-Tyrone or South Donegal. Figures for the Covenant are unreliable for specific figures due to how date has been captured.

51 It is worth noting here that Monaghan showed remarkable enthusiasm for the Covenant and had one of the highest engagement rates anywhere in Ulster, see Dooley, *Monaghan*, p. 20.

52 Grant, *Derry*, pp 30–1.

53 CI Fermanagh, Oct. 1912 (TNA, CO 904/88).

54 *Ulster Herald* (hereafter *UH*), 28 Sept. 1912.

55 CI Fermanagh, Dec. 1912 (TNA, CO 904/88).

56 Ibid., Feb. 1913 (TNA, CO 904/89).

57 Ibid.

58 Frank Thompson, 'The Land War in Fermanagh' in Murphy & Roulston (eds), *Fermanagh*, p. 293.

59 Barton, 'Unionism in Fermanagh', p. 317.

60 Gerard Michael Farrell, 'The Ulster Volunteer Force, 1912–14' (MA thesis, National University of Ireland, Maynooth, 2006), p. 20.

61 Alvin Jackson, *Ireland 1798–1998: war, peace and beyond* (Oxford, 1999), pp 233–4.

62 CI Fermanagh, July 1913 (TNA, CO 904/90).

63 Fitzpatrick, *Descendancy*, p. 244. All data calculated by David Fitzpatrick and originally taken from Mac Giolla Choille, *Intelligence notes*, pp 16–37.

64 Barton, 'Unionism in Fermanagh', p. 325.

65 Ibid.

66 Barton, *Brookeborough: the making of a prime minister* (Belfast, 1988), p. 14.

67 CI Fermanagh, Apr. 1913 (TNA, CO 904/89).

68 Timothy Bowman, 'The North began: but when? The formation of the Ulster Volunteer Force', *History Ireland*, 21:2 (Mar.–Apr. 2013), 29.

69 Barton, 'Unionism in Fermanagh', p. 326.

70 Bowman, 'The North began', 29.

71 Timothy Bowman, *Carson's army: the Ulster Volunteer Force, 1910–22* (Manchester, 2007), p. 51.

72 Alvin Jackson, 'Unionist myths', *Past & Present*, 136 (Aug. 1992), 172.

73 Flyer signed by Trimble, 24 May 1913, Papers relating to the Enniskillen Horse (TNA, CO 904/27/1).
74 Report on gathering of Enniskillen Horse, 10 Oct. 1913 (ibid.).
75 CI Fermanagh, Oct. 1913 (TNA, CO 904/91).
76 Ibid.
77 Mac Giolla Choille, *Intelligence notes*, pp 32–4.
78 CI Fermanagh, July 1913 (TNA, CO 904/90).
79 Ibid., Aug. 1913 (ibid.).
80 Ibid.
81 CI Fermanagh, Oct. 1913 (TNA, CO 904/91).
82 Ibid., Nov. 1913 (ibid.).
83 Ibid., Jan. 1914 (TNA, CO 904/92).
84 *IT*, 6 Dec. 1913.
85 Ibid.
86 CI Fermanagh, July 1914 (TNA, CO 904/94).
87 *IT*, 10 Mar. 1914.
88 Mac Giolla Choille, *Intelligence notes*, p. 33.
89 Ibid., p. 33.
90 Travers, *Donegal*, p. 26; Dooley, *Monaghan*, pp 24–6.
91 CI Fermanagh, July 1913 (TNA, CO 904/90).
92 Ibid., Apr. 1914 (TNA, CO 904/93).
93 Ibid., May 1914 (ibid.).
94 Ibid., Apr. 1913 (TNA, CO 904/89).
95 George Irvine (BMH WS 265, p. 1).
96 Joseph Connell, 'Founding of the Irish Volunteers', *History Ireland*, 21:6 (Nov.–Dec. 2013), 16.
97 Peadar Livingstone, *The Fermanagh story* (Enniskillen, 1969), pp 272–4.
98 CI Fermanagh, Mar. 1914 (TNA, CO 904/92).
99 Francis O'Duffy (BMH WS 654, p. 3).
100 Ibid.
101 CI Fermanagh, Dec. 1913 (TNA, CO 904/91).
102 Mac Giolla Choille, *Intelligence notes*, pp 109–11.
103 Figures calculated based on Volunteer membership by county as on 31 Sept. 1914; Mac Giolla Choille, *Intelligence notes*, pp 109–11; Grant, *Derry*, pp 53–5.
104 CI Fermanagh, May 1914 (TNA, CO 904/93).
105 Ibid., July 1914 (TNA, CO 904/94).
106 Francis O'Duffy (BMH WS 654, p. 2).
107 Nicholas Smyth (BMH WS 721, p. 1).
108 John Connolly (BMH WS 598, p. 1).
109 CI Fermanagh, May 1914 (TNA, CO 904/93).
110 Ibid.
111 CI Fermanagh, June 1914 (TNA, CO 904/93).
112 George Irvine (BMH WS 265, p. 1).
113 Francis O'Duffy (BMH WS 654, p. 1).
114 George Irvine (BMH WS 265, p. 2).
115 Dooley, *Monaghan*, pp 29–30; Travers, *Donegal*, pp 30–1.

CHAPTER THREE *'Bury the hatchet and take up the rifle': the First World, 1914–16*

1 CI Fermanagh, June 1914 (TNA, CO 904/93).
2 Ibid., Aug. 1914 (TNA, CO 904/94).

3 Terence Dooley, 'County Monaghan, 1914–1918: recruitment, the rise of Sinn Féin and the partition crisis', *Clogher Record*, 16:2 (1998), 144.

4 Timothy Bowman, 'The Ulster Volunteer Force and the formation of the 36th (Ulster) Division', *Irish Historical Studies*, 32:128 (Nov. 2001), 500–1.

5 *Report on recruiting in Ireland, 1914–16* (Cd. 8168).

6 Bowman, 'The Ulster Volunteer Force', 505.

7 *Belfast Newsletter* (hereafter *BN*), 7 Sept. 1914.

8 CI Fermanagh, Sept. 1914 (TNA, CO 904/94).

9 *BN*, 23 Sept. 1914.

10 Ibid.

11 Bowman 'The Ulster Volunteer Force', 510.

12 Ibid.

13 *BN*, 7 Nov. 1914.

14 Ibid., 17 Nov. 1914.

15 Ibid., 12 Nov. 1914.

16 CI Fermanagh, Aug. 1914 (TNA, CO 904/94).

17 Ibid., Oct. 1914 (TNA, CO 904/95).

18 Ibid., Sept. 1914 (TNA, CO 904/94); CI Fermanagh, Oct. 1914 (TNA, CO 904/95); *FH*, 10 Oct. 1914.

19 David Fitzpatrick, 'The logic of collective sacrifice: Ireland and the British army, 1914–18', *Historical Journal*, 38:4 (1995), 1026.

20 CI Fermanagh, Dec. 1914 (TNA, CO 904/95).

21 Francis O'Duffy (BMH WS 654, p. 3).

22 *BN*, 12 Nov. 1914.

23 Maurice Moore to James Rogers, 1 Oct. 1914 (NLI, Maurice Moore papers, MS 10548/6).

24 *FH*, 5 Sept. 1914.

25 Livingstone, *Fermanagh*, p. 273.

26 Francis O'Duffy (BMH WS 654, p. 2); CI Fermanagh, Oct. 1914 (TNA, CO 904/95).

27 CI Fermanagh, Nov. 1914 (TNA, CO 904/95).

28 Ibid., Dec. 1914 (ibid.).

29 *BN*, 5 Mar. 1915.

30 Ibid., 19 Apr. 1915.

31 Ibid., 12 Mar. 1915.

32 CI Fermanagh, May 1915 (TNA, CO 904/97).

33 Bowman, 'The UVF and the Ulster Division', 507.

34 *BN*, 19 Apr. 1915; *FH*, 19 June 1915.

35 Livingstone, *Fermanagh*, p. 273.

36 Ibid.

37 *Irish Independent* (hereafter *II*), 22 July 1915.

38 *Freeman's Journal* (hereafter *FJ*), 27 July 1915.

39 *II*, 12 June 1915.

40 Ibid.

41 *BN*, 6 Sept. 1914.

42 Ibid., 3 July 1915.

43 Timothy Bowman, William Butler & Michael Wheatley, *The disparity of sacrifice: Irish recruitment to the British armed forces, 1914–1918* (Oxford, 2020), p. 116.

44 Irish Red Cross service records accessed online at https://vad.redcross.org.uk/ (accessed 12 Dec. 2021).

45 Fionnuala Walsh, *Irish women and the Great War* (Cambridge, 2020), p. 145.

46 *BN*, 11 Nov. 1915.

47 Ibid.
48 Ibid., 3 July 1915.
49 Ibid.
50 *Drogheda Independent*, 24 July 1915.
51 *FH*, 29 Jan. 1915.
52 Ibid., 6 Nov. 1915.
53 Barton, 'Unionism in Fermanagh', p. 331.
54 *FJ*, 22 July 1915.
55 CI Fermanagh, Aug. 1915 (TNA, CO 904/97).
56 Ibid., May 1915 (TNA, CO 904/97).
57 Figures provided by David Fitzpatrick; Mac Giolla Choille, *Intelligence notes*, pp 100, 110–12.
58 CI Fermanagh, Sept. 1914 (TNA, CO 904/94), Dec. 1915 (TNA, CO 904/98).
59 Travers, *Donegal*, pp 54–5; McCluskey, *Tyrone*, pp 51–3.
60 CI Fermanagh, Dec. 1914 (TNA, CO 904/94).
61 Figures provided by David Fitzpatrick; Mac Giolla Choille, *Intelligence notes*, pp 100, 110–12.
62 Eligibility is defined as males over 18 in the 1911 census who are not employed in agriculture. McCluskey, *Tyrone*, pp 50–5; Dooley, *Monaghan*, pp 35–6, 38.
63 CI Fermanagh, Jan. 1915 (TNA, CO 904/96).
64 Ibid., Sept. 1915 (TNA, CO 904/98).
65 Ibid., Nov. 1915 (ibid.).
66 John Connolly (BMH WS 598, p. 1).
67 James J. Smyth (BMH WS 559, p. 1).
68 Francis O'Duffy (BMH WS 654, pp 2–5).
69 Ibid.
70 Peadar Livingstone, *The Monaghan story* (Enniskillen, 1979), p. 363; Dooley, *Monaghan*, pp 33–4.
71 Ibid.
72 Ibid.
73 'Sinn Féin meetings', 1915 (TNA, CO 904/23/2).
74 Francis O'Duffy (BMH WS 654, p. 5).
75 Ibid.; O'Duffy was convinced of this opinion by Michael O'Hanrahan of Volunteer headquarters who was later executed for his part in the 1916 Rising.
76 CI Fermanagh, Nov. 1914 (TNA, CO 904/95).
77 Fermanagh Irish National Volunteers secretary to Maurice Moore, 4 Dec. 1914 (NLI, Moore papers, MS 10,548/6).
78 CI Fermanagh, Apr. 1915, May 1915 (TNA, CO 904/96).
79 Joost Augusteijn, *From public defiance to guerrilla warfare: the experience of ordinary volunteers in the Irish War of Independence, 1916–1921* (Dublin, 2006), p. 28.
80 CI Fermanagh, Apr. 1915 (TNA, CO 904/96), July 1915 (TNA, CO 904/97), Nov. 1915 (TNA, CO 904/98).

CHAPTER FOUR *'Rebels, traitors and pro-Germans': the rise of Sinn Féin and the unionist response, 1916–18*

1 *FH*, 30 Apr. 1966.
2 Francis O'Duffy (BMH, WS 654), pp 3–4; McCluskey, *Tyrone*, pp 57–8.
3 Ibid.
4 CI Fermanagh, Apr. 1916 (TNA, CO 904/99).
5 The biographies of these individuals are detailed in the publication Fermanagh 1916 Centenary Association, *Fearless but few: Fermanagh and the Easter Rising* (Castleblayney, 2015).
6 Ibid., p. 57.
7 George Irvine (BMH WS 265, pp 3–4).

8   Ibid., p. 4; *Fearless but few*, pp 63–4.
9   George Irvine (BMH WS 265, pp 4–5).
10   *Fearless but few*, p. 65.
11   Ibid., pp 105–6.
12   Livingstone, *Fermanagh*, p. 279.
13   *Fearless but few*, p. 22.
14   Ibid., p. 42.
15   Pension application of Michael Love (IMA, MSPC, 24SP11754); *Fearless but few*, p. 76.
16   Francis Tummon (BMH WS 820, pp 1–2).
17   *Fearless but few*, pp 14–15.
18   CI Fermanagh, Apr. 1916 (TNA, CO 904/99).
19   Francis Tummon (BMH WS 820, p. 2).
20   *FH*, 6 May 1916.
21   Ibid.
22   Ibid.
23   Note: there is some contention about whether Crockett died immediately as was recorded by
     his commanding officer or a few days later of his wounds as was recorded locally in Derry.
24   Eunan O'Halpin & Daithí Ó Corráin, *The dead of the Irish Revolution* (London & New Haven,
     2020), p. 56; Find a Grave Memorial 139067497, https://www.findagrave.come (accessed 25
     Jan. 2021).
25   Find a Grave Memorial 161588907 (ibid.).
26   Francis Tummon (BMH WS 820, pp 1–2).
27   Nicholas Smyth (BMH WS 721, p. 2); Francis Tummon (BMH WS 820, pp 1–2).
28   CI Fermanagh, May 1916 (TNA, CO 904/100).
29   McRoe, 'Honest Pat', 546.
30   Alan O'Day, *Irish home rule, 1867–1921* (Manchester, 1998), p. 271.
31   Dooley, 'County Monaghan, 1914–1918', 28.
32   A.C. Hepburn, *Catholic Belfast and nationalist Ireland in the era of Joe Devlin, 1871–1934*
     (Oxford, 2008), p. 179.
33   Livingstone, *Fermanagh*, p. 281.
34   Ibid.
35   CI Fermanagh, July 1916 (TNA, CO 904/100).
36   Ibid., June, July 1916 (ibid.).
37   Ibid., Oct. 1916, Dec. 1916 (TNA, CO 904/101).
38   David W. Savage, 'The attempted home rule settlement of 1916', *Éire-Ireland*, 3:2 (1967), 133–
     4.
39   *FH*, 20 May 1916.
40   Ibid.
41   Ibid.
42   CI Fermanagh, Aug. 1916 (TNA, CO 904/100).
43   Livingstone, *Fermanagh*, p. 281.
44   CI Fermanagh, Sept. 1916 (TNA, CO 904/101).
45   Ibid., Feb. 1917 (TNA, CO 904/102).
46   Ibid., May 1917 (TNA, CO 904/103).
47   Francis O'Duffy (BMH WS 654, p. 4).
48   Ibid., Oct. 1917 (TNA, CO 904/104).
49   Ibid., Nov. 1917 (ibid.).
50   Ibid., Jan. 1917 (TNA, CO 904/102).
51   Ibid., Feb. 1917 (ibid.).
52   Ibid., May 1917 (TNA, CO 904/103).

53   CI Fermanagh, Mar. 1918 (TNA, CO 904/105).
54   Ibid.
55   CI Fermanagh, Dec. 1918 (TNA, CO 904/107).
56   Francis O'Duffy (BMH WS 654, pp 4–5).
57   Livingstone, *Fermanagh*, p. 282.
58   Pension application of Ellen J. McGrath (IMA, MSPC, MSP34REF10260).
59   Pension application of Alice Cashel (IMA, MSPC, MSP34REF55390).
60   Pension application of Cissie McGovern (IMA, MSPC, 34REF47744).
61   CI Fermanagh, Mar. 1918 (TNA, CO 904/105).
62   *FH*, 8 Dec. 1917, 29 June 1918.
63   Ibid., 29 June 1918.
64   *Fearless but few*, p. 65.
65   *FH*, 7 July 1917.
66   *Fearless but few*, p. 65.
67   Livingstone, *Fermanagh*, p. 283.
68   Ibid.
69   Ibid.
70   CI Fermanagh, Nov. 1918, Dec. 1918 (TNA, CO 904/107).
71   *IR*, 24 May 1917.
72   It seems likely this 'Moloney' is actually G.V. Maloney, law agent for Arthur Griffith in the
     East Cavan by-election, as there are no other solicitors in Cavan, Monaghan or Fermanagh for
     which we have a record and 'Moloney' is recorded as having offices in Cootehill.
73   *IR*, 7 Mar. 1918.
74   Ibid., 1 Nov. 1917.
75   Ibid., 18 Jan. 1917.
76   Ibid., 8 Feb. 1917.
77   Ibid.
78   Ibid., 10 May 1917.
79   Ibid.
80   Ibid., 8 Nov. 1917.
81   CI Fermanagh, Nov. 1917 (TNA, CO 904/104).
82   *IR*, 24 May 1917.
83   Ibid., 11 Jan. 1923.
84   Kevin O'Shiel (BMH WS 1170, pp 22–4).
85   *IR*, 19 Oct. 1919.
86   Ibid., 23 Nov. 1922.
87   Livingstone, *Fermanagh*, p. 268.
88   *IR*, 19 Oct. 1919.
89   Ibid., 18 Apr. 1918.
90   Livingstone, *Fermanagh*, p. 283.
91   *Hansard (Commons)*, 17 Jan. 1918, vol. 101, col. 556.
92   Alan J. Ward, 'Lloyd George and the 1918 Irish conscription crisis', *Historical Journal*, 17:1
     (Mar. 1974), 111.
93   Kevin O'Shiel (BMH WS 1170, p. 736).
94   CI Fermanagh, Apr. 1918 (TNA, CO 904/105).
95   Ibid., May 1918 (TNA, CO 904/106).
96   Ibid., Apr. 1918 (TNA, CO 904/105).
97   Ibid.
98   *FH*, 27 Apr. 1918.
99   *Anglo-Celt*, 20 Apr. 1918.

100 Jim Quinn, 'Labouring on the margins: trade union activity in Enniskillen, 1917–1923', *Saothar*, 15 (1990), 59.
101 Ibid., 58.
102 *FH*, 27 Apr. 1918.
103 *FT*, 18 Apr. 1918.
104 CI Fermanagh, May 1918 (TNA, CO 904/106).
105 Ibid., Apr. 1918 (TNA, CO 904/105).
106 Ibid., May 1918 (TNA, CO 904/106).
107 *IR*, 18 Apr. 1918.
108 Phoenix, 'Cahir Healy', 37.
109 *FH*, 18 May 1918.
110 *IR*, 5 Sept. 1918.
111 CI Fermanagh, May 1917 (TNA, CO 904/103), Feb. 1918 (TNA, CO 904/105).
112 Ibid., Mar. 1918 (TNA, CO 904/105).
113 Francis Tummon (BMH WS 820, pp 5–6).
114 Nicholas Smyth (BMH WS 721, pp 2–3).
115 Francis Tummon (BMH WS 820, pp 5–6).
116 Pension application of Patrick McNulty (IMA, MSPC, 24SP3133).
117 CI Fermanagh, Mar. 1918 (TNA, CO 904/105).
118 Laffan, *Resurrection*, pp 142–4.
119 *FH*, 25 May 1918.
120 Francis Tummon (BMH WS 820, pp 9–10).
121 *FH*, 11 May 1918.
122 *IR*, 18 July 1918.
123 Ibid.
124 Ibid.
125 *IT*, 20 July 1918.
126 *FH*, 19 Oct. 1918.
127 *IR*, 5 Sept. 1918.
128 Ibid., 18 July 1918.
129 Ibid., 5 Sept. 1918.
130 Ibid., 14 Nov. 1918.
131 *FT*, 14 Nov. 1918.
132 *IT*, 19, 20 Oct. 1916.
133 Ibid., 28 Oct.1916.
134 *IR*, 28 Nov. 1918.
135 Ibid., 5 Dec. 1918.
136 Aisling Walsh, 'Michael Cardinal Logue, 1840–1924', *Seanchas Ardmhacha*, 18:1 (1999), 181.
137 *IR*, 5 Dec. 1918.
138 McRoe, 'Honest Pat', 547.
139 *IR*, 5 Dec. 1918.
140 Kevin O'Shiel (BMH WS 1170, pp 813–14).
141 Ibid., p. 795.
142 Ibid., p. 815; Livingstone, *Fermanagh*, p. 272.
143 Kevin O'Shiel (BMH WS 1170, pp 818–19).
144 Eda Sagarra, *Kevin O'Shiel: Tyrone nationalist and Irish state-builder* (Dublin, 2013), p. 108.
145 Kevin O'Shiel (BMH WS 1170, p. 820).
146 Ibid., p. 822.
147 *IR*, 19 Dec. 1918.
148 Ibid., 5 Dec. 1918.

149 *FT*, 12 Dec. 1918.
150 Kevin O'Shiel (BMH WS 1170, p. 824).
151 Ibid.
152 *IR*, 12 Dec. 1918.
153 *FT*, 9 Jan. 1919.
154 Livingstone, *Fermanagh*, p. 273.
155 Kevin O'Shiel (BMH WS 1170, pp 779–80).
156 *FT*, 28 Nov. 1918.
157 Ibid., 29 Jan. 1919.
158 Ibid.
159 *IR*, 9 Jan. 1919.

CHAPTER FIVE *'There was little sign to be seen of the war': the War of Independence, 1919–20*

1 McCluskey, *Tyrone*, pp 89–92; Dooley, *Monaghan*, pp 81–100; Travers, *Donegal*, pp 101–10.
2 Livingstone, *Fermanagh*, p. 285; CI Fermanagh, Mar. 1919 (TNA, CO 904/108).
3 *An tÓglach*, 31 Jan. 1919.
4 *IR*, 13 Mar. 1919.
5 Joseph V. Lawless (BMH WS 1043, pp 314–15).
6 Livingstone, *Fermanagh*, p. 284.
7 Phoenix, 'Cahir Healy', 37.
8 Livingstone, *Fermanagh*, p. 284.
9 Kevin O'Shiel (BMH WS 1170, p. 866).
10 Ibid.
11 Gary Evans, 'The raising of the first internal Dáil Éireann loan and the British responses to it, 1919–1921' (MLitt, Maynooth University, 2012), p. 154; Travers, *Donegal*, p. 88; Dooley, *Monaghan*, p. 74.
12 Kevin O'Shiel (BMH WS 1170, pp 866–7).
13 Ibid.
14 Michael Hopkinson, *The Irish War of Independence* (Dublin, 2002), pp 15–16.
15 4th South Donegal Brigade Nominal Rolls (IMA, Nominal Rolls, RO/375–9A).
16 2nd Tyrone Brigade Nominal Rolls (IMA, Nominal Rolls, RO/455–8).
17 Livingstone, *Fermanagh*, p. 285.
18 Fermanagh Brigade Nominal Rolls (IMA, Nominal Rolls, RO/593–7); James J. Smyth (BMH WS 559, pp 6–7).
19 Lawrence William White, 'Francis Carney (1896–1932)', *DIB*.
20 Ibid.
21 James J. Smyth (BMH WS 559, pp 1–2).
22 Seán Sheehan to Department of Defence in military service pension application of Frank Carney (IMA, MSPC, 28APB560).
23 James J. Smyth (BMH WS 559, p. 2).
24 Pension application of Cissie McGovern (IMA, MSPC, MSP34REF47744).
25 *Belfast Telegraph*, 5 May 1920.
26 Sheehan to Department of Defence in military service pension application of Frank Carney (IMA, MSPC, 28APB560).
27 Ibid.
28 Charles Townshend, 'The Irish Republican Army and the development of guerrilla warfare, 1916–19', *English Historical Review*, 94:371 (1971), 329.
29 Grant, *Derry*, p. 104; Travers, *Donegal*, p. 106.
30 Livingstone, *Fermanagh*, p. 286.

31 Francis Tummon (BMH WS 820, p. 10).
32 Ibid.
33 John Connolly (BMH WS 598, p. 7).
34 Francis Tummon (BMH WS 820, pp 10–13).
35 Livingstone, *Fermanagh*, p. 287.
36 Townshend, 'The IRA', 322.
37 James J. Smyth (BMH WS 559, pp 4–5).
38 John Connolly (BMH WS 598, p. 1).
39 *Anglo-Celt*, 20 Mar. 1920.
40 Ibid., 28 Feb. 1920.
41 McCluskey, *Tyrone*, pp 71–4; Dooley, *Monaghan*, pp 87–9.
42 *FH*, 4 Jan. 1919.
43 Ibid., 2 Aug. 1919.
44 Ibid., 16 Aug. 1919.
45 'Summary of destruction of Income Tax offices in Fermanagh' (IMA, Brigade activity reports, MA/MSPC/A/71).
46 Ibid.
47 Livingstone, *Fermanagh*, p. 288; 'Summary of attack on Belleek barracks' (IMA, Brigade activity reports, MA/MSPC/A/71).
48 James J Smyth (BMH WS 559, p. 4).
49 Livingstone, *Fermanagh*, p. 289.
50 Joseph Murray (BMH WS 1566, pp 14–16); 'Summary of attack on Belleek barracks' (IMA, Brigade activity reports, MA/MSPC/A/71).
51 'Summary of attack on Belleek barracks' (IMA, Brigade activity reports, MA/MSPC/A/71); O'Halpin & Ó Corráin, *Dead of the Irish Revolution*, pp 201–2.
52 Livingstone, *Fermanagh*, p. 289.
53 Pension application of Cissie McGovern (IMA, MSPC, MSP34REF47744).
54 *IR*, 10 June 1920; *Skibbereen Eagle*, 12 June 1920; *FT*, 17 June 1920.
55 Arthur Hezlet, *The 'B' Specials: a history of the Ulster Special Constabulary* (London, 1972), p. 17; *Ulster Herald*, 6 Nov. 1920; *IR*, 10 June 1920.
56 James J. Smyth (BMH WS 559, pp 2–3).
57 Ibid., p. 3.
58 Hezlet, *'B' Specials*, pp 16–17.
59 *IR*, 10 June 1920.
60 Brian Barton, 'Sir Basil Brooke' in Jack Johnston (ed.), *The Brookeborough story: Aghalun in Aghavea* (Brookeborough, 2004), p. 47.
61 Hezlet, *'B' Specials*, pp 16–17.
62 Michael Farrell, *Arming the Protestants: the formation of the Ulster Special Constabulary and the Royal Ulster Constabulary, 1920–7* (Belfast, 1983), p. 13.
63 Viscountess Brookeborough to General Macready, July 1920 (PRONI, Brookeborough papers, D3004/C/2).
64 Mervyn Dane, *The Fermanagh 'B' Specials* (Enniskillen, 1970), p. 4.
65 Barton, *Brookeborough*, p. 33.
66 Dane, *Fermanagh 'B' Specials*, p. 4.
67 Barton, *Brookeborough*, p. 32.
68 Cormac Moore, *The border: the impact of partition in Ireland* (Dublin, 2019), p. 30.
69 Correspondence on Fermanagh Vigilance Force, 1920 (PRONI, Ernest Clark papers, D1022/2/3).
70 Dane, *Fermanagh 'B' Specials*, p. 4.

71 Ibid.
72 'Summary of activities in Fermanagh 1920–1921' (IMA, Brigade activity reports, MSPC/ A/71).
73 *IR*, 19 Sept. 1920.
74 Ibid., 9 Dec. 1920.
75 Francis Tummon (BMH WS 820, p. 14).
76 James J. Smyth (BMH WS 559, pp 4–5).
77 *IR*, 10 June 1920.
78 Ibid., 30 Sept. 1920.
79 CI Fermanagh, June 1920 (TNA, CO 904/112).
80 *IR*, 10 June 1920, 1 July 1920.
81 *FH*, 9 Oct. 1920.
82 Dane, *Fermanagh 'B' Specials*, pp 30–2.
83 James J. Smyth (BMH WS 559, pp 4–6); *IR*, 25 Nov. 1920.
84 Livingstone, *Fermanagh*, p. 238.
85 'Summary of attack on Belleek barracks' (IMA, Brigade activity reports, MSPC/A/71); O'Halpin & Ó Corráin, *Dead of the Irish Revolution*, pp 201–2.
86 CI Fermanagh, Oct. 1920 (TNA, CO 904/113).
87 *IR*, 16 Sept. 1920.
88 Ibid., 18 Nov. 1920.
89 Ibid., 25 Nov. 1920.
90 Ibid., 30 Sept. 1920.
91 James J. Smyth (BMH WS 559, pp 5–6).
92 Eunan O'Halpin, 'Price, Ivon Henry', *DIB*.
93 CI Fermanagh, Oct. 1920 (TNA, CO 904/113).
94 Ibid., Jan. 1920 (TNA, CO 904/111).
95 Francis Tummon (BMH WS 820, p. 27).
96 Ibid., pp 27–8.
97 Cahir Healy, 'First Republican courts in North' (PRONI, Cahir Healy papers, D2991/C/3).
98 Dáil Éireann Publicity Department, 'Map showing Irish towns and villages wholly or partly wrecked by English forces from Sept. 9th, 1919 to March 1st, 1921' (UCDA, p. 0150-1336).
99 Francis Tummon (BMH WS 820, p. 25).
100 Hezlet, *'B' Specials*, p. 21.
101 *BN*, 17 Nov. 1920.
102 Dane, *Fermanagh 'B' Specials*, p. 4.
103 Barton, *Brookeborough*, p. 35.
104 Moore, *The border*, pp 84–5.
105 Barton, *Brookeborough*, p. 39.
106 Dane, *Fermanagh 'B' Specials*, p. 5.
107 Barton, 'Basil Brooke', p. 48.
108 Barton, *Brookeborough*, p. 43.
109 McCluskey, *Tyrone*, pp 93–5.
110 Hezlet, *'B' Specials*, p. 22.
111 Ibid., p. 21.
112 Ibid., p. 19.
113 *BN*, 8 Dec. 1920.
114 *IT*, 13 Dec. 1920.
115 Brooke to Fermanagh USC, 23 Nov. 1920 (PRONI, Falls and Hanna papers, D1390/19).
116 *FT*, 2 Dec. 1920.
117 McCluskey, *Tyrone*, p. 99.

118 *IR*, 23 Dec. 1920.
119 *FT*, 30 June 1921.
120 Livingstone, *Fermanagh*, p. 311.
121 Nicholas Smyth (BMH WS 721, pp 24–5).
122 Livingstone, *Fermanagh*, p. 301.
123 Ibid., p. 280.
124 *IR*, 23 Dec. 1920.
125 *FH*, 25 Dec. 1920.
126 *IR*, 6 Jan. 1921.
127 *IT*, 25 Jan. 1921; O'Halpin & Ó Corráin, *Dead of the Irish Revolution*, p. 279.
128 Hezlet, *'B' Specials*, p. 30.
129 *BN*, 26 Jan. 1921; *II*, 25 Jan. 1921.
130 CI Fermanagh, Oct. 1920 (TNA, CO 904/113).
131 Ibid., Dec. 1920.
132 Quinn, 'Labouring on the margins', 58.
133 Quinn lists the initial representatives as the Irish National Teachers' Organisation, the
     Discharged Soldiers' and Sailors' Federation, the National Union of Railwaymen, the
     Drapers' Assistants Association, the Co-operative Society, the Typographical Association, the
     Postal Telegraph Society, the Postmen's Federation, the NAUL, the National Union of Life
     Assurance Agents, and the Amalgamated Society of Tailors and Tailoresses. These were later
     joined by the Amalgamated Society of Woodworkers, the Manchester Unity Operative
     Bricklayers, and the House and Ship Painters' Association of Manchester.
134 Quinn, 'Labouring on the margins', 59.
135 *FH*, 20 Dec. 1919.
136 Quinn, 'Labouring on the margins', 60.
137 *FH*, 5 Nov. 1921.
138 Ibid.
139 *FT*, 29 Jan. 1920.
140 *FH*, 5 Nov. 1921.
141 *FT*, 29 Jan. 1920.
142 Ibid.
143 Charlie McGuire, 'Socialist political thinking in revolutionary Ireland, 1912–1923', *Socialist
     History*, 55 (2019), 62.
144 Quinn, 'Labouring on the margins', 61.
145 Ibid.
146 Grant, *Derry*, pp 94–5.
147 Correspondence with UUC secretary, including letters of resignation, May 1920 (PRONI,
     UUC papers, D1327/18/30).
148 *FT*, 20 Mar. 1920; Delegates extracted from UUC annual reports (PRONI, J. Milne Barbour
     papers, D972/17).
149 *FT*, 25 May 1920.
150 Representation on behalf of the three counties, Apr. 1920 (PRONI, UUC papers,
     D1327/18/28).
151 Correspondence with UUC secretary, including letters of resignation, May 1920 (PRONI,
     UUC papers, D1327/18/30).
152 *IR*, 17 Aug. 1922.
153 *FT*, 10 Nov. 1921.
154 Ibid., 22 Apr. 1920.
155 Doran to Dawson Bates, Apr. 1920 (PRONI, UUC papers, D1327/18/28).
156 Ibid., 9 Dec. 1920.

157 *FT*, 22 Apr. 1922.
158 Ibid., 28 Nov. 1918.
159 James Loughlin, 'Creating "A social and geographical fact": regional identity and the Ulster question, 1880s–1920s', *Past and Present*, 195 (May 2007), 159–60.
160 *IR*, 9 Dec. 1920.
161 Ibid., 27 June 1918.
162 *FT*, 27 Jan. 1921.
163 *IR*, 9 Dec. 1920.
164 Ibid., 4 July 1919.
165 *FT*, 8 Sept. 1921.
166 *IR*, 24 Nov. 1921.
167 *FH*, 21 Feb. 1920.
168 *IR*, 15 Jan. 1920.
169 *FH*, 10 Jan. 1920.
170 *IR*, 15 Jan. 1920.
171 *FH*, 1 Jan. 1920.
172 Ibid.
173 *FH*, 29 May 1920.
174 *IR*, 15 Jan. 1920.
175 Ibid.
176 *FT*, 29 Jan. 1920.
177 *FH*, 7 Feb. 1920.
178 Ibid., 24 Jan. 1920.
179 *BN*, 11 June 1920.
180 Ibid., 5 June 1920.
181 *IR*, 24 June 1920.
182 *BN*, 5, 11 June 1920; *IR*, 3, 24 June 1920.
183 *IR*, 10 June 1920.
184 *FH*, 12 June 1920.
185 *IR*, 24 June 1920.
186 *FH*, 26 June 1920.
187 Ibid.
188 Ibid.
189 *IT*, 15 Nov. 1920.
190 Augusteijn, *Public defiance*, p. 303.
191 *FH*, 11 Sept. 1920.
192 *Ulster Herald*, 6 Mar. 1920.
193 *BN*, 3 Mar. 1920.
194 *FH*, 28 Feb. 1920.
195 Ibid., 24 Dec. 1921; *IR*, 24 June 1920.
196 *IR*, 24 June 1920.
197 *FH*, 12 July 1919.
198 Ibid.
199 *Anglo-Celt*, 22 May 1920.
200 *FH*, 2 Aug. 1919.
201 *FJ*, 18 Sept. 1919.
202 *FH*, 11 Dec. 1920.
203 *IR*, 2 Nov. 1921.
204 Ibid.
205 *Northern Standard*, 2 Dec. 1920.

206 *IR*, 9 Aug. 1921.
207 Ibid., 2 Aug. 1921.
208 Livingstone, *Fermanagh*, p. 312.
209 *IR*, 18 Aug. 1921. The members were James McCorry, John Cassidy, John McLoughlin, Cahir Healy and James McGrath. McHugh the chairman did not sign.
210 *IR*, 25 Aug. 1921.
211 Livingstone, *Fermanagh*, p. 312.

CHAPTER SIX *'A unionist coup': Fermanagh and the Treaty in 1921*

1 As with many cases in Northern Ireland, the divisions between the Catholic and Protestant communities in Roslea were pronounced enough to even manifest themselves in placenames. The case of Roslea is particularly egregious given the miniscule differences insisted upon as the terms of distinction. Roslea can be categorized as the Catholic spelling of the name while the addition of an s transforms the place to a very Protestant Rosslea. When writing about the place here we shall use Roslea, primarily because of its predominance across the sources consulted. See also Cooneen or Coonian, Ederney or Ederny, Aghadrumsee or Adrumsee and Bellanaleck or Belnaleck.
2 CI Fermanagh, Jan. 1921 (TNA, CO 904/114).
3 Ibid., Feb. 1921 (ibid.).
4 Hezlet, *'B' Specials*, p. 25.
5 Ibid., p. 24.
6 Ibid., p. 25.
7 Ibid., p. 26.
8 *Northern Standard*, 25 Feb. 1921; *IR*, 24 Feb. 1921.
9 *FT*, 24 Feb. 1921.
10 CI Fermanagh, Aug. 1921 (TNA, CO 904/116).
11 Ibid.
12 Patrick McMeel (BMH WS 520, pp 5–6); John McKenna (BMH WS 552, pp 9–10).
13 John Connolly (BMH WS 598, pp 2–3).
14 *Northern Standard*, 25 Feb. 1921.
15 *IT*, 24 Feb. 1921.
16 *IR*, 24 Feb. 1921; George Lunt, 'Family life on the Fermanagh–Monaghan border', https://www.borderroadmemories.com/search-border-crossings/memories/family-life-on-the-fermanagh-monaghan-border/ (accessed 25 Jan. 2018).
17 James Mulligan copybook (Monaghan County Museum, Marron papers).
18 Ibid.; *II*, 28 Apr. 1921.
19 *II*, 23 Feb. 1921.
20 *IR*, 7 July 1921.
21 *Northern Standard*, 25 Feb. 1921.
22 John Connolly (BMH WS 598, p. 4).
23 *II*, 23 Feb. 1921.
24 Ibid., 28 Apr. 1921.
25 *Northern Standard*, 25 Feb. 1921; *IR*, 24 Feb. 1921.
26 *IR*, 24 Feb. 1921.
27 *FT*, 24 Feb. 1921.
28 John Connolly (BMH WS 598, pp 4–5).
29 James McKenna (BMH WS 1028, pp 10–11).
30 John Connolly (BMH WS 598, pp 4–5); James McKenna (BMH WS 1028, pp 11–13).
31 James McKenna (BMH WS 1028, p. 10).

32 Ibid., p. 11.
33 Tim Wilson, 'The strange death of loyalist Monaghan' in Senia Paseta (ed.), *Uncertain futures: essays about the Irish past for Roy Foster* (Oxford, 2016), p. 184.
34 Philip Marron (BMH WS 657, p. 8).
35 James McKenna (BMH WS 1028, p. 10).
36 Pension application of Mary McGurk (IMA, MSPC, MSP34REF60384).
37 Wilson, 'Strange death', p. 184; Patrick McMeel (BMH WS 520, pp 7–8).
38 Statement of James McKenna (Monaghan County Museum, Marron papers); the raid is also recounted in Patrick McMeel (BMH WS 520, pp 7–8). The man is likely to have been William Leary of Kilcorran in Monaghan, an Anglican farmer with three sons, who would have been 57 at the time.
39 Ibid.
40 Philip Marron (BMH WS 657, p. 8); Statement of James McKenna (Monaghan County Museum, Marron papers).
41 Philip Marron (BMH WS 657, p. 10); *IR*, 24 Mar. 1921.
42 *Anglo-Celt*, 2 Apr. 1921.
43 George Lunt, 'Family life'.
44 CI Fermanagh, Mar. 1921 (TNA, CO 904/114).
45 George Lunt, 'Family life'.
46 CI Fermanagh, Feb. 1921 (TNA, CO 904/114).
47 *Anglo-Celt*, 2 Apr. 1921.
48 Statement of Harry Macklin (Monaghan County Museum, Marron papers).
49 *Anglo-Celt*, 2 Apr. 1921; *FH*, 26 Mar. 1921.
50 *FH*, 26 Mar. 1921.
51 Ibid.
52 John Connolly (BMH WS 598, p. 6).
53 *Anglo-Celt*, 2 Apr. 1921.
54 Ibid., 26 Mar. 1921.
55 *FT*, 24 Mar. 1921; *Anglo-Celt*, 26 Mar. 1921.
56 *Anglo-Celt*, 2 Apr. 1921.
57 George Lunt, 'Family life'.
58 *Northern Standard*, 22 Apr. 1921.
59 *Anglo-Celt*, 11 Aug. 1921.
60 CI Fermanagh, Mar. 1921 (TNA, CO 904/114).
61 Ibid.
62 O'Halpin & Ó Corráin, *Dead of the Irish Revolution*, p. 353.
63 *FH*, 9 Apr. 1921.
64 *Northern Standard*, 10 June 1921.
65 *IR*, 30 Mar. 1921.
66 Ibid., 4 May 1922.
67 *IR*, 4 May 1922.
68 Ibid., 12 May 1921.
69 Ibid.
70 James J. Smyth (BMH WS 559, pp 5–6).
71 Paul Bew, *Ideology and the Irish question: Ulster unionism and nationalism, 1912–16* (Oxford, 1994), pp 32–5.
72 Terence Dooley, 'From the Belfast boycott to the Boundary Commission: fears and hopes in County Monaghan, 1920–26', *Clogher Record*, 15:1 (1994), 91.
73 Gemma Clark, *Everyday violence in the Irish Civil War* (Cambridge, 2014), pp 45–6.
74 Dooley, *Monaghan*, p. 96.

75 *FH*, 18 Sept. 1920.

76 *IR*, 23 Sept. 1920.

77 *FH*, 11 Nov. 1920.

78 Dooley, *Monaghan*, pp 96–8.

79 John Connolly (BMH WS 598, p. 2).

80 Livingstone, *Fermanagh*, p. 293.

81 Francis Tummon (BMH WS 820, p. 25).

82 Ibid., p. 27.

83 D.S. Johnson, 'The Belfast boycott, 1920–1922' in J.M. Goldstrom and L.A. Clarkson (eds), *Irish population, economy and society: essays in honour of the late K.H. Connell* (Oxford, 1982), p. 190.

84 CI Fermanagh, Aug. 1921 (TNA, CO 904/116).

85 Ibid., Sept. 1921 (ibid.).

86 *IR*, 8 Sept. 1921.

87 CI Fermanagh, June 1921 (TNA, CO 904/115).

88 *IR*, 11 Aug., 8 Sept. 1921.

89 Ibid., 11 Aug. 1921.

90 Ibid., 1 Dec., 8 Sept. 1921.

91 Donal Hall, *Louth: the Irish Revolution, 1912–23* (Dublin, 2019), p. 73.

92 Brian Hughes, *Defying the IRA: intimidation, coercion, and communities during the Irish Revolution* (Liverpool, 2019), p. 89.

93 Dooley, *Monaghan*, p. 97; McCluskey, *Tyrone*, pp 86–7.

94 *IR*, 11 Aug. 1921.

95 Ibid., 8 Sept. 1921.

96 Ibid., 11 Aug. 1921.

97 Ibid., 6 Oct. 1921.

98 Ibid., 17 Nov. 1921.

99 Ibid., 10 Nov. 1921.

100 Livingstone, *Fermanagh*, p. 295.

101 Barton, 'Basil Brooke', p. 42; Hezlet, *'B' Specials*, p. 31.

102 Dane, *Fermanagh 'B' Specials*, p. 26; Hezlet, *'B' Specials*, p. 31.

103 Barton, 'Basil Brooke', p. 42.

104 Barton, *Brookeborough*, p. 43.

105 CI Fermanagh, Mar. 1921 (TNA, CO 904/114).

106 Ibid.

107 CI Fermanagh, May 1921 (TNA, CO 904/115).

108 Ibid., June 1921 (ibid.).

109 Ibid.

110 *FH*, 18, 25 June 1921; *IR*, 16 June 1921.

111 Livingstone, *Fermanagh*, p. 295.

112 Ibid., p. 313.

113 *FH*, 5 Nov. 1921.

114 Livingstone, *Fermanagh*, p. 314.

115 *FH*, 5 Nov. 1921.

116 *FH*, 12 Nov. 1921.

117 *IR*, 9 Mar. 1922.

118 McCluskey, *Tyrone*, pp 102–3.

119 Grant, *Derry*, p. 116.

120 McCluskey, *Tyrone*, p. 102.

121 Robert Lynch, *Revolutionary Ireland, 1912–1925* (London, 2015), p. 97.

122 *IR*, 12 May 1921.
123 *FH*, 21 May 1921.
124 *FT*, 21 May 1921.
125 Ibid.
126 Livingstone, *Fermanagh*, p. 296.
127 *FH*, 4 June 1921.
128 Ibid., 18 June 1921.
129 Ibid., 5 Nov. 1921.
130 Ibid.
131 *FH*, 30 Apr. 1921.
132 *BN*, 30 May 1921.
133 *FT*, 2 June 1922.
134 Barton, *Brookeborough*, p. 39.
135 McCluskey, *Tyrone*, pp 104–7.
136 Livingstone, *Fermanagh*, p. 297.
137 Barton, *Brookeborough*, p. 44.
138 Farrel, *Arming the Protestants*, p. 62.
139 Hezlet, *'B' Specials*, p. 50.
140 McCluskey, *Tyrone*, p. 103.
141 Ibid.
142 Livingstone, *Fermanagh*, p. 296.
143 Hezlet, *'B' Specials*, p. 45.
144 McCluskey, *Tyrone*, p. 105.
145 NI cabinet minutes, 1 Dec. 1921 (PRONI, CAB/4/14/28).
146 Livingstone, *Fermanagh*, p. 297.
147 Moore, *The border*, p. 69.
148 Eoin MacNeill to de Valera, 1 Dec. 1921 (UCDA, Éamon de Valera papers, P150/1492).
149 McCluskey, *Tyrone*, p. 130.
150 *FJ*, 28 Dec. 1921.
151 Phoenix, 'Cahir Healy', 38.
152 *II*, 3 Jan. 1922.
153 Margaret O'Callaghan, 'Old parchment and water: the Boundary Commission of 1925 and the copperfastening of the Irish border', *Bullan: an Irish Studies Journal*, 5:2 (Nov. 2000), 33.
154 *FJ*, 28 Dec. 1921.
155 *Ulster Herald*, 13 Sept. 1923.
156 Phoenix, 'Cahir Healy', 38.
157 *FH*, 31 Dec. 1921.
158 *II*, 31 Dec. 1921.
159 Petitions from representative bodies in Fermanagh and Tyrone (NLI, Seán O'Mahony papers, MS 24,468).
160 Petition from Rossinure More SF club (ibid.).
161 Petition from Magheraveely SF club (ibid.).
162 *Dáil Éireann debates*, 4 Jan. 1922, vol. T, no. 11.
163 Petition from Arney SF club (NLI, O'Mahony papers, MS 24,468).
164 Éamon Phoenix, *Northern nationalism: nationalist politics, partition and the Catholic minority in Northern Ireland, 1890–1940* (Belfast, 1994), p. 163; McCluskey, *Tyrone*, pp 115–17.
165 White, 'Francis Carney'.
166 *Fearless but few*, p. 57.
167 James J. Smyth (BMH WS 559, p. 7).
168 Phoenix, *Northern nationalism*, p. 163.

169 Ibid., p. 164.
170 McCluskey, *Tyrone*, p. 113.

CHAPTER SEVEN *'Ulster is awake': the establishment of the northern state, 1922–3*

1   Travers, *Donegal*, pp 123–6.
2   Michael Hopkinson, 'The Craig-Collins pacts of 1922: two attempted reforms of the Northern Ireland government', *Irish Historical Studies*, 27:106 (Nov. 1990), 149; Michael Hopkinson, *Green against green: the Irish Civil War* (Dublin, 1988), p. 28.
3   Hezlet, *'B' Specials*, p. 51.
4   Robert Lynch, 'The Clones affray, 1922: massacre or invasion?', *History Ireland*, 12:3 (2004), 34.
5   Those arrested were Dan Hogan, Clones; James Brannagan, Monaghan; James McKenna, Clones; James Murphy, Clones; Thomas Quigley, Clones; Thomas Donnelly, Clones; James Winters, Clones; Edward O'Carroll, Clones; Thomas Mason, Carrickmacross; and P. McCrory, Glaslough. For a detailed account of the arrest see files relating to arrest of Monaghan footballers (PRONI, Cabinet files, CAB/6/34).
6   Files relating to the kidnapping of Specials by Enniskillen (PRONI, Home Office files, HA 5/166).
7   *FH*, 11 Feb. 1922.
8   James J. Smyth (BMH WS 559, pp 4–6); Nicholas Smyth (BMH WS 721, pp 19–20); Dane, *Fermanagh 'B' Specials*, p. 22.
9   Dane, *Fermanagh 'B' Specials*, p. 10.
10 *FH*, 29 Apr. 1922.
11 *IR*, 9 Feb. 1922.
12 Livingstone, *Fermanagh*, p. 305.
13 Dane, *Fermanagh 'B' Specials*, p. 10.
14 Peter Leary, *Unapproved routes: histories of the Irish border, 1922–1972* (Oxford, 2016), pp 7–9; Files relating to arrest of Monaghan footballers (PRONI, Cabinet files, CAB/6/34).
15 John Connolly (BMH WS 598, pp 8–9).
16 *Northern Standard*, 10 Feb. 1922.
17 Ibid.
18 John Connolly (BMH WS 598, pp 8–9).
19 Robert Lynch, *The Northern IRA and the early years of partition, 1920–1922* (Dublin, 2006), p. 53.
20 *IR*, 9 Feb. 1922.
21 Ibid.
22 Ibid., 16 Feb. 1922.
23 Dane, *Fermanagh 'B' Specials*, p. 5.
24 *FT*, 16 Feb. 1922.
25 *IR*, 16 Feb. 1922.
26 Barton, *Brookeborough*, p. 46.
27 Ibid., pp 46–7.
28 *IR*, 23 Feb. 1922.
29 Ibid., 11 Apr. 1922.
30 Dooley, *Monaghan*, p. 105.
31 Hezlet, *'B' Specials*, p. 53.
32 *FT*, 16 Feb. 1922; *IR*, 16 Feb. 1922.
33 *IR*, 13, 27 July 1922.
34 *Northern Standard*, 10 Feb. 1922.

35 *IR*, 9 Feb. 1922.
36 Ibid.
37 *FT*, 16 Feb. 1922.
38 Dane, *Fermanagh 'B' Specials*, p. 27.
39 Ibid.
40 *FH*, 1 Apr. 1922; *Ulster Herald*, 1 Apr. 1922.
41 *FH*, 25 Feb. 1922.
42 Ibid.
43 Livingstone, *Fermanagh*, p. 306.
44 *FH*, 18 Feb., 29 Apr. 1922; *FJ*, 16 Feb. 1922; *II*, 16 Feb. 1922.
45 Bernard Hughes application to the Irish Grants Committee (TNA, CO 762/178/16).
46 Hopkinson, 'The Craig–Collins pacts of 1922', 151.
47 Hopkinson, *Green against green*, p. 84.
48 Barton, *Brookeborough*, p. 48.
49 Farrell, *Arming the Protestants*, p. 64.
50 Hopkinson, 'The Craig–Collins pacts of 1922', 152.
51 *FH*, 28 Jan. 1922.
52 *IR*, 16 Feb. 1922.
53 *FH*, 28 Jan. 1922.
54 *II*, 4 May 1922.
55 *FJ*, 22 Mar. 1922; *IR*, 30 Mar., 22 June 1922.
56 *IR*, 3 Aug. 1922.
57 *FH*, 8 Apr. 1922.
58 *II*, 4 May 1922.
59 *FJ*, 22 Mar. 1922.
60 *FH*, 6 Oct. 1922.
61 Ibid., 24 June 1922.
62 *IR*, 4 Jan. 1923.
63 *FH*, 24 June 1922.
64 *Cork Examiner*, 3 May 1923.
65 *FH*, 24 June 1922.
66 *IR*, 4 Jan. 1923.
67 *FH*, 24 June 1922.
68 Ibid.
69 Report on Pettigo-Belleek (NAI, North Eastern Boundary Bureau files, TAOIS/NEBB/1/1/6).
70 *IR*, 8 Feb. 1923.
71 *FH*, 24 June 1922.
72 *IR*, 22 Aug. 1922.
73 *Cork Examiner*, 3 May 1923.
74 *FH*, 24 June 1922.
75 Ibid., 16 July 1921.
76 Dane, *Fermanagh 'B' Specials*, p. 22.
77 Hezlet, *'B' Specials*, p. 56.
78 Ibid., p. 57.
79 Dane, *Fermanagh 'B' Specials*, p. 5.
80 Liam Ó Duibhir, *Donegal & the Civil War: the untold story* (Cork, 2011), pp 87–8.
81 Dane, *Fermanagh 'B' Specials*, p. 19.
82 Barton, *Brookeborough*, p. 49.
83 *IR*, 13 Apr. 1922.

84 Livingstone, *Fermanagh*, p. 307.
85 Ó Duibhir, *Donegal*, p. 89.
86 Tim Wilson, *Frontiers of violence: conflict and identity in Ulster and Upper Silesia, 1918–1922* (Oxford, 2010), p. 122.
87 Livingstone, *Fermanagh*, p. 307.
88 Hezlet, *'B' Specials*, p. 55.
89 Ibid., p. 82.
90 Ibid.
91 Dane, *Fermanagh 'B' Specials*, p. 28.
92 *IR*, 22 June 1922; *Northern Standard*, 23 June 1922.
93 'Bertie Kerr' in Tom Brady (ed.), *Borderlines: personal stories and experiences from the border counties* (Dublin, 2006), p. 55.
94 For examples see the cases of James Mullan, Emyvale (NAI, FIN/COMP/2/18/187); Patrick Fox, Tullynahattina (NAI, FIN/COMP/2/18/170); John McKenna, Emyvale (NAI, FIN/COMP/2/18/121), and Patrick Kerr, Emyvale (NAI, FIN/COMP/2/18/108). See also files relating to the death of Robert Scott (PRONI, Cabinet files, CAB 9B/42(7)/1).
95 *IR*, 6 Jan. 1921.
96 *Northern Standard*, 31 Mar. 1922.
97 Ibid., 24 Mar. 1922.
98 *IR*, 13 July, 15 June 1922.
99 Livingstone, *Fermanagh*, pp 308–9.
100 Ibid.; *FH*, 10 June 1922.
101 Nicholas Smyth (BMH WS 711, pp 1–2); Travers, *Donegal*, pp 123–4.
102 Barton, *Brookeborough*, p. 154.
103 Livingstone, *Fermanagh*, p. 308.
104 Hezlet, *'B' Specials*, p. 60.
105 Ibid.
106 Ellen J. McGrath pension application (IMA, MSPC, MSP34REF10260); Bridget Cleary pension application (IMA, MSPC, MSP34REF35152).
107 Hezlet, *'B' Specials*, p. 61.
108 Ibid.
109 Compensation claims for Pettigo–Belleek (PRONI, Cabinet files, CAB/9/W/1/1).
110 Farrell, *Arming the Protestants*, p. 133.
111 Hezlet, *'B' Specials*, p. 61.
112 Farrell, *Arming the Protestants*, p. 133.
113 Ibid.
114 Travers, *Donegal*, pp 125–6.
115 Livingstone, *Fermanagh*, p. 310.
116 *FT*, 25 Jan. 1923.
117 Ibid., 31 Aug. 1922.
118 *Donegal Democrat*, 8 Sept. 1922; *BN*, 14 Dec. 1922; *IR*, 14 Dec. 1922.
119 *IR*, 15 June 1922.
120 *BN*, 21 May 1922.
121 *IR*, 15 June 1922.
122 *FT*, 8 June 1922.
123 *IR*, 15 June 1922.
124 *FH*, 11 June 1922.
125 Report on Pettigo–Belleek (NAI, North Eastern Boundary Bureau files, TAOIS/NEBB/1/1/6).
126 *Ulster Herald*, 10 June 1922.
127 *IR*, 22 Dec. 1922.

128 *FT*, 25 Jan. 1923.
129 Ibid., 11 Jan. 1923.
130 *IR*, 1 June 1922.
131 *FT*, 8 June 1922.
132 *IR*, 8 June 1922.
133 Ibid., 1 June 1922.
134 *IR*, 15 June 1922.
135 Ibid., 15 June 1922.
136 Ibid.
137 *IR*, 8 June 1922.
138 Ibid., 15 June 1922.
139 *FT*, 20 June 1922.
140 Barton, *Brookeborough*, p. 49.
141 Farrell, *Arming the Protestants*, p. 196.
142 Barton, *Brookeborough*, p. 52.
143 Ibid.
144 Hezlet, *'B' Specials*, p. 60.
145 Farrell, *Arming the Protestants*, p. 111.
146 Hezlet, *'B' Specials*, p. 80.
147 *IR*, 9 and 16 Mar. 1922; *Northern Standard*, 10 Mar. 1922.
148 Barton, *Brookeborough*, p. 46.
149 *Northern Standard*, 10 Mar. 1922.
150 Livingstone, *Fermanagh*, p. 300.
151 John Furniss Potter, *A testimony to courage: the regimental history of the Ulster Defence Regiment, 1969–1992* (London, 2001), p. 5.
152 Livingstone, *Fermanagh*, p. 300.
153 Dane, *Fermanagh 'B' Specials*, p. 5.
154 *IR,* 14 Dec. 1922.
155 Ibid., 26 May 1921, 29 June 1922, 4 Jan. 1923; for examples in the *FT* see 16 Feb. 1923, 29 June 1922.
156 *FT,* 20 Apr., 4 May 1922.
157 *IR*, 6 July 1922.
158 *FT*, 9 Mar. 1922. These are selected lines only; the full poem is 40 lines.
159 *FH*, 24 June 1922.
160 Quinn, *Labouring beside Lough Erne*, p. 34.
161 *FH*, 16 Sept. 1922.
162 Ibid., 23 Sept. 1922.
163 *IR*, 22 Jan. 1922.
164 Livingstone, *Fermanagh*, p. 311.
165 *FH*, 31 Dec. 1921.
166 Ibid., 4 Feb. 1922.
167 *FH*, 31 Dec. 1921; Livingstone, *Fermanagh*, p. 312.
168 *FH*, 7 Jan. 1922; *IR*, 5 Jan. 1922.
169 *FH*, 7 Jan. 1922.
170 *IR*, 5 Jan. 1922.
171 Ibid., 22 June 1922.
172 *FH*, 1 July 1922; *IR*, 8 Feb. 1923.
173 *FH*, 10 Feb. 1923.
174 Quinn, *Labouring beside Lough Erne*, p. 37.
175 Ibid., p. 38.

176 *FH*, 19 Feb. 1922.
177 Quinn, *Labouring beside Lough Erne*, p. 38.
178 *FH*, 19 Feb. 1922.
179 Ibid., 28 Jan. 1922.
180 *FH*, 28 Jan. 1922.
181 Quinn, *Labouring beside Lough Erne*, p. 38.
182 Ibid.
183 *FH*, 27 Jan. 1923.
184 Quinn, *Labouring beside Lough Erne*, p. 39.
185 Ibid., p. 40.
186 Ibid., p. 41.
187 Ibid.
188 *IR*, 16 June 1921.
189 *Hansard (Commons)*, 8 Feb. 1922, vol. 150, col. 188.
190 Barton, *Brookeborough*, p. 49; Phoenix, 'Cahir Healy', 39–40.
191 Ibid.
192 Barton, *Brookeborough*, p. 49.
193 Phoenix, 'Cahir Healy', 39.
194 Livingstone, *Fermanagh*, p. 312.
195 Ibid., p. 315.
196 *IR*, 3 Nov. 1922.
197 Livingstone, *Fermanagh*, p. 315.
198 *Strabane Chronicle*, 25 Nov. 1922.
199 Research on 1923 Northern Ireland election (NAI, North Eastern Boundary Bureau files, TAOIS/NEBB/1/1/6).
200 Ibid.
201 *FH*, 25 Nov. 1922, 15 Dec. 1923.
202 Ibid., 15 Dec. 1923.
203 Research on 1923 Northern Ireland Election (NAI, North Eastern Boundary Bureau files, I TAOIS/NEBB/1/1/6).
204 *Derry Journal*, 7 Dec. 1923; *II*, 7 Dec. 1923; *FH*, 15 Dec. 1923.
205 Livingstone, *Fermanagh*, pp 299–300.
206 Ibid.
207 *FH*, 24 May 1924.
208 *FJ*, 7 Nov. 1923.
209 Ibid.; *Nenagh Guardian*, 10 Nov. 1923.
210 *FJ*, 7 Nov. 1923.
211 Farrell, *Arming the Protestants*, p. 197.
212 Barton, *Brookeborough*, p. 45.
213 *IR*, 13 Oct. 1923.
214 Dane, *Fermanagh "B" Specials*, p. 17.
215 Grant, *Derry*, p. 140.

CHAPTER EIGHT *Fermanagh in 1923 and beyond*

1 Travers, *Donegal*, p. 134.
2 Kieran J. Rankin, *The creation and consolidation of the Irish border*, IBIS working paper no. 48 (Belfast, 2005), p. 20.
3 Ibid.
4 Moore, *The border*, p. 126.

5   Paul Murray, 'Partition and the Irish Boundary Commission: a northern nationalist perspective', *Clogher Record* 18:2 (2004), 182–3.
6   Terence Dooley, 'Protestant migration from the Free State to Northern Ireland, 1920–25: a private census for Co. Fermanagh', *Clogher Record*, 15:3 3 (1996), 87–132.
7   Earl of Belmore evidence (TNA, Boundary Commission files, CAB 61/30).
8   William Cassidy statement, Fermanagh County Council evidence (TNA, Boundary Commission files, CAB 61/65).
9   Phoenix, 'Cahir Healy', p. 370.
10 Ibid.
11 Ibid., p. 371.
12 Geoffrey Hand (ed.), *Report of the Irish Boundary Commission* (Dublin, 1969), pp 106–7, 140–3.
13 Murray, 'Irish Boundary Commission', 185.
14 Phoenix, 'Cahir Healy', p. 370.
15 Ibid.
16 Marie Coleman, *The Irish Revolution, 1916–1923* (Abingdon, 2013), pp 98–9.
17 Phoenix, 'Cahir Healy', p. 372.
18 Ibid.
19 Jim Quinn, *Labouring beside Lough Erne*, pp 46–9.
20 Ibid.
21 Gerry McElroy, 'Archdale, Sir Edward Mervyn (1853–1943)', *DIB*.
22 John F. Harbinson, *The Ulster Unionist Party, 1882–1973: its development and organization* (Belfast, 1973), p. 205.
23 Brian Barton, 'Brooke, Basil Stanlake', *DIB*.
24 McCluskey, *Tyrone*, p. 113.
25 Petitions from representative bodies in Fermanagh and Tyrone (NLI, O'Mahony papers, MS 24,468).
26 McCluskey, *Tyrone*, pp 89–92; Travers, *Donegal*, pp 101–10.
27 CI Fermanagh, Dec. 1914 (TNA, CO 904/95); Francis O'Duffy (BMH WS 654, p. 3).
28 Townshend, 'The IRA', 329.
29 Jackson, *Ireland, 1798–1998*, pp 233–4.
30 Rankin, *Creation and consolidation*, pp 15–18.
31 Livingstone, *Fermanagh*, p. 273.
32 Murray, 'Irish Boundary Commission', 185–9.
33 McCluskey, *Tyrone*, p. 130.
34 Fr Eugene Coyle to Ernest Blythe, 15 Sept. 1925 (UCDA, Ernest Blythe papers, P24/49).

Select bibliography

PRIMARY SOURCES

A. MANUSCRIPTS

Belfast
Public Records Office of Northern Ireland
Brookeborough papers
Cabinet papers
Cahir Healy papers
Carson papers
Sir Ernest Clark papers
Falls & Hanna papers
Irish Unionist Alliance papers
J. Milne Barbour papers
Ministry of Home Affairs papers
Ulster Solemn League and Covenant
Ulster Unionist Council papers

Dublin
Irish Military Archives
Bureau of Military History
Brigade activity reports
Michael Collins papers
Cumann na mBan nominal rolls
IRA nominal rolls
Military Service Pensions Collection

National Archives of Ireland
Chief Secretary's Office registered papers
Department of the Taoiseach files
Finance Compensation (post-truce) files
North Eastern Boundary Bureau records

National Library of Ireland
Maurice Moore papers
Seán O'Mahony papers
William Copeland Trimble papers

UCD Archives
Ernest Blythe papers
Éamon de Valera papers
Richard Mulcahy papers

London
National Archives, London
Boundary Commission papers
Cabinet Office papers
Colonial Office papers
Home Office papers
War Office papers

Monaghan
Monaghan County Museum
Fr Laurence Marron papers

B. OFFICIAL RECORDS

Census of Ireland 1901, 1911
Census of Ireland (Reports) 1926
Census of Northern Ireland (Reports) 1926
Dáil Éireann, parliamentary debates
Hansard House of Commons parliamentary debates
Report on Recruitng in Ireland, 1914–16 (col. 8168)

C. NEWSPAPERS AND PERIODICALS

Anglo-Celt
An tÓglach
Belfast and Province of Ulster Directory
Belfast Newsletter
Belfast Telegraph
Cork Examiner
Derry Journal
Donegal Democrat
Drogheda Independent
Fermanagh Herald
Fermanagh Times

Freeman's Journal
Impartial Reporter
Irish Independent
Irish Times
Nenagh Guardian
Northern Standard
Skibbereen Eagle
Strabane Chronicle
Thom's Directory
Ulster Herald

D. PRINTED PRIMARY MATERIAL

Hand, Geoffrey (ed.), *Report of the Irish Boundary Commission* (Dublin, 1969).
Irish Claims Compensation Association, *The campaign of fire. Facts for the public: a record of some mansions and houses destroyed, 1922–3* (Westminster, 1924).
Hajducki, S. Maxwell, *A railway atlas of Ireland* (Newton Abbott, 1974).
Mac Giolla Choille, Breandán, *Chief Secretary's Office Dublin Castle Intelligence notes, 1913–1916* (Dublin, 1966).

SECONDARY SOURCES

E. PUBLISHED WORKS

Augusteijn, Joost, *From public defiance to guerrilla warfare: the experience of ordinary volunteers in the Irish War of Independence* (Dublin, 1996).

Barton, Brian, *Brookeborough: the making of a prime minister* (Belfast, 1988).

——, 'Sir Basil Brooke' in Jack Johnston (ed.), *The Brookeborough story: Aghalun in Aghavea* (Brookeborough, 2004), pp 35–47

——, The origins and development of unionism in Fermanagh, 1885–1914' in Eileen M. Murphy & William J. Roulston (eds), *Fermanagh history and society: interdisciplinary essays on the history of an Irish county* (Dublin, 2004), pp 307–37.

Bell, Jonathan, 'Changing farming methods in County Fermanagh' in Murphy & Roulston (eds), *Fermanagh history and society*, pp 501–23.

Bew, Paul, *Ideology and the Irish question: Ulster unionism and nationalism, 1912–16* (Oxford, 1994).

Bowman, Timothy, 'The Ulster Volunteer Force and the formation of the 36th (Ulster) Division', *Irish Historical Studies*, 32:128 (Nov. 2001), 498–518.

——, *Carson's army: the Ulster Volunteer Force, 1910–22* (Manchester, 2007).

——, 'The North began: but when? The formation of the Ulster Volunteer Force', *History Ireland*, 21:2 (Mar.–Apr. 2013), 28–31.

——, William Butler & Michael Wheatley, *The disparity of sacrifice: Irish recruitment to the British armed forces, 1914–1918* (Oxford, 2020).

Brady, Tom (ed.), *Borderlines: personal stories and experiences from the border counties* (Dublin, 2006).

Chambers, George, 'The rise and fall of an indigenous industry: milk processing in County Fermanagh from the seventeenth century until the present day' in Murphy & Roulston (eds), *Fermanagh history and society*, pp 525–50.

Clark, Gemma, *Everyday violence in the Irish Civil War* (Cambridge, 2014).

Coleman, Marie, *The Irish Revolution, 1916–1923* (Abingdon, 2013).

Connell, Joseph, 'Founding of the Irish Volunteers', *History Ireland*, 21:6 (Nov.–Dec. 2013), 66.

Dane, Mervyn, *The Fermanagh 'B' Specials* (Enniskillen, 1970).

Dooley, Terence, 'From the Belfast boycott to the Boundary Commission: fears and hopes in County Monaghan, 1920–26', *Clogher Record*, 15:1 (1994), 90–106.

——, 'Protestant migration from the Free State to Northern Ireland, 1920– 25: a private census for Co. Fermanagh', *Clogher Record*, 15:3 (1996), 87–132.

——, 'The organization of Unionist opposition to home rule in Counties Monaghan, Cavan and Donegal, 1885–1914', *Clogher Record*, 16:1 (1997), 46–70.

——, 'County Monaghan, 1914–1918: recruitment, the rise of Sinn Féin and the Partition Crisis', *Clogher Record*, 16:2 (1998), 144–58.

——, *The plight of Monaghan Protestants, 1912–26* (Dublin, 2000).

——, *Monaghan: the Irish Revolution, 1912–23* (Dublin, 2017).

Farrell, Michael, *Northern Ireland: the Orange state* (London, 1976).

——, *Arming the Protestants: the formation of the Ulster Special Constabulary and the Royal Ulster Constabulary, 1920–7* (Belfast, 1983).

Fermanagh 1916 Centenary Association, *Fearless but few: Fermanagh and the Easter Rising* (Castleblayney, 2015).

Fitzpatrick, David, 'The geography of Irish nationalism 1910–1921', *Past & Present*, 78 (1978), 113–44.

——, 'The logic of collective sacrifice: Ireland and the British army, 1914–1918', *Historical Journal*, 38:4 (1995), 1017–30.

——, *Descendancy: Irish Protestant histories since 1795* (Cambridge, 2014).

Gibbon, Peter, *The origins of Ulster unionism: the formation of popular Protestant politics and ideology in nineteenth-century Ireland* (Manchester, 1975).

Grant, Adrian, *Derry: the Irish Revolution, 1912–23* (Dublin, 2018).

Hall, Donal, *Louth: the Irish Revolution, 1912–23* (Dublin, 2019).

Harbinson, John F., *The Ulster Unionist Party, 1882–1973: its development and organization* (Belfast, 1973).

Hepburn, A.C., *Catholic Ireland and nationalist Belfast in the era of Joe Devlin, 1871–1934* (Oxford, 2008).

Hezlet, Arthur, *The 'B' Specials: a history of the Ulster Special Constabulary* (London, 1972).

Hopkinson, Michael, *Green against green: the Irish Civil War* (Dublin, 1988).

——, 'The Craig–Collins pacts of 1922: two attempted reforms of the Northern Ireland government', *Irish Historical Studies*, 27:106 (Nov. 1990), 145–58.

——, *The Irish War of Independence* (Dublin, 2002).

Hughes, Brian, *Defying the IRA? Intimidation, coercion, and communities during the Irish Revolution* (Liverpool, 2016).

Jackson, Alvin, *The Ulster Party: Irish Unionists in the House of Commons, 1884–1911* (Oxford, 1989).

——, 'Unionist myths, 1912–85', *Past and Present*, 136 (Aug. 1992), 164–85.

——, *Ireland, 1798–1998: war, peace and beyond* (Oxford, 1999).

——, '"Tame Tory hacks"? The Ulster Party at Westminster, 1922–72', *Historical Journal*, 54:2 (2011), 453–75.

Johnson, D.S., 'The Belfast boycott 1920–1922' in J.M. Goldstrom & L.A. Clarkson (eds), *Irish population, economy and society: essays in honour of the late K.H. Connell* (Oxford, 1982), pp 287–307.

Johnston, Jack (ed.), *The Brookeborough story: Aghalun in Aghavea* (Brookeborough, 2004).

Laffan, Michael, *The partition of Ireland* (Dublin, 1983).

——, *The resurrection of Ireland: the Sinn Féin party, 1916–1923* (Cambridge, 1999).

Leary, Peter, *Unapproved routes: histories of the Irish border, 1922–1972* (Oxford, 2016).

Livingstone, Peadar, *Cuimhneachain Mhuineachain, 1916–1966* (Enniskillen, 1966).

——, *The Fermanagh story* (Enniskillen, 1969).

——, *The Monaghan story* (Enniskillen, 1979).

Loughlin James, 'Creating "A social and geographical fact": regional identity and the Ulster question, 1880s–1920s', *Past and Present*, 195 (May 2007), 159–96.

Lynch, Robert, 'The Clones affray, 1922: massacre or invasion?', *History Ireland*, 12:3 (2004), 33–7.

——, *The Northern IRA and the early years of partition, 1920–1922* (Dublin, 2006).

——, *Revolutionary Ireland, 1912–1925* (London, 2015).

McCluskey, Fergal, 'Unionist ideology in Tyrone, 1911–1924', *Clogher Record*, 21:1 (2012), 65–89.

——, *Tyrone: the Irish Revolution, 1912–23* (Dublin, 2014).

McGuire, Charlie, 'Socialist political thinking in revolutionary Ireland, 1912–1923', *Socialist History*, 55 (2019), 47–68.

McGuire, James & James Quinn (eds), *Dictionary of Irish biography* (9 vols, Cambridge, 2009).

McMinn, Richard, Éamon Phoenix & Joanne Biggs, 'Jeremiah Jordan M.P. (1830–1911): Protestant home ruler or "Protestant renegade"'?, *Irish Historical Studies*, 36:143 (2009), 349–67.

McRoe, Malachy, '"Honest Pat" – Patrick Crumley DL, MP', *Clogher Record*, 20:3 (2011), 541–50.

Moore, Cormac, *The border: the impact of partition in Ireland* (Dublin, 2019).

Murphy, Eileen M. & William J. Roulston (eds), *Fermanagh history and society: interdisciplinary essays on the history of an Irish county* (Dublin, 2004).

Murray, Paul, 'Partition and the Irish Boundary Commission: a Northern nationalist perspective', *Clogher Record*, 18:2 (2004), 181–218.

——, *The Irish Boundary Commission and its origins, 1886–1925* (Dublin, 2011).

Newmann, Kate (ed.), *Dictionary of Ulster biography* (Belfast, 1993).

Ó Duibhir, Liam, *Donegal & the Civil War: the untold story* (Cork, 2011).

O'Callaghan, Margaret, 'Old parchment and water: the Boundary Commission of 1925 and the copperfastening of the Irish border', *Bullan: an Irish Studies Journal*, 5:2 (Nov. 2000), 27–55.

O'Day, Alan, *Irish home rule, 1871–1921* (Manchester, 1998).

O'Halpin, Eunan & Daithí Ó Corráin, *The dead of the Irish Revolution* (London & New Haven, 2020).

Phoenix, Éamon, *Northern nationalism: nationalist politics, partition and the Catholic minority in Northern Ireland, 1890–1940* (Belfast, 1994).

——, 'Cahir Healy (1877–1970): Northern nationalist leader', *Clogher Record*, 18:1 (2003), 32–52.

——, 'Cahir Healy and nationalist politics in Co. Fermanagh, 1885–1970' in Murphy & Roulston (eds), *Fermanagh history and society*, pp 357–86.

Potter, John Furniss, *A testimony to courage: the regimental history of the Ulster Defence Regiment, 1969–1992* (London, 2001).

Quinn, Jim, 'Labouring on the margins: trade union activity in Enniskillen, 1917–1923', *Saothar*, 15 (1990), 57–64.

——, *Labouring beside Lough Erne: a study of the Fermanagh Labour movement, 1826–1932* (Enniskillen, 2019).

Rankin, Kieran, *The creation and consolidation of the Irish border*, IBIS working paper no. 48 (Belfast, 2005).

——, 'The search for statutory Ulster', *History Ireland*, 17:3 (2009), 28–32.

Sagarra, Eda, *Kevin O'Shiel: Tyrone nationalist and Irish state-builder* (Dublin, 2013).

Savage, David W., 'The attempted home rule settlement of 1916', *Éire-Ireland*, 2:3 (1967), 132–45.

Thompson, Frank, 'The Land War in Fermanagh' in Murphy & Roulston (eds), *Fermanagh history and society*, pp 287–301.

Townshend, Charles, 'The Irish Republican Army and the development of guerrilla warfare, 1916–19', *English Historical Review*, 94:371 (1971), 318–45.

——, *Easter 1916: the Irish Rebellion* (Dublin, 2005).

Travers, Pauric, *Donegal: the Irish Revolution, 1912–23* (Dublin, 2022).

Urquhart, Diane (ed.), *The minutes of the Ulster Women's Unionist Council and executive committee, 1911–40* (Dublin, 2001).

Walker, Brian, *Parliamentary election results in Ireland, 1801–1922* (Dublin, 1978).

Walsh, Aisling, 'Michael Cardinal Logue, 1840–1924, part 2', *Seanchas Ardmhacha*, 18:1 (1999), 163–95.

Walsh, Fionnuala, *Irish women and the Great War* (Cambridge, 2020).

Ward, Alan J., 'Lloyd George and the 1918 Irish conscription crisis', *Historical Journal*, 17:1 (1974), 107–29.

Wilson, Tim, *Frontiers of violence: conflict and identity in Ulster and Upper Silesia, 1918–1922* (Oxford, 2010).

——, 'The strange death of loyalist Monaghan' in Senia Paseta (ed.), *Uncertain futures: essays about the Irish past for Roy Foster* (Oxford, 2016), pp 174–87.

F. THESES AND UNPUBLISHED WORK

Evans, Gary, 'The raising of the first internal Dáil Éireann loan and the British responses to it, 1919–21' (MLitt, Maynooth University, 2012).

Farrell, Gerard Michael, 'The Ulster Volunteer Force, 1912–4' (MA, NUI Maynooth, 2006).

Lynch, Robert, 'The Northern IRA and the early years of partition' (DPhil, University of Sterling, 2003).

G. ONLINE SOURCES

Find a grave; https://www.findagrave.com

George Lunt, 'Family life on the Fermanagh-Monaghan border', https://www.borderroadmemories.com

Irish Red Cross service records, https://vad.redcross.org.uk

Index

Abraham, Joseph, 119
Abraham, Robert, 23
abstention, 107, 115, 145, 146, 149
Achingham, George, 23
Agar-Robartes, Thomas, 18
Aghadrumsee, 26, 70
Aghafin, 99, 100
Aghavea, 122
Aiken, Frank, 98
All-for-Ireland League, 53
Allingham family, 117
An tÓglach, 65
Ancient Order of Hibernians (AOH), 5, 9, 16, 18, 26, 32, 38, 41, 46, 48
Anderson family, 69
Anderson, Albert, 129
Andrews, William, 100
Anglican, 1, 5, 21, 31, 41, 42, 49, 62, 128
Anglo-Celt, 54, 100
Anglo-Irish Treaty, 95, 110–16, 123, 124, 126, 127, 139, 142–5, 147–50; Article 12, 112, 115; support in Fermanagh, 139, 140
Antrim, County, 9, 19, 22, 36, 45, 60, 61, 84, 90, 137
Archdale (Archdall) family, 6, 22, 23
Archdale, Capel, 81
Archdale, Edward Mervyn, 6, 12, 13, 15, 16, 19, 31, 33, 35, 52, 57, 58, 60–2, 89, 90, 108, 110, 146, 149, 150, *plate 3*
Argenta, 137, 138
armistice, 58, 74
arms raids, 69, 70, 73, 96, 98, 100
Arney, 68, 70, 113
arson, 56, 70–3, 76, 78, 92, 95–100, 105, 120, 123, 128
Asquith, Herbert Henry, 14, 16, 28, 45, 47
Augusteijn, Joost, 38

Bailey, Patrick, 51
Ballinamallard, 1, 2, 4, 13, 25, 33, 51, 57, 61, 66, 77, 109, 120, 122, 123, 139

Ballybay, 41, 130
Ballytrain barracks, 56, 70
Barton, Brian, 6, 15, 22, 75, 76, 79, 126, 137, 140
Barton, Ffoliott Warren, 12
Barton, Robert, 77
Battersby, Thomas, 16
Beatty, Rowland, 98
Belcoo, 5, 15, 49, 48–50, 65, 68, 72, 76, 113, 123, 125, 144
Belfast and Province of Ulster Directory, 2
Belfast Convention, 40, 45–7
Belfast Telegraph, 33
Belfast, 4, 5, 25, 46–65, 70, 75–8, 82, 85–90, 100, 112, 126, 137–9, 147, 149
Belleek: porcelain, 2, *plate 18*; attack on barracks, 71–3, 76; Pettigo–Belleek affair, 116, 125–9, 131, 141, 148
Belmore, earls of, *see* Lowry-Corry family
Bigger, Francis Joseph, 17
Black, James, 122
Bloomfield, Constance, 24
Blythe, Ernest, 37, 41, 102
Boa Island, 66, 129
boards of guardians, 92, 146; Enniskillen, 16, 47, 51, 77, 83, 86, 88, 91, 106, 133–6; Ballyshannon, 106; Clones, 106; Lisnaskea, 106, 112, 133; Irvinestown, 106
Boho, 15, 22, 36, 42, 48, 67
Bonar Law, Andrew, 53, 141
border, 66, 95, 104; Cavan border, 1, 2, 20, 37, 69; Monaghan border, 2, 5, 73, 96, 97, 100, 102, 103, 125; Donegal border, 20, 26, 49, 125; cross-border raiding, 96, 116–18, 121, 124, 141; creation, 118, 130, 131, 142–5; cross-border firing, 124, 125, 127; Leitrim border, 125
Bowman, Timothy, 30, 31
boycotting, 15, 110, 134; Belfast boycott, 95, 96, 101–5, 116, 123

Boyd, Humphrey, 23
Bracken, William, 23
Bradley, Sam, 134
Breagho, 68
Breen, Philip, 74, 77
Britain, 15, 35, 52, 65, 144; British
    Empire, 80, 91
British army, 22, 30, 32, 35, 38, 51, 65, 68,
    99, 116, 127; Inniskilling Dragoons,
    23, 31, 40, *plate 12*; Ulster Division,
    31, 33; Royal Irish Rifles, 31; Royal
    Inniskilling Fusiliers, 31, 32, 68;
    Connaught Rangers, 32; Royal
    Dublin Fusiliers, 32, 44
British League for the Support of Ulster
    and the Union, 33
Brooke Family, 6, 22, 23
Brooke hotel, 68
Brooke, Basil, 6, 10, 20, 118, 123, 124,
    129–31, 141, 142, 146, 147, *plate 28*;
    'Fermanagh Vigilance', 74–6; UVF
    career, 79–81, 105, 110
Brooke, Cynthia, 75
Brookeborough, 4, 6, 20, 26, 76, 85, 140
Brookeborough, Lord, *see* Brooke, Basil
Brown Morrell, Henry, 24
Brown, William J., 59, 92, 134
Buck Island, 126
Bundoran, Co. Donegal, 4, 25, 72
Burns, Robert, 71
Butler, Major Hal, 79

Campling, Walter, 82, 83, 106, 132
Carlare, 105
Carlow, County, 37
Carney, Frank, 56, 66–9, 72, 73, 74, 82,
    83, 106, 114, 132, 134, 148, *plate 21*
Carngreen, 70, 76
Carraher, Dr John, 77
Carrickroe, 96
Carron, Anne, 97
Carson, Edward, 12, 13, 15, 18–21, 23, 27–
    31, 34, 45, 46, 49, 50, 76, 140, 149
Carson, F.R., 91, 92
Carson, Francis, 23
Carson, Ivan, 117

Carson, Michael, 139
Carty, Liam, 65
Carty, Seán, 65
Casement, Roger, 17
Cashel, Alice, 49
Cassidy, Peter, 113
Cassidy, Philip, 41–3
Cassidy, William (nationalist), 119
Cassidy, William (Unionist), 143
Castle Coole, 6
Castleblaney, 130
Castlesaunderson, 69, 125
Cathcart, Archibald, 12, 90
Catholic, 26, 27, 45, 58, 62, 63, 66, 87, 88,
    91–3, 100, 104, 106, 130, 136, 142–4,
    150; population profile, 1–5, 19;
    church and clergy, 9, 40, 46–8, 53,
    54, 59, 60, 70, 97, 101, 102; anti-
    Catholicism, 15, 33, 51, 52, 75–8, 80,
    81, 83–5, 98, 105, 107, 120–3, 147;
    enlistment, 34, 36
Caulfield, Fr Terence, 48, 53, 65, 113
Cavan, County, 1, 2, 9, 18–22, 36, 37, 42,
    67, 69, 73, 85, 92, 95, 106, 113, 123,
    124, 130, 131
Cavanacross, 26, 68
Ceannt, Éamonn, 41
Cecil, Lord Hugh, 19
Census (1911 Irish), 2–5, 144
Central Recruiting Committee, 33
chicanery, 60
Chittick, George, 119
Churchill, Winston, 127
Civil War, 114, 116, 128, 49, 56, 64, 67–
    94, 101, 103, 148
Clark, Gemma, 102
Clark, Sir Ernest, 79, 80, 102
Clarke, Samuel, 88
Clarke, Thomas, 42
Clarke, William, 53, 54, 82, 83, 107, 134,
    135
Cleghorn Hogg, David, 16
Clonaroo, 105
Clones, 2, 4–7, 31, 67, 81, 97, 100, 103,
    108, 111, 118, 125, 129, 131, 144,
    148; Clones affray, 118–21, 123, 124

Coa, 26, 68

Coalter, Robert, 105

Cole family, 6, 9, 22, 23; Cole, Lowry, 4th Earl, 8, 12, 19, 24; Cole, John Henry Michael, Viscount Cole, 79, 110; Cole, Lady Florence Mary, Lady Erne, 12, 13, 31

Colebrooke, 4, 6, 74

Collins, Michael, 65, 128, 107, 112, 114, 116, 120, 121, 137, 139, 141, 144

Collins–Craig pact, 116–17, 120–1, 137, 139

Collum, Arthur, 13

Collum, John, 33

Compston, Robert, 96

Congested Districts Board, 50

Connolly, Annie, 105

Connolly, Fr Peter, 65, 124

Connolly, Fr, 124

Connolly, Frank, 100

Connolly, James, 42

Connolly, John, 27, 37, 69, 96–8, 100, 117

Connolly, John, 27, 37, 70, 96, 97, 100, 117

conscription crisis, 52–5, 57, 58; Labour, 82, 83, 134; support for, 35, 38, 39

Conservative Party, 19, 47, 53

Convery, J.P., 47

Cooper census, 143

Cooper, James, 8, 12, 17, 59–61, 63, 81, 83, 84, 89–91, 103, 104, 107–9, 117, 121, 126, 135, 143; Cooper private census, 143

Coote, William, 57, 62, 107, 108, 118, 121

Cootehill, 130

Corrigan, Edmund, 86, 87, 106

Corrigan, Thomas, 93, 133, 137

Coulter, Thomas, 105

courthouse burnings, 70–1

Courtney, Francis, 68

Coyle, Fr Eugene, 112, 123, 140, 150

Craig, James, 12, 13, 15, 19, 30, 78, 79, 105, 110, 111, 116, 120, 121, 130, 137, 140

creameries, 3, 124

Crichton family, 6, 8; Crichton, John, 4th Earl, 6, 8, 12, 19, 22, 23

Crockett, Charles Love, 44

Crom, 5, 19, 22, 24, 25, 31

Crossmaglen, 96

Crozier, John, 46, 47, 51, 91

Crumley, Patrick, 16, 17, 32, 33, 35, 38, 44, 46, 51, 59, 60, 70, 71, 91, 92

Cullinan, Fr Patrick, 65, 113

Cullinan, Patrick, 65, 113

Cumann na mBan, 24, 48, 49, 68, 73, 75, 98, 126; pin badge, *plate 17*

Dáil loan, 65, 66

Dáil, 114–16, 133, 147

Dane, Richard, 7

D'Arcy-Irvine, C.C., 84

Davidson, John, 125

Dawson Bates, Richard, 85

de Valera, Eamon, 41, 42, 53, 107, 108, 111, 114, 139, 145

Dernawilt, 70

Derry, County, 4, 8

Derry Sentinel, 102

Derrybrusk, 74

Derrycormick, 42

Derryelvin, 78

Derrygonnelly, 26, 46, 49, 53, 82, 113, 122

Derrylin, 16, 20, 37, 40, 46, 68, 70, 113, 120, 144

Devenish West, 65, 109

Devlin, Joseph, 38, 46, 107, 145, 146

Dillon, John, 47, 53, 55

Dobbyn, Seamus, 37

Dobson, Thomas, 127

Dolan, Charles, 18

Donnelly, Alexander, 145

Donnelly, Patrick, 66

Donnelly, P.J., 71

Dooley, Terence, 14, 25, 45, 102

Doon Cross, 72

Doonan, Patrick, 105

Doran, Colonel Robert, 84, 85

Dougherty, William, 119

Douglas, James, 99, 100

Down, County, 9, 19, 22, 45, 59, 84, 140

drilling, 15, 19, 21, 22, 24, 26, 27, 38, 78, 110

Drugan, Patrick, 123
Drumavaughan, 120
Drumharvey, 119
Drummully, 126
Dublin, 11, 13, 20,25,26, 28, 40–6, 54, 59, 64
Duffy, Frank, 67
Duffy, Joseph, 41
Dundalk, 4, 41
Dundas, James, 15

Easter Rising, 18, 37, 40–4, 47–9, 51, 52, 59, 68, 78
elections: UK general elections (1885–6), 6; UK general election (1895), 9; UK general election (1906), 9, 13; UK general elections (1910), 9, 11–13; UK general election (1918), 40, 58–63, 64, 70, 71, 84, 147, 149; UK general election (1922), 138, 139, 147, 149; UK general election (1923), 138, 139; UK general election (1924), 145; NI general election (1921), 95, 107–10; NI general election (1925), 145; local elections (1914), 17, 149; local elections (1920), 64, 82–4, 86–90, 111; Derry City by-election (1912), 16; North Leitrim by-election (1908), 18; East Cavan by-election (1918), 49; South Longford by-election (1918), 50; South Armagh by-election (1918), 50
electoral violence, 61, 64, 138
Ely, marquesses of, *see* Loftus family
Enniskillen: ambulance kidnappings, 117, 118; boycott committee, 103, 104, East ward, 2, 52, 88; Labour Union, 53, 54; Model School, 41; North ward, 2, 88, 146; Orange Hall, *plate 14*; South ward, 2, 88; Trades and Labour Council, 82; town hall, *plate 9*
Enniskillen, earls of, *see* Cole family
Enniskillen Horse, 18, 19, 21–5, 29, 31, 34, 81, 148, *plate 11*
Erne, earls of, *see* Crichton family

Falls, Charles, 20, 31, *plate 6*
Farrell, Michael, 75
Feetham, Richard, 143, 144, 150
Fermanagh: Fermanagh militia tradition, 21, 74, 80; Fermanagh Recruiting Committee, 33, 34; Fermanagh Ladies Recruiting Committee, 34, 35; Fermanagh Women's Unionist Committee, 34; Fermanagh Vigilance, 74, 75, 76, 79, 148
Fermanagh County Council, 8, 16, 26, 27, 33, 52, 55, 58, 83–6, 88–90, 93, 95, 102, 106–9, 111–16, 133, 137–9, 143, 149–51; emergency committee, 89, 90; finance committee, 89
Fermanagh Herald, 5, 43, 47, 49, 55, 56, 80, 83, 88
Fermanagh Times, 5, 22, 32, 35, 61, 62, 63, 80, 83, 85
Fetherstonhaugh, Godfrey, 12, 13, 19, 20, 24, 33, 58, *plate 5*
Figgis, Darrell, 50
Finegan, Samuel, 97, 98
Finlay, John, 124
Finnegan, Matthew, 97
Finner Camp, 31, 34
First World War/Great War, 11, 29, 30, 32, 39, 58, 81, 86, 132
Fisher, J.R., 143
Fitzgerald, Seán, 66
Fitzpatrick, David, 14, 32
Fitzpatrick, Edward, 105, 123
Fitzpatrick, Frank, 70
Florencecourt, 5, 20, 24, 44, 79, 82, 89, 108, 109, 122, 137, 139
Flynn, James, 97
Forthill, 75
Free State, 118, 125–31, 137–40, 143–5, 148

GAA, 17, 18, 32, 49, 50
Gaelic League, 17, 18, 26, 28, 37, 41, 49
Gallagher, Alfonsus, 120
Gallagher, Daniel, 66
Gallagher, James, 66
Gallagher, Jane, 128

Gallagher, Michael, 66
Garrison, 3, 26, 49, 65, 112, 123, 126,
     131, 140, 144
Gavin, Thomas, 26
Geddis, Joseph, 106, 133
George V, 29, 93, 110, 128
German Plot, 56, 64
Germany, 32, 52, 56, 64
gerrymandering, 51, 109, 111, 109, 136,
     146, 150
Gillin, J.P., 17, 26, 33, 53, 55, 56, 58, 60,
     81, 88–90, 107, 108, 114, 133, 146
Gilmurray, Thomas, 51
Gilroy, Patrick, 122, 123
Glan Lower, 68
Glan Upper, 68
Glenawley, 23, 57
Glendenning, Billy, 74
Glengreen, 117
Godler, George, 105
Goodwin, J., 122
Gordon, Thomas, 88, 106
Gordon, William, 99–101
Government of Ireland Act, 95, 104, 107
Grant, Adrian, 20, 69, 141
Grant, F.W., 105
Gray, Edward, 68
Green, James, 122, 123
Greene, Owen, 41–43
Greenwood, Hamar, 76
Griffith, Arthur, 17, 48–50, 60, 108, 112–
     15, 139, 141, 144, *plate 19*

Hackett, James, 122, 123
Hall, Donal, 104
Hall, John, 105
Hanna, Samuel, 47, 48, 56, 78
Harbison, Thomas, 138, 145, 149
Harte, Patrick, 113
Healy, Cahir, 10, 37, 41, 65, 78, 117, 142,
     148, 149, *plate 4*; early years, 17, 18,
     55; local politics, 86, 89, 93, 102,
     104, 132; partition, 110, 140, 144–6;
     pro-treaty, 112–14; interment, 137,
     140; elections, 138, 145
Hegarty, William, 17, 37

Herbert, Dick, 61
Hewitt, Johnston, 131
Hezlett, Arthur, 81, 96
Hibernians, *see* Ancient Order of
     Hibernians (AOH)
Hobson, Bulmer, 26, 41
Hogan, Dan, 67, 114, 117, 148
Holywell, 20, 54
home rule, 11–21, 23, 25, 27–31, 35, 37,
     45, 47, 53, 56, 57, 63
Hopkinson, Michael, 66, 121
housing, 4, 82, 107, 146
Houston, Tommie, 70
Hughes, Bernard, 120, 121
Hughes, Brian, 104
Hughes, John (CI), 36
Hughes, John, 120
hunger strike, 68

Impartial Reporter, 5, 32, 43, 51, 52, 59,
     60, 69, 76, 80
Inglis bakery, 103
Innisrath, 79
internment, 114
Irish Anti-Conscription Committee, 53
Irish Citizen Army, 41, 42
Irish National Foresters, 53, 82
Irish Nation League, 47
Irish Parliamentary Party (IPP), 11, 13,
     14, 102, 107–9; pre-1912, 5–11;
     troubles post-Jordan, 16–18, 25, 26,
     29; Great War, 30, 32–7; republican
     opponents, 37, 38; post-1916, 40,
     45–61; perseverance, 64, 71, 84,
     86–92; Anglo-Irish Treaty, 112–14;
     post-partition, 138, 140, 145, 146,
     147–9
Irish Recruiting Council, 58
Irish Republican Army (IRA), 28, 37, 43,
     49, 64–82, 86, 92, 95–111, 114–29,
     134, 138, 139, 141, 148, 149; Roslea
     Company, 37, 67, 70, 98; Fermanagh
     IRA structure, 66–9; 1st Northern
     Division, 66, 68, 124, 144; 2nd
     Northern Division, 66, 96; 1st
     Monaghan Brigade, 66, 98, 103, 36,

Irish Republican Army (IRA), *(continued)*
  37, 42, 54, 68, 80, 81, 104, 105, 107,
  110, 111, 116, 124, 133–7; 1st
  Midland Division, 67; 2nd Tyrone
  Brigade, 66; GHQ, 66, 121;
  Lisnaskea Battalion, 67, 68, 72; 5th
  Northern Division, 67, 114, 117
Irish Republican Brotherhood (IRB), 17,
  18, 25, 26, 27, 28, 37, 38, 40, 41
Irish Transport and General Workers
  Union (ITGWU), 54, 83
Irish Unionist Alliance, 12
Irish Volunteers, 11, 25–7, 30, 32, 37–43,
  48, 49, 56–8, 65, 67, 68, 71–3, 76,
  103, 116, 148; Easter Rising, 40, 41
Irvine, George, 27, 28, 41–3, 49, 60, 61,
  70, 108, 114
Irvine, Georgina, 12
Irvine, Thomas, 112
Irvinestown, 2, 3, 6, 15, 20, 22, 25, 26, 31,
  37, 54, 66, 82, 104, 106, 119

Jackson, Alvin, 22, 148
Johnston, James, 32, 97
Johnston, John, 100
Jordan, Jeremiah, 2, 9, 14, 16, 61, 148,
  plate 2

Keenan, Bernard, 26, 82, 83, 106, 132, 134
Keenan, Edward, 81
Keenan, John, 53
Kelly, Francis, 119
Kelly, James, 132
Keown, John, 120
Kerr, Samuel, 13, 14
Kettle, Tom, 34–6
Kickham, Cathal, 26
Kiflosher, 68
Kilcorrin, 100
Killeyrover, 67, 68
Killanin, Lord (Martin Morris), 86
Killinagh, 68
Killyrover, 67, 68
Kilmainham, 42
Kiltylogher, 124
Kinawley, 26, 68, 104, 131

Kingarrow, 68
Kinturk, 117
Kitchener, 30
Knight, Michael, 101
Knocknagun, 67, 68
Knox, Francis William, 44

labour, 9, 53, 54; labourers, 4, 21, 23, 27,
  34, 35, 82, 104, 107, 136; pre-
  partition, 64, 81–3, 87–90, 106, 107;
  Labour Party, 82, 146; post-
  partition, 132–6, 141, 146, 147
Lack, 112
Lady of the Lake/HMS *Pandora*, 126,
  plate 26
Laffan, Michael, 18
Laird, Samuel, 117, 119
land agitation, 21, 48, 104, 123
Land and Labour League, 9
Larne gun-running, 25, 27, 74, 79, 148
Lawless, Joseph, 65
Leary, William, 100
Leitrim, County, 5, 18, 19, 26, 67, 73,
  104, 110, 125
Lendrum, Alan, 77
Leonard, Felix, 55, 56, 58
Leonard, Patrick, 50, 56, 58
Leslie, Colonel John, 33
Lester, George, 95–9, 149
Lester, Thomas, 96, 98, 100, 117, 118
Letterbreen, 42, 70, *plate 24*
Lewis, James, 119
Liberal Party, 11, 14, 16, 18
Liddle, George Edwin, 74
Lisbellaw, 2, 4, 24, 31, 57, 62, 70, 82, 139;
  battle of Lisbellaw, 73–7, 80; attack
  on Hughes Brothers, 119–21
Little, William, 105
Livingstone, Peadar, 42, 48, 65, 69, 92,
  102, 107, 112, 124
Lloyd George, David, 28, 45–7, 52, 53,
  57, 84, 116, 127, 142
Local Government Act 1898, 7
Local Government Board (LGB), 51, 87,
  90, 91, 92, 93, 109, 136
lockout, 42

Loftus family, 6
Londonderry, Lady, 25
Lough Erne Fishery Company, 2
Lough Erne, 1, 5, 6, 57, 85, 92, 125–7, 131
Loughkillygreen, 125
Loughlin, James, 85
Love, Michael, 41, 43
Lowry, Henry, 105
Lowry, Hugh, 105
Lowry-Corry family, 5, 6, 8; Lowry-Corry, Armar, 5th Earl, 12, 33, 88–92, 102, 106, 138, 143; Lowry-Corry, Cecil, 84; Lowry-Corry, Margaret, Lady Belmore, 34; Lowry-Corry, Somerset, 4th Earl, 12, 19
Lucas, Sgt. Samuel, 72, 77
Lurganboy, 81
Lynch, Louis, 5
Lynch, Robert, 117

Mac Eoin, Sean, 67, 114
MacCool, Sean, 66
MacDonagh, Thomas, 43
MacEntee, Seán, 48, 102, 108, 109
Macklin, Harry, 99
MacNeill, Eoin, 26, 37, 48, 50, 112, 114, 143, 144
Macready, General Neville, 75, 76, 127
MacSwiney, Terence, 120
Madden, Colonel James, 93
Magee, James, 122, 123
Magheraveely, 113
Maghermeena Castle, 126
Maguire, Francis, 139
Maguire, Peter, 67
Maguire, William, 50, 51
Maguiresbridge, 4, 20, 26, 31, 57, 58, 61, 76, 109
Mallin, Michael, 42
Markievicz, Constance, 42, 43, 51
Marlbank, 139
Marrinan, Patrick, 50
Marron, Philip, 98, 99
Maxwell, Cissie, 49
Maxwell, Thomas, 51
McCaffrey, Hugh, 97

McCarvill, Fr Michael, 48
McClean Family, 98, 99
McCluskey, Feargal, 112, 115, 150
McCreery, Samuel, 74
McCullough, James, 81
McElgunn, John, 112
McElvaney, J., 97
McEntee, Dan, 97
McGarvey, Frank, 122
McGilligan, Patrick, 7
McGinn, Michael Conway, 41, 43
McGinn, Patrick Romauld, 41
McGovern, Cissie, 68, 73
McGovern, James, 51, 91
McGovern, Kate, 122
McGrath, Ellen J., 48, 49
McGuinness, Joseph, 50
McGuire, John, 15, 19, 23
McGuire, Patrick, 41
McHugh, James, 120
McHugh, John, 17, 33, 35, 46, 58, 80, 89, 90, 92, 102, 110, 112, 114, 120, 132
McKegney, E.W., 128
McKenna, Bishop Patrick, 17, 48, 138
McKenna, James, 66, 98, 99
McKenna, John, 96
McLaughlin, Edward, 119
McMahon, James, 97
McMahon, Robert, 119
McManus, Hugh, 56
McMeel, Patrick, 96
McMullen, Felix, 68
McNeill, Robert, 111, 132, 133
McNulty, Patrick, 56
McPhail, Jack, 43
Methodism, 2, 5, 9, 21, 118
Miller, William Thomas, 108
Milroy, Sean, 108, 113–15
Moen's Cross, 67, 68
Monaghan, County, 2, 4, 5, 9, 14, 18–20, 36, 45, 46, 63, 64, 70, 73, 77, 78, 81, 92, 95–8, 101–4, 117–19, 123, 125, 126, 130, 131, 148; footballers, 117–18; town, 130
Monaghan, John, 105
Monea, 26, 32, 67

Moore, Colonel Maurice, 32
Moore, Cormac, 79, 111, 143
motor permit, 109
Mulcahy, Richard, 66
Mullaghdun, 43, 54, 68
Mullaglass, 100
Mulleek, 48, 66
Mulligan, James, 97
Murnaghan, George, 138
Murphy, Dominick, 120
Murray, Paul, 143

National Amalgamated Union of Labour
    (NAUL), 54, 81, 82, 83, 84, 134, 135
National Federation of Building Trade
    Operatives, 134
National Union of Life Assurance
    Workers, 82
National Volunteers, 30, 32–8
Nationalist Election Association, 83
Nawn, Frederick, 74
Nelson, Edward, 100
Nethercott, Mollie, *plate 23*
Nethercott, Seán, 82, 137, *plate 23*
Newbliss, 96
Newtownbutler, 19, 43, 44, 56, 57, 67, 70,
    73, 79, 81
Nixon, Samuel, 99–101
North-Eastern Advisory Committee, 137
North-Eastern Boundary Bureau, 138–40,
    144
Northern Ireland cabinet, 121, 130
Northern Ireland senate, 110, 118, 146
Northern Ireland, 1, 6, 10, 131, 139, 145;
    'six counties', 9, 46, 59, 104, 105,
    130, 137–9; establishment, 84–6, 91,
    95, 19, 74, 80, 110, 112, 123, 131,
    134, 138; parliament, 110, 111, 132,
    84, 140, 143, 146; attacks on, 116–21,
    125–9; post-1923, 144–50
Northern Irish Horse, 23
Nugent, Colonel Oliver, 22
Nulty, Patrick, 56, 68

Ó Ciaráin, Fr Lorcáin, 65, 72, 111, 114,
    126, 148

O'Brien, Fr. William, 123
O'Daly, Fr James, 40, 122
O'Daly, Fr, 122
O'Duffy, Eoin, 67, 73, 96–8, 100, 102,
    148, *plate 21*
O'Duffy, Francis, 27, 28, 32, 37, 38, 40,
    41, 48, 53, 54, 56, 60
O'Flanagan, Fr Michael, 86
O'Hara, Robert, 92
O'Hart, Patrick, 113
O'Kelly, Seamus G., 40, 43
Omagh, 4, 5, 31, 47, 51, 54, 109
O'Mahony, Seán, 56, 59, 61, 64, 65, 108,
    111, 113–15, 145, 147, *plate 8*
Orange Order, 5, 8, 14–16, 18, 22, 62,
    Orange Order Derrygonnelly Star of
    Freedom, *plate 7*
O'Reilly, John, 81
O'Shiel, Kevin, 9, 51, 53, 60–2, 65, 66,
    70, 108, 109, 140, 144, 146

Parliament Act 1911, 14
parliamentary constituencies: Fermanagh
    (South), 1, 6, 9, 11, 14, 17, 20, 40, 59,
    63, 84, 85, 108, 140; Fermanagh
    (North), 1, 6, 7, 11–14, 19, 20, 40, 54,
    58, 60, 62, 63, 66, 70, 146–9; South
    Tyrone, 57, 62; Cavan (East), 60;
    North West Tyrone, 59, 84; North
    East Tyrone, 59, 84; Fermanagh-
    Tyrone, 112, 115, 132, 138, 149
partition, 1, 9, 17, 30, 47, 52, 86, 93, 94,
    96, 106, 110, 111, 115, 126, 138,
    141–50; four-county, 18, 19; nine-
    county, 28, 29, 85; six-county, 29,
    43–5, 60, 84, 93, 141, 147, 149; anti-
    partition, 62, 83, 91, 108, 109, 138
Pearse, Patrick, 17, 18, 37, 43
Pettigo, 26, 65, 66, 77, 78, 84, 123, 144
Phoenix, Eamon, 17, 114, 137, 143
Pim, Herbert, 50
Plumb, James, 124
Plymouth Brethren, 42
Porter-Porter, John, 6, 12, 19, 20, 22, 33,
    35, 57, 80, 110, 146
Portora Hill, 19

Portora Royal School, 41
Presbyterian, 5, 21
Price, Ivon Henry, 78
proportional representation, 89
Protestant Defence Association, 122
Protestant, 18, 19, 21–4, 34, 53, 58, 84,
    120, 128, 136, 137, 140; population
    profile, 1–4; relationship with
    Catholics, 15, 59, 61, 66, 75, 80, 92,
    93, 100–2, 104, 117, 120–4, 131, 146,
    147; recruitment, 36, 57;
    Republicans, 41, 42, 46, 49, 60;
    Protestantism of Fermanagh, 52, 62,
    63, 85, 86, 150; labour activism, 54,
    83, 84

Quinn, Jim, 54, 82–3, 106, 134, 135, 146
Quinn, Thomas, 106

railway, 4, 5, 19, 43, 70, 73, 74, 103, 118–
    20, 126, *plate 22*; Great Northern
    Railway (GNR), 4
Rankin, Kieran, 143
rates, 7, 8, 82, 86, 87, 91, 107
Rathkeevan, 99
recruitment, 15, 18, 22, 24, 26, 30–8, 56,
    57, 77, 79, 80, 96, 121
Redistribution of Seats Act 1885, 6
Redmond, John, 30, 28, 47, 29, 16, 45, 11,
    40, 46, 9, 51, 148, 50, 56
Redmondism, 55, 138
Reform Act, 6
Reid, William, 15
Reilly, David, 132
Representation of the People Act 1884, 6
Representation of the People Act 1918, 58
reprisals, 120, 121, 130, 149, 150
Ricardo, Brigadier General Ambrose, 84
Richardson, Colonel Henry, 79
Richardson, Guy, 79
Richardson, Phyllis, 34
Rickerby, Albert, 126
Ritchie, William, 5
Riversdale, 6
Robinson, Sir Henry, 93
Rogers, James, 32

Roslea/Rosslea, 2, 16, 20, 26, 27, 69, 70,
    77, 117, 119, 131, 140, 144, 148, 149;
    sack of, 56, 96–101, 111, 129, 149,
    plate 20
Rossinure More, 67, 113
Rosslea, *see* Roslea
Rough Island, 127
Royal Irish Constabulary (RIC), 18, 41,
    43, 81, 93, 100, 105, 111, 125, 126,
    132, *plate 16*; Intelligence Reports,
    14, 21, 23, 26, 27, 32, 33, 38, 47, 48–
    51, 96; County Inspector, 15, 16, 18,
    19, 21–33, 36, 41, 43, 44, 47, 50, 55,
    56, 76–8, 95, 100, 103, 110, 117, 124;
    response to IRA, 57, 66, 77, 78, 103;
    attacks on, 65, 69–74, 77, 110;
    Protestant suspicions of, 75, 79, 80, 130
Royal Ulster Constabulary (RUC), 130
Rural District Council, 33, 140;
    Enniskillen, 2, 7, 8, 20, 40, 84, 88,
    89, 92, 106, 111, 136; Clones No. 2,
    7, 88, 106, 111; Belleek, 2–7, 17, 20,
    26, 48, 65, 66, 109, 106, 111, 140,
    144; Lisnaskea, 2–4, 26, 31, 49, 57,
    65, 67, 88, 91, 111, 136; Clogher, 51;
    Irvinestown, 88, 106, 136, 140
Russelite Unionists, 11, 13, 14

Sagarra, Eda, 61
Scollan, John Joe, 41
Scotshouse, 98
Scotstown, 67, 117
Scott, William, 41, 42
Sears, Jack, 24
sectarianism, 15, 18, 69, 80, 83, 98, 101–
    5, 122, 131, 139, 147
Shan Von Vocht, 17
Shaun McDermott SF Club, 113
Sheehan, Seán, 67, 68, 71, 73, 74
Sheemuldoon, 66
Sheridan, Frank, 70
Sinn Féin, 17–19, 28–30, 37–43, 46–65,
    70, 75–8, 82, 85–90, 100, 112, 126,
    137–9, 145–9; members, 49, 50, 66,
    97, 100, 103, 105, 107–14, 118, 119,
    133, 134

Slavin, Joseph, 72
Smith, Pat, 103
Smithborough, 97, 98, 101
Smyth, James J., 65, 67, 68, 72, 78, 114
Smyth, Joseph, 68, 72, 78, 114
Smyth, Nicholas, 27, 44
Solly-Flood, Arthur, 130
Soloheadbeg, 65
South Dublin Union, 42
Spender, Wilfrid, 79
St Michael's church, Enniskillen, 53, 81
St Michael's Intermediate School, 27, 37
Stack, Revd William, 25
Stopford Green, Alice, 17
Stranorlar, 66
Strathearn, R.W., 84
Sweeney, Joseph, 66

Tattymore, 99
Teemone, 105
Tempo, 20, 25, 26, 31, 57, 72, 73, 76, 77,
    123
Thomas McDonagh, 43
Thompson, John Alexander, 44
'Three County Unionism', 18, 25, 28, 66,
    84, 85
Tierney, Archdeacon John, 52, 133, 140,
    144
Tievegarrow, 143
Tipperary, 65
Toal, Thomas, 101
Toneyglaskin, 68
Townshend, Charles, 69, 70, 72, 148
Trade Union Congress, 82
Trainor, Joseph, 72
Trainor, Philip, 97
Travers, Pauric, 14, 20, 25, 69
Traynor, John, 42
Trillick, 51, 52, 68, 70, 119
Trimble, Egbert, 43
Trimble, William Copland, 5, 12, 23, 24,
    31, 55, 76, 84, 85, 86, 101, 121, 150,
    plate 1
Trinity College Dublin, 41
Tripartite Agreement, 144
Trotter, Thomas, 82, 83, 106

Tully, 97, 117
Tully, Patrick, 97
Tullyrain, 120
Tummon, Francis, 43, 44, 56, 57, 69, 73,
    76, 78, 103
Tummon, John, 78
Turkington, James, 83, 134
Twaddell, William, 125, 137
Tyrell, Frederick, 78, 100, 124
Tyrone, County 2, 4, 6, 8, 9, 14, 18–29,
    34, 36, 40, 44–7, 51, 62, 68, 70, 79,
    80, 88, 95, 97, 104, 107–15, 117, 119,
    121, 125

Ulster: Fermanagh's place in, 1–2, 5, 8, 9,
    36, 45, 60, 62, 66; Ulster Club, 11,
    14–6, 18–24, 85; Ulster Women's
    Unionist Council (UWUC), 13, 20,
    34, 49, *plate 10*; Ulster Campaign,
    18; Ulster Day, 19, 21, 29, 50; idea
    of, 64, 85–6, 122, 123, 129, 147;
    Ulster Workers' Union, 83, 84, 134,
    133, 138, 139, 146; Ulster Defence
    Association, 122
Ulster Covenant, 11, 18–22, 45; women's
    Declaration, 19, 20
Ulster Herald, 5, 21
Ulster Special Constabulary (USC), 1,
    10, 64, 74, 75, 78–81, 94, 95–101,
    103–5, 110, 111, 114–31, 141, 148–
    50; A Special, 79, 80, 96, 100, 120,
    124–6; B Special, 79, 95–7, 105,
    117–18, 122, 125–6, 129–30, 135,
    139, *plates 24, 25*; C Special, 79, 80;
    accidental deaths, 96, 131
Ulster Unionist Council (UUC), 11–14,
    21–4, 28, 45, 46, 79, 84, 86, 93, 149,
    150
Ulster Volunteer Force (UVF), 10, 11, 77,
    69, 146, 148, 149; home rule crisis,
    21–7; Easter War recruitment, 31–6;
    Rising, 41; reestablishment, 72, 75–
    9, 96, 97, 110; 3rd Battalion of UVF
    Enniskillen, *plate 15*
Union Flag/Jack, 19, 93, 100, 109, 127,
    141

United Irish League, 9, 16, 18, 32, 38, 46, 47, 50, 53, 56

Urban District Council, 9, 57; Enniskillen, 8, 17, 26, 33, 35, 47, 51, 52, 81–3, 88, 90–2, 95, 106, 107, 111, 117, 132–7, 146, 136; Belturbet, 50, 51

Vintners' Assistants Association, 82

Walsh, Fionnuala, 34
War of Independence, 28, 37, 43
Ward, Richard, 117
Warrington Family, 69
Wattlebridge, 56, 57, 67, 69, 70, 72, 73, 76, 78, 103
West, W.H., 93
Whalley, George, 88, 91
Wheathill, 68

White, Lawrence, 68
Whitechurch, 68
Whitehill, 122
Whittaker, Alexander, 136
Wickham, Sir Charles George, 80, 130
Wicklow, 44, 77
William Copeland Trimble, 5, 12, 23, 24, 31, 43, 55, 76, 84–6, 101, 122, 150
Wilson, Henry, 133
Wilson, Tim, 98, 124
Woobally, 68
Worrell, Robert, 117
Wray, Catherine, 34
Wray, John, 26, 32, 33
Wylie, Robert, 23
Wyse Power, Nancy, 49

Yeats, William Butler, 17